A BIBLIOGRAPHY OF WORKS IN ENGLISH ON EARLY RUSSIAN HISTORY TO 1800

A BIBLIOGRAPHY OF
WORKS IN ENGLISH ON

EARLY RUSSIAN
HISTORY

TO 1800

Compiled by

PETER A. CROWTHER

NEW YORK
BARNES & NOBLE
1969

First published in The United States, 1969
by Barnes & Noble, Inc.
New York, New York

389–01009–X

PRINTED IN GREAT BRITAIN

CONTENTS

PREFACE

The subject of this Bibliography was originally suggested by Mr. J. S. G. Simmons, who first made me aware of the need for a bibliography of works in English on early Russian history. The only major bibliography of English-language material on Russian history was D. M. Shapiro's work, which is restricted to the period 1801–1917. With Mr. Shapiro's encouragement I started compiling the present bibliography in December 1964. Since that date it has occupied most of my spare time, and would undoubtedly have taken much longer to complete had I not received the grant of a month's study leave in August last year, which enabled me to visit the Bodleian Library and the British Museum. I should like to express my thanks to the University of Birmingham, and its Librarian for the opportunity thus afforded.

Almost all the references which together make up the Bibliography were verified in three libraries : the Library of the University of Birmingham, the Birmingham Reference Library and the Bodleian Library. My thanks are due to the Librarians and staff of all these institutions.

It would be impracticable to list all those people who have helped in one way or another to make this Bibliography possible, but I should like to express a particular debt of gratitude to Dr. K. W. Humphreys, Librarian of the University of Birmingham Library, for his support and encouragement; also to Mr. J. S. G. Simmons of the Taylor Institute, Oxford, Mr. D. M. Shapiro of the Department of Government, University of Essex, and to Professor R. E. F. Smith of the Department of Russian, University of Birmingham, all of whom read the original draft and contributed much in the way of indicating omissions and making useful suggestions for its improvement. Needless to say I am myself responsible for whatever errors and defects remain in the work.

My thanks are also due to Mr. J. Wall and Mr. R. Beesley

of the Bodleian Library, Mr. M. Young of the Birmingham Reference Library and Mr. T. H. Bowyer of the University of Birmingham Library; similarly to Miss A. Totney and Mrs. K. Burke who typed the manuscript. Last but by no means least I must thank my wife, Jan, whose active contribution to this Bibliography has been scarcely less than my own.

May, 1968   P.A.C.

INTRODUCTION

Western research on Russia and Russian history has grown in
bulk and importance since the end of the First World War, coin-
ciding with the emergence of the Soviet Union as a world power.
At the same time, Russian studies have tended to be far more
concerned with the events of the immediate past than with the
earlier, formative period. The extent of this imbalance can be
seen if one examines almost any recent general survey of Russian
history. As often as not, more than one third of the book is
devoted to the last fifty years, a little less than that to the nineteenth century and the remainder to the centuries before 1800.

The present bibliography has been compiled in the hope
that it may encourage students of Russian history, at whatever
level, to turn their attention to this earlier period, and in the
belief that only by doing so can they fully understand the more
recent developments of tsarist and Soviet history.

As a bibliography of works in English it is intended primarily
but not exclusively for those unable to read Russian. Readers
with a knowledge of Russian have at their disposal the reasonably
comprehensive Soviet bibliography of Russian history: *Istoriya
SSSR: ukazatel' sovetskoy literatury, 1917–1952* (Moscow,
1956–8; 2t. in 4) and the history section of the selective and
annotated bibliography of works in Russian on Russia and the
Soviet Union edited by Paul L. Horecky: *Basic Russian Publications* (Univ. of Chicago Press, 1962). For those who are
concerned with Russian history but unable to read Russian there
are two recent general bibliographies of Western- and English-
language publications on Russia, viz., Paul L. Horecky, ed.
Russia and the Soviet Union (13), and the annual *American
Bibliography of Russian and East European Studies* (16).
Whilst both of these works contain sections on the history of
Russia the only recent English-language bibliography devoted
exclusively to general Russian history is D. M. Shapiro's *A
Select Bibliography of Works in English on Russian History,*

1801–1917 (Oxford, 1962). The present bibliography is intended as a companion volume to this work and closes at the point in time at which it begins.

SCOPE

The Bibliography, which covers both separately published material and articles in periodicals and collective works, aims at comprehensiveness in those sections most pertinent to the central theme of Russian history, e.g. the sections on general and chronological history, foreign relations, and social and economic history; it is more selective in those sections dealing with the history of Russia's borderlands, whilst the language section does not pretend to include more than a selection of those works most relevant to the historian.

Publications in certain categories have been omitted. First, British state papers have been excluded as deserving a more specialized study; secondly, obviously popular works of little scholarly or research value have been left out; and thirdly, manuscripts, doctoral dissertations and other unpublished material are not covered. It should be pointed out, however, that though the actual doctoral dissertations have not been listed, bibliographies relating to them have been included.

On the other hand the Cambridge histories and major collections of travels such as those compiled by Richard Hakluyt and Samuel Purchas have been searched for relevant material.

The present (1967) boundaries of the Soviet Union have been taken as the geographical limits of the bibliography; chronologically it extends from the earliest times to 1800. The bibliography covers material published down to 31 July 1967. A list of addenda covering the period from August 1967 to December 1968 is appended.

ARRANGEMENT

Entries have been classified into twenty separate divisions, which have been further subdivided into sections according to the requirements of the subject and the amount of material available. Each section is prefaced by a short introduction explaining its arrangement, indicating specific topics and drawing attention to the more significant works. Cross-references are given to related material.

The arrangement of items within each section is based primarily on the principle of proceeding from the general to the more specific; thus, works covering the subject of the section as a whole are listed before works on specific events or topics. The latter are arranged either on the same principle or chronologically, whichever is more appropriate to the subject matter.

Sub-arrangement of the group of general works and works on a specific topic is by date of publication. Further sub-arrangement, if required, is by coverage (i.e. a comprehensive treatise on a particular topic would precede a short periodical article on the same topic if both were published in the same year). Bibliographies and works of historiography are placed at the beginning of a sequence. At the end of the section will be found works dealing with the subject as represented in the history of Russia's borderlands, arranged geographically by regions in the order in which they are listed in the section (19) on regional and local history.

General surveys of Russian history (5A) are listed by date of publication of the first edition; contemporary descriptive works and travellers' accounts (20B) are listed chronologically.

FORM OF ENTRY

Individual entries are listed as far as possible under the name of the person or corporate body chiefly responsible for their original production. In cases of doubt the heading selected is that which has been found to be generally adopted in most library catalogues and bibliographies.

Alternative forms of an author's name are given in parentheses to facilitate retrieval. When an item has been found to be entered under a variety of headings, e.g. editor, translator or sponsoring corporate body, the names of these have been included in the text of the entry and also in the index. It is hoped that readers will thus be enabled to locate a desired item irrespective of which heading has been selected for entry in the particular catalogue that they may be consulting. Similarly in the case of a work which has been published as a separate monograph or volume of a serial publication, and which may be entered in a catalogue only under the name of the serial, the latter has been given in parentheses, together with the volume number, in the text of the entry.

Russian names, appearing in the heading but not in the text of an entry, have been transliterated in accordance with a modified version of the system used by the Library of Congress.[1] However in the case of persons of Russian origin living in the West and writing in the English language, no change has been made from the author's own adopted usage, regardless of the transliteration scheme on which this has been based. Cross-references have been given in all doubtful cases.

Although entries have been described as succinctly as possible, titles and sub-titles have normally been cited in full. It is hoped that the additional information as to a work's contents which may be given by this means will compensate for the lack of individual annotations. Successive editions are enumerated with details of place of publication (or university press where applicable), date of publication, pagination and bibliography. Pagination is omitted when the work is in two or more volumes. Reprints are noted (except in the case of modern textbooks of Russian history) and all items have been checked in the 1967 edition of Whitaker's *Paperbacks in Print*.

Approximately ninety-five per cent of all entries have been examined personally. The remainder have been verified in published library catalogues, chiefly in those of the British Museum and the Library of Congress. When personal examination of one-volume works has not been possible the pagination has been derived from bibliographies or catalogues and the statement of pagination is enclosed in parentheses. In some instances it has not proved possible to establish the pagination and it has had to be omitted. In the case of works in two or more volumes a note indicates that the work has not been personally examined.

References are given to reviews of the more significant or controversial works.

PERIODICALS

Approximately 200 titles have been inspected in the course of compiling the bibliography; nearly half this number have been examined from cover to cover for relevant material, the remainder were consulted only to verify specific references. The

---

[1] я and ю have been rendered as *ya* and *yu* respectively. й when occurring as a terminal letter has been ignored, elsewhere it is represented by *y*.

list of periodicals given below includes only those to which abbreviations have been allocated. Less frequently cited journals and those having only one word in the title are quoted in full. A comprehensive list of relevant current English-language periodicals is given in no. 16.

Titles of periodical articles are given in inverted commas, followed by the name of the periodical, or its abbreviation, the volume, year and page numbers. No reference is made to individual parts of a volume except when the pagination is that of the part and not the volume.

ABBREVIATIONS

AA	*Artibus Asiae* (Ascona).
AATSEEL Jnl	*American Association of Teachers of Slavic and East European Languages Journal* (afterwards *SEEJ*).
AHR	*American Historical Review.*
AJA	*American Journal of Archaeology.*
Am Anthrop	*American Anthropologist.*
ASEER[1]	*American Slavic and East European Review* (afterwards *Slavic Rev*).
AUA	*Annals of the Ukrainian Academy of Arts and Sciences in the U.S.*
BK	*Bedi Kartlisa* (Paris).
BSOAS	*Bulletin of the School of Oriental and African Studies.*
Byz Met	*Byzantina-Metabyzantina* (New York).
Byz Zeit	*Byzantinische Zeitschrift* (Munich).
CAH	*Cambridge Ancient History.*
CAR	*Central Asian Review.*
CEH	*Cambridge Economic History of Europe.*
CH	*Church History.*
CHJ	*Cambridge Historical Journal.*
C Med H	*Cambridge Mediaeval History.*
C Mod H	*Cambridge Modern History.*
C Q Rev	*Church Quarterly Review.*
CR	*Caucasian Review* (Munich).
CSS	*California Slavic Studies.*
DOP	*Dumbarton Oaks Papers.*
Econ HR	*Economic History Review.*
EHR	*English Historical Review.*
ESA	*Eurasia Septentrionalis Antiqua* (Helsinki).
HSS	*Harvard Slavic Studies.*
IJSLP	*International Journal of Slavic Linguistics and Poetics.*
JAOS	*Journal of the American Oriental Society.*
JCEA	*Journal of Central European Affairs.*
JEBH	*Journal of Economic and Business History.*
JEH	*Journal of Economic History.*
JHI	*Journal of the History of Ideas.*
JMH	*Journal of Modern History.*

JRAI	*Journal of the Royal Anthropological Institute of Great Britain and Ireland.*
JRAS	*Journal of the Royal Asiatic Society.*
✓*New C Mod H*	*New Cambridge Modern History.*
OCP	*Orientalia Christiana Periodica* (Rome).
OSP	*Oxford Slavonic Papers.*
PHR	*Pacific Historical Review* (Berkeley, Cal.).
Pol R	*Polish Review.*
RCAJ	*Royal Central Asian Journal.*
✓*Rus R*	*Russian Review* (New York).
Rus R (Liverpool)	*Russian Review* (Liverpool).
SEEJ	*Slavic and East European Journal* (formerly *AATSEEL Jnl*).
SEER²	*Slavonic and East European Review.*
✓*Slavic Rev*	*Slavic Review* (formerly *ASEER*).
Trans APS	*Transactions of the American Philosophical Society.*
Trans RHS	*Transactions of the Royal Historical Society.*
Ukr Qly	*Ukrainian Quarterly.*
Ukr Rev (L)	*Ukrainian Review* (London).
Ukr Rev (Munich)	*Ukrainian Review* (Munich).

Notes 1. Vols. 1–3 constitute vols. 20–22 of *SEER*. From vol. 20, no. 3, 1961 became *Slavic Review*.

2. Vols. 1–6 entitled: *Slavonic Review*; vols. 20–22 constitute vols. 1–3 of *ASEER*.

OTHER ABBREVIATIONS

Bibl.	Bibliography.
C.	Cambridge.
cf.	Compare.
Comp.	Compiler.
C.U.P.	Cambridge University Press.
Ed.	Edition, Editor.
et seq.	And what follows.
L.	London.
No(s).	Number(s).
N.Y.	New York.
O.	Oxford.
O.U.P.	Oxford University Press.
Pbk.	Paperback.
Pp.	Pages.
Pt(s).	Part(s).
Rev.	Reviewed.
Trans.	Translated.
U.P.	University Press.
Vol(s).	Volume(s).

I

BIBLIOGRAPHY

Bibliography of bibliographies, 1–3; library catalogues, 4–5; general bibliographies, arranged by date, 6–13; annual surveys, 14–16; theses, 17–19; library resources, 20–27; other special, 28–30.
Particularly recommended as examples of the modern approach to subject bibliography, **3** and **13**. Now available as a facsimile reprint, **4** is still a useful source of rare or little-known material. Bibliographies on special topics are classed with the topic, e.g.: Slavs, **107–108**; Khazars, **270–272**; Peter the Great, **398**; archaeology, **909–910**; anthropology, **1024**; art and literature, **1309**; language, **1406–1407**; Slavic folk literature, **1485**; Baltic states, **1619–1620**; Latvia, **1627**; Estonia, **1630**; Lithuania, **1635**; Belorussia, **1654**; Ukraine, **1661–1662**; Circassia, **1753**; Siberia and North-eastern Asia, **1817–1818**; voyages and travels, **1024** and **1869–1871**.

1 KERNER, ROBERT J., 'The Foundations of Slavic Bibliography', *Papers of the Bibliographical Society of America,* vol. 10, no. 1, 1916, pp. (3–39).

2 NEW YORK. *Public Library. Slavonic Division.* A Bibliography of Slavonic Bibliography in English. N.Y., 1947. Pp. 11.
Originally published in the *Bulletin of the New York Public Library,* April 1947.

3 MAICHEL, KAROL. Guide to Russian Reference Books. Edited by J. S. G. Simmons. Vol. 1– Stanford Univ., 1962–
In progress. Vols. 1–2 published to date [i.e. 1967]. To be completed in 6 vols. (Vol. 1: General bibliographies and reference books. Vol 2: History, ethnography, geography. Vol. 3: Social sciences, religion, philosophy, military and library science. Vol. 4: Humanities. Vol. 5: Science, technology and medicine. Vol. 6: Supplementary material and cumulative index.)

4 ST. PETERSBURG. *Imperial Public Library.* Catalogue de la Section des Russica; ou, Écrits sur la Russie en Langues

Étrangères. 2 vols. St. Petersburg, 1873. Reprinted Amsterdam, 1964.

5 NEW YORK. *Public Library. Slavonic Division.* Dictionary Catalog of the Slavonic Collection. 26 vols. Boston, Mass., 1959.

6 KERNER, ROBERT J. Slavic Europe: a Selected Bibliography in the Western European Languages. Harvard U.P., 1918. Pp. xxiv, 402.

7 YAKOBSON, S. *and* EPSTEIN, F. 'A List of Books in English on Russia Published in 1935', *SEER,* vol. 15, 1936–7, pp. 482–90.

8 LOEWENSON, LEO. 'Some Recent Books on Russian History', *History,* vol. 28, 1943, pp. 207–15.

9 MORLEY, CHARLES. Guide to Research in Russian History. Syracuse U.P., 1951. Pp. xiii, 227.

10 KEEP, JOHN L. H., *comp.* 'Verzeichnis des englischsprachigen Schrifttums (ausser USA), 1939–1952 zur Geschichte Osteuropas und Südosteuropas', *Forschungen zur Osteuropäischen Geschichte,* vol. 5, 1957, pp. 119–62.

11 FISHER, HAROLD H., *ed.* American Research on Russia. Indiana U.P., 1959. Pp. xiv, 240.

12 KEEP, JOHN L. H. 'Verzeichnis des amerikanischen Schrifttums 1939–1952 zur Geschichte Osteuropas und Südosteuropas', *Forschungen zur Osteuropäischen Geschichte,* vol. 7, 1959, pp. 397–446.

13 HORECKY, PAUL L., *ed.* Russia and the Soviet Union: a Bibliographical Guide to Western-Language Publications. U. of Chicago P., 1965. Pp. xxiv, 473.

14 'Bibliography of Books and Articles on Russia, 1941–58', *Rus. R.,* vols. 1–18. Published annually, listing previous years' publications, as follows: – 1941: vol. 1, no. 2, 1941–2, pp. 116–23; 1942: vol. 2, no. 2, 1942–3, pp. 113–21; 1943: vol. 3, no. 2, 1943–4, pp. 119–28; 1944: vol. 4, no. 2, 1944–5, pp. 104–19; 1945; vol. 5, no. 2, 1945–6, pp. 116–29; 1946: vol. 6, no. 2, 1946–7, pp. 101–15; 1947: vol. 7, no. 2, 1947–8, 103–14; 1948: vol. 8, 1949, pp. 253–64; 1949: vol. 9, 1950, pp. 243–59; 1950; vol. 10, 1951, pp. 234–50; 1951: vol. 11, 1952, pp. 177–95; 1952: vol. 12, 1953, pp. 206–22; 1953: vol. 13, 1954, pp. 224–42; 1954: vol. 14, 1955, pp. 275–91;

1955 : vol. 15, 1956, pp. 218–32; 1956 : vol. 16, no. 3, 1957, pp. 70–90; 1957 : vol. 17, no. 3, 1958, pp. 229–48; 1958 : vol. 18, 1959, pp. 257–75.

15 GRIERSON, PHILIP. 'Books and pamphlets on Russia, 1942–50', *SEER*, vols. 24–9. Published annually as follows :– 1942–5 : vol. 24, 1946, pp. 133–47; 1946–7 : vol. 25, 1946–7, pp. 508–17; 1947 : vol. 26, 1947–8, pp. 512–8; 1948 : vol. 27, 1948–9, pp. 556–62; 1949 : vol. 28, 1949–50, pp. 486–92; 1950 : vol. 29, 1950–1, pp. 550–7.
   The compiler's earlier work : *Books on Soviet Russia, 1917–1942*, L., 1943 is confined to the Soviet period.

16 AMERICAN BIBLIOGRAPHY OF RUSSIAN AND EAST EUROPEAN STUDIES. 1956– Indiana U.P., 1957–
   The interval between date of coverage and date of publication has extended to two or more years in recent issues.

17 KERNER, ROBERT J. 'Bibliography of American Doctoral Dissertations on Slavonic Studies, 1914–1924', *SEER*, vol. 3, 1924–5, pp. 745–9.

18 DOSSICK, JESSE J. Doctoral Research on Russia and the Soviet Union. N.Y.U.P., 1960. Pp. 248.

19 DOSSICK, JESSE J. 'Doctoral Dissertations on Russia and the Soviet Union Accepted by American, British and Canadian Universities, 1960–1966', *Slavic Rev.*, vols. 23–5. Published annually as follows :– 1960–4 : vol. 23, 1964, pp. 797–812; 1964–5 : vol. 24, 1965, pp. 752–61; 1965–6 : vol. 25, 1966, pp. 710–17.
   The two most recent articles include dissertations on Eastern Europe.

20 RUGGLES, MELVILLE J. *and* MOSTECKY, VACLAV. Russian and East European Publications in the Libraries of the United States. Columbia U.P., 1960. Pp. xv, 396. Bibl.

21 MORLEY, CHARLES. 'Major Russian Collections in American Libraries', *SEER*, vol. 29, 1950–1, pp. 256–66. Also in **9**.

22 HORECKY, PAUL L. 'The Slavic and East European Resources and Facilities of the Library of Congress', *Slavic Rev.*, vol. 23, 1964, pp. 309–27.

23 GRIMSTED, PATRICIA K. 'Soviet Archives and Manu-

script Collections : a Bibliographical Introduction', *Slavic Rev.*, vol. 24, 1965, pp. 105–20.

24   BURTSEV, VLADIMIR. 'Russian Documents in the British Museum', *SEER*, vol. 4, 1925–6, pp. 669–85.

25   LOEWENSON, LEO. 'Russian Documents in the British Museum, I', *SEER*, vol. 14, 1935–6, pp. 380–8.

26   LOEWENSON, LEO. 'Russian Documents in the British Museum, II : 17th Century—the MSS. of Englebert Kämpfer', *SEER*, vol. 14, 1935–6, pp. 661–9.

27   DJAPARIDZÉ, DAVID. Mediaeval Slavic Manuscripts : a Bibliography of Printed Catalogues. Cambridge, Mass., 1957. Pp. xv, 134.

28   RAPOPORT, SEMEN. 'Mohammedan Writers on Slavs and Russians', *SEER*, vol. 8, 1929–30, pp. 80–98.
Surveys 9th–10th centuries Arabian sources on Kiev Rus; cf. **82, 269, 296.**

29   FERGUSON, ALAN D. 'A Bibliography of the Works of Professor George Vernadsky', *OSP*, vol. 5, 1954, pp. 32–40.

30   FERGUSON, ALAN D. 'Bibliography of the Works of George Vernadsky', in **83**, pp. xiii–xxv.
cf. **74.**

2

HISTORIOGRAPHY

Western historiography, **31–36**; Soviet historiography and commentaries by Western historians, **37–52**; periodization of Russian history, **53–56**; the Eurasian movement, **57–59**; Ukrainian and Great Russian views of Russian history contrasted, **60–63**; individual historians, A–Z, **64–74**;regional schools of history, **75–76**. Arrangement is chronological within each of the above-mentioned topics, with the exception of the sections on individual historians and regional schools of history.

There is an obvious need for a comprehensive, scholarly treatise on Russian historiography; **35** is not wholly satisfactory. A good introduction to Soviety historiography is provided by **37** in the form of an anthology of the writings of a selection of Soviet historians.

The historiography of special events, topics or areas is classed with the subject, e.g. ancient history, **242**; Kiev Rus', **281–283**; Ivan IV, **343**; social development, **818**; Lithuania, **1636–1638**; Belorussia, **1655–1657**; Ukraine, **1663–1670** and **1690**.

31   MILYUKOV, PAVEL N. 'The Chief Currents of Russian Historical Thought', *American Historical Association Annual Report,* 1904 (Washington, 1905), pp. 109–14.

32   REDDAWAY, WILLIAM F. Introduction to the Study of Russian History. (Helps for Students of History, no. 25.) L., 1920. Pp. 32.

33   GAPANOVICH, I. I. Russian Historiography outside Russia : an Introduction to the Study of Russian History. Peiping, 1935. Pp. 187.

34   MAZOUR, ANATOLE G. 'Modern Russian Historiography', *JMH,* vol. 9, 1937, pp. 169–202.

35   MAZOUR, ANATOLE G. An Outline of Modern Russian Historiography. U. of California P., 1939. Pp. viii, 130. Bibl. 2nd ed. : Modern Russian Historiography. Princeton, 1958. Pp. xii, 260. Bibl.

Rev.: M. Szeftel in *ASEER*, vol. 18, 1959, pp. 250–252; Jesse D. Clarkson in *Rus R*, vol. 18, 1959, pp. 247–248.

36 MANNING, CLARENCE A. A History of Slavic Studies in the United States. Marquette U.P., 1957. Pp. ix, 118.

37 BLACK, CYRIL E., *ed*. Rewriting Russian History: Soviet Interpretations of Russia's Past. N.Y., 1956, L., 1957. Pp. xvi, 413.
     Rev.: Raymond H. Fisher in *ASEER*, vol. 17, 1958, pp. 234–235.

38 GREKOV, B. D. 'The Development of Historical Science in the U.S.S.R.', *Anglo-Soviet Journal*, vol. 5, no. 1, 1944, pp. 17–22.

39 CARSON, GEORGE B. 'Changing Perspectives in Soviet Historiography', *South Atlantic Quarterly*, vol. 47, 1948, pp. 186–95.

40 YAKOBSON, SERGIUS. 'Postwar Historical Research in the Soviet Union', *Annals of the American Academy of Political and Social Science*, vol. 263, May, 1949, pp. 123–33.

41 SCHLESINGER, RUDOLF. 'Recent Soviet Historiography. Pts. I–IV', *Soviet Studies*, vol. 1, 1949–50, pp. 293–312 and vol. 2, 1951, pp. 3–21, 138–62, 265–88.

42 MAZOUR, ANATOLE G. *and* BATEMAN, HERMAN E. 'Recent Conflicts in Soviet Historiography', *JMH*, vol. 24, 1952, pp. 56–68.

43 OHLOBLYN, ALEKSANDR P. 'Soviet Historiography', in *Academic Freedom under the Soviet Regime: a Symposium* . . . N.Y., 1954, pp. 69–77.

44 YARESH, LEO A., *pseud*. [A. Moskalenko]. Two Essays in Soviet Historiography: 1. The Centralized Russian State of the 17th Century. 2. The Age of Catherine II. (Trans. from Russian.) N.Y., 1955. Pp. (61).

45 DALLIN, ALEXANDER. 'Recent Soviet Historiography', *Problems of Communism*, vol. 5, no. 6, 1956, pp. 24–30.

46 LABEDZ, LEOPOLD. 'Soviet Historiography between the Thaw and the Freeze', *Soviet Survey*, no. 15, May, 1957, pp. 2–13.

47 AESSON, A. 'Slavic History in the Eyes of the Soviets', *CR*, vol. 4, 1957, pp. 86–95.

48 YARESH, LEO A., *pseud*. [A. Moskalenko]. 'The "Peasant

Wars" in Soviet Historiography', *ASEER*, vol. 16, 1957, pp. 241–59.

49 URBAN, P. 'Changing Trends in Soviet Historiography', *CR*, vol. 9, 1959, pp. 11–24.

50 SHTEPPA, KONSTANTIN F. Russian Historians and the Soviet State. Rutgers U.P., 1962. Pp. xiv, 437.
Rev.: Ralph T. Fisher in *Rus R*, vol. 22, 1963, pp. 420–423.

51 ANDREYEV, NIKOLAY. 'Recent Soviet Studies of Russian History and Culture before 1462', *Slavic Rev.*, vol. 21, 1962, pp. 336–42.

52 MENDEL, ARTHUR P. 'Current Soviet Theory of History: New Trends or Old?', *AHR*, vol. 72, 1966, pp. 50–73.

53 ROZANOV, VASILY V. 'On the Epochs of Russian History', *SEER*, vol. 8, 1929–30, pp. 164–75.

54 KOROSTOVETZ, VLADIMIR DE. 'Continuity in Russian History', *Contemporary Review*, vol. 170, 1946, pp. 145–8.

55 DAVIES, ROBERT W. 'The Discussion of Periodisation of Russian History and its Place in the Development of Soviet Historiography', *Anglo-Soviet Journal*, vol. 12, no. 4, 1951, pp. 4–12.

56 SCHLESINGER, RUDOLF. 'Recent Discussion of the Periodization of History', *Soviet Studies*, vol. 4, 1952–3, pp. 152–69.

57 MIRSKY, DMITRI S. 'The Eurasian Movement', *SEER*, vol. 6, 1927–8, pp. 311–9.

58 ISHBOLDIN, BORIS, 'The Eurasian Movement', *Rus R*, vol. 5, no. 2, 1945–6, pp. 64–73.

59 RIASANOVSKY, NICHOLAS V. 'The Emergence of Eurasianism', *California Slavic Studies*, vol. 4, 1967, pp. 39–72.

60 VOLKONSKI, ALEKSANDR, *Prince* (Wolkonsky). The Ukrainian Question: the Historic Truth versus Separatist Propaganda. (Trans. from French.) Rome, 1920. Pp. 239.

61 CHUBATY, NICHOLAS D. (Czubatyj). 'The Meaning of "Russia" and "Ukraine"', *Ukr Qly.*, vol. 1, 1944–5, pp. 351–64.
cf. **297–298**.

62 CHUBATY, NICHOLAS D. (Czubatyj). 'The Ukrainian and

Russian Conceptions of the History of Eastern Europe',
*Proceedings of the Shevchenko Scientific Society, Histor-
ical-Philosophical Section,* vol. 1, 1951, pp. 10–25.
cf. **1668**.

63 SIMPSON, GEORGE W. The Names Rus, Russia, Ukraine
and their Historical Background. Winnipeg, 1951. Pp. 24.
Bibl.
cf. **289–290**.

64 LOEWENSON, LEO. 'The Historian Alexander Brückner,
1834–1896 : a Neglected Page of Russian Historiography', *SEER,* vol. 25, 1946–7, pp. 149–58.

65 CROSS, ANTHONY. 'Karamzin Studies. For the Bicenten-
ary of the Birth of N. M. Karamzin, 1766–1966', *SEER,*
vol. 45, 1967, pp. 1–11; Bibl.

66 PIPES, RICHARD. 'Karamzin's Conception of the
Monarchy', HSS, vol. 4, 1957, pp. 35–58.

67 McGREW, R. E. 'Notes on the Princely Role in
Karamzin's *Istorija Gosudarstva Rossijskago*', *ASEER,*
vol. 18, 1959, pp. 12–24.

68 MALIA, MARTIN E. 'M. M. Karpovich', *Rus R.,* vol. 19,
1960, pp. 60–71.

69 MAKLAKOV, BASIL. 'Klyuchevsky', *SEER,* vol. 13,
1934–5, pp. 320–9.

70 JAGIĆ, V. 'Klyuchevsky and his *Course of Russian
History*', *SEER,* vol. 1, 1922–3, pp. 504–24.

71 KARPOVICH, MICHAEL. 'Klyuchevski and Recent Trends
in Russian Historiography', *SEER,* vol. 21, no. 1, 1943,
pp. 31–9.

72 LOEWENSON, LEO. 'Karl Stählin, 1865–1939 : a Chapter
of German Historiography on Russia', *SEER,* vol. 28,
1949–50, pp. 152–60.

73 CLARKSON, JESSE D. 'Toynbee on Slavic and Russian
History', *Rus R,* vol. 15, 1956, pp. 165–72.
cf. **1150**.

74 OBOLENSKY, DMITRI. 'George Vernadsky as a Historian of Ancient and Medieval Russia' in **83**, pp. 1–17; Bibl.
cf. **29–30** and **201–202**.

75 BILMANIS, ALFRED. 'Latvia's Contribution to Historical
Science', *ASEER,* vol. 4, nos. 3–4, 1945, pp. 163–73.

76 LASHAURI, MINDIA. 'The State of Historical Science
in the Georgian SSR', *CR,* vol. 1, 1955, pp. 93–9.

3

GENERAL WORKS

Encyclopaedias, **77–82**; collections and anthologies, **83–86**; pictorial histories, **87–90**; maps and atlases, **91–97**; auxiliary sciences of history, chiefly numismatics, **98–106**.

77 McGRAW-HILL ENCYCLOPEDIA OF RUSSIA AND THE SOVIET UNION. Edited by Michael T. Florinksy. N.Y., 1961. Pp. xiv, 624.
> Rev.: Paul L. Horecky in *Slavic Rev*, vol. 21, 1962, pp. 786–788.

78 UTECHIN, S. V., *comp.* Everyman's Concise Encyclopaedia of Russia. L., N.Y., 1961, Pp. xxvi, 623.
> Rev.: R. V. Allen in *Slavic Rev*, vol. 21, 1962, pp. 187–188; Jerry F. Hough in *Rus R*, vol. 21, 1962, pp. 192–193.

79 STRAKHOVSKY, LEONID I., *ed.* A Handbook of Slavic Studies. Harvard U.P., 1949. Pp. xxii, 753. Bibl.
> Rev.: Gojko Ružičić in *ASEER*, vol. 9, 1950, pp. 139–141; John C. Adams in *Rus R*, vol. 9, 1950, pp. 67–68.

80 ROUCEK, JOSEPH S., *ed.* Slavonic Encyclopaedia. N.Y., 1949. Pp. xi, 1445.
> Rev.: Philip E. Mosely in *ASEER*, vol. 9, 1950, pp. 141–143; R. R. Betts in *SEER*, vol. 28, 1949–50, pp. 294–296.

81 VLAHOVIĆ, VLAHO S., *ed.* Slavonic Personalities, Past and Present. N.Y., 1940. Pp. (96).

82 AL-MASUDI, *885–956* A.D. (Alî b. al-Husain). El-Mas'údí's Historical Encyclopaedia, Entitled: Meadows of Gold and Mines of Gems. (Trans. from Arabic by A. Sprenger.) Vol. 1. L., 1841. Pp. lxxii, 464.

83 FERGUSON, ALAN D. *and* LEVIN, ALFRED, *ed.* Essays in Russian History: a Collection Dedicated to George Vernadsky. Hamden, Conn., 1964. Pp. xxv, 317.
> Rev.: Jesse D. Clarkson in *Rus R*, vol. 24, 1965, pp. 412–414.

84 WALSH, WARREN B., *comp.* Readings in Russian History. Syracuse U.P., 1948. Pp. 549. 2nd ed. 1950. Pp. 638. 3rd ed. 1959. Pp. 702. 4th ed. 3 vols. 1963.
> Rev.: Ralph T. Fisher in *Slavic Rev*, vol. 23, 1964, pp. 578–579.

85 HARCAVE, SIDNEY S., *ed.* Readings in Russian History. 2 vols. N.Y., 1962.
Rev.: Arthur E. Adams in *Slavic Rev*, vol. 22, 1963, pp. 329–330.

86 DMYTRYSHYN, BASIL, *ed.* Medieval Russia: a Source Book, 900–1700. N.Y., 1967. Pp. (viii, 312). Bibl.

87 HOWARD, ALEXANDER *and* NEWMAN, ERNEST. Pictorial History of Russia . . . L., N.Y., 1943. Pp. 216. (500 illus.)

88 MARTIN, JOHN S., *ed.* A Picture History of Russia. N.Y., 1945, L., 1947. Pp. (376). (500 illus.)

89 CARMICHAEL, JOEL. An Illustrated History of Russia. N.Y., 1960. Pp. 305.

90 DUNCAN, DAVID D. The Kremlin: a Pictorial Record of the History of Russia from the 11th Century. L., 1960. Pp. 170. Bibl.

91 SOVIET RUSSIA IN MAPS: its Origin and Development. Edited by George Goodall. L., 1942. Pp. 33. Other Editions: 1943, 1947, 1949, 1954 and 1961.
From 1947 entitled: *Soviet Union in Maps etc.*; 1961 edition edited by H. Fullard.

92 ADAMS, ARTHUR E., *and others.* An Atlas of Russian and East European History. N.Y., 1966, L., 1967. Pp. xi, 204. Bibl.

93 CHEW, ALLEN F. An Atlas of Russian History: Eleven Centuries of Changing Borders. Yale U.P., 1967. Pp. x, 113.

94 JAŻDŻEWSKI, KONRAD. Atlas to the Prehistory of the Slavs. 2 pts. (Łódzkie Towarzystwo Naukowe. Wydział 2. Acta Praehistorica Universitatis Łodziensis, nr. 1.) Łódz, 1948–9.

95 A DESCRIPTIVE ATLAS, Illustrative of the Seats of War and Exhibiting the Vast Increase of the Russian Territories from the Accession of Peter the Great to the Present Time. L., 1854. Pp. 24.

96 MOLL, HERMAN. Russia or Muscovy with its Acquisitions and Conquests in Sweden. Map no. 4 of *Atlas Minor*. 2nd ed. L., 1732.

97 ELLIS, GEORGE. Memoir of a Map of the Countries . . . between the Black Sea and the Caspian. With an Account of the Caucasian Nations . . . L., 1788. Pp. ii, 80 + Map.

98 DOLGORUKOV, PETR V., *Prince*. A Handbook of the Principle Families in Russia. (Trans from French.) L., 1858. Pp. vi, 192.

99 ALEF, GUSTAVE. 'The Adoption of the Muscovite Two-Headed Eagle: a Discordant View', *Speculum*, vol. 41, 1966, pp. 1–21.

100 SNYDERMAN, I. 'Outline of Russian Numismatic History', *Numismatist*, vol. 40, 1942, pp. (99–102).

101 SEVERIN, H. M., *comp*. The Silver Coinage of Imperial Russia, 1682–1917: a Compilation of all Known Types and Varieties. Basle, 1967. Pp. (276).

102 ALEF, GUSTAVE. 'The Political Significance of the Inscriptions on Muscovite Coinage in the Reign of Vasili II', *Speculum*, vol. 34, 1959, pp. 1–19.

103 HASSE, JOHN. The Coins etc. of Russia: Being an English Translation of *De Moneta Russica*, Elzevier, 1630 ... Edited by Edmund Goldsmid. (Bibliotheca Curiosa, vol. 47.) Edinburgh, 1886. Pp. 7. Also in **1872b,** Entitled: 'The Coines, Weights and Measures Used in Russia, Written in the Yere 1554', vol. 2, p. 278.

104 KELPSH, A. E. 'Rubles of Peter the Great', *Numismatist*, vol. 62, March, 1949, pp. 161–74.

105 LANG, DAVID M. Studies in the Numismatic History of Georgia in Transcaucasia. (Numismatic Notes and Monographs, no. 130.) N.Y., 1955. Pp. x, 138. Bibl.
    Rev.: Cyril Toumanoff in *ASEER*, vol. 15, 1956, pp. 429–430.

106 LANG, DAVID M. 'Numismatic Data for the History of Georgia', *BK*, New Series, vols. 19–20, 1965, pp. 173–7.

4

THE SLAVS, EARLY PANSLAVISM

Bibliography, **107–108** (cf. **1–2, 5–6**); general works, **109–117**; conversion to Christianity, **118–120**; Juraj Križanić and early Panslavism, **121–125**; the name "Slav", **126–127**.

This section contains only the most general works on Slavic history and civilization. Slavic encyclopaedias, **79–81;** ancient settlements, **263–269**; anthropology, **1028;** mythology and folklore, **1072–1079.**

107 EPSTEIN, FRITZ T., *comp.* 'A Short Working Bibliography on the Slavs', *SEER,* vol. 22, no. 3, 1944, pp. 110–9.

108 LENCEK, RADO L., *comp.* A Bibliographical Guide to the Literature on Slavic Civilizations. N.Y., 1966. Pp. xiv, 52.

109 DVORNIK, FRANCIS. The Slavs: their Early History and Civilization. Boston, Mass., 1956. Pp. 394. Bibl.
Rev.: J. Stauber in *Études Slaves,* vol. 1, 1956, pp. 189–190; R. R. Betts in *SEER,* vol. 35, 1956–57, pp. 584–587.

110 DVORNIK, FRANCIS. The Slavs in European History and Civilization. Rutgers U.P., 1962. Pp. xxviii, 688. Bibl.
Rev.: Imre Boba in *Slavic Rev,* vol. 22, 1963, pp. 547–548; Charles Jelavich in *Rus R,* vol. 22, 1963, pp 315–316.

111 CROSS, SAMUEL H. Slavic Civilization through the Ages. Harvard U.P., 1948. Pp. vi, 195. Reprinted N.Y., 1965.
Rev.: Frank Friedeberg Seeley in *SEER,* vol. 27, 1948–49, pp. 302–308.

112 BARTOL'D, VASILI V. (Barthold). 'Slavs', in *Encyclopaedia of Islam,* vol. 4, Leyden, 1934, pp. 467–8; Bibl.

113 BIDLO, JAROSLAV. 'The Slavs in Medieval History', *SEER,* vol. 9, 1930–31, pp. 34–55.

114 DVORNIK, FRANCIS. The Making of Central and Eastern Europe. L., 1949. Pp. iv, 350. Bibl.
Rev.: R. R. Betts in *SEER,* vol. 28, 1949–50, pp. 547–554.

115 MACARTNEY, C. A. 'Eastern Europe', *New C. Mod H*, vol. 1, C.U.P., 1957, Chapter 13, pp. 368–94.
Covers the period from 1460 onwards.

116 DVORNIK, FRANCIS. 'Western and Eastern Traditions of Central Europe', *Review of Politics*, vol. 9, 1947, pp. 463–81.

117 NOWAK, FRANK. Medieval Slavdom and the Rise of Russia. N.Y., 1930. Pp. (xii, 132). Bibl.

118 JAGIĆ V. 'Conversion of the Slavs', *C Med H*, vol. 4, C.U.P., 1923, Chapter 7B, pp. 215–29; Bibl.: pp. 822–5.
cf. **1156**.

119 DVORNIK, FRANCIS. 'The Significance of the Missions of Cyril and Methodius', *Slavic Rev.*, vol. 23, 1964, pp. 196–211.
cf. **1155**.

120 SHEVCHENKO, IHOR. 'Three Paradoxes of the Cyrillo-Methodian Mission', *Slavic Rev.*, vol. 23, 1964, pp. 220–36.

121 HALECKI, OSCAR. 'The Renaissance Origin of Panslavism', *Pol R*, vol. 3, nos. 1–2, 1958, pp. 7–19.

122 SHMURLO, E. 'From Križanić to the Slavophils', *SEER*, vol. 6, 1927–8, pp. 321–35.

123 PETROVICH, MICHAEL B. 'Juraj Križanić: a Precursor of Pan-Slavism, ca. 1618–83', *ASEER*, vol. 6, no. 2, 1947, pp. 75–92; Bibl.

124 LAVRIN, JANKO. 'Yury Krizhanich', *Rus R*, vol. 25, 1966, pp. 369–82.

125 KADIĆ, ANTE. 'Križanić's Formative Years', in *American Contributions to the 5th International Congress of Slavists, Sofia, 1963*, vol. 2, The Hague, 1963, pp. 167–200.

126 RUDNYĆKYJ, J. B. 'Slaves or Glorious Ones? the Origin of the Name "Slav"', *Names*, vol. 8, 1960, pp. 65–74.

127 LOZINSKI, B. PHILIP. 'The Name "Slav"', in **83**, pp. 19–32.

5

GENERAL HISTORY

Chronicles are listed at the head of the sequence; general works follow, arranged by date of first edition.

Of the rich collection of early Russian chronicles available to Russian speakers in the multi-volume *Polnoe sobranie russkikh letopisey* currently being published in the Soviet Union, only two have been translated into English, **129–131.**

English works on Russia before the 19th century, **132–139,** generally took the form of accounts and contemporary descriptions of travellers or temporary residents in Russia; see section 20.

The rather full list of 19th-century histories given here, **140– 170,** will have little interest for the general student of Russian history, but is presented nevertheless for the more bibliographically minded and those researching into the history of Russian historical studies in Britain or America. It is interesting, for example, to note the number of occasional works published at the time of the Crimean and Second World Wars, catering for the sudden upsurge of popular interest in Russia, whether as an adversary or an ally.

Twentieth-century works, **171–241.** Many of the earlier works in this section though somewhat outdated are still readable and contain proportionately more text on the early period. Two works from this group merit special mention: **177,** the classic Russian work, and **200,** a work of historical geography, particularly valuable for an understanding of the background to early Russian history. Early Marxist works in translation: **192** and **194;** Soviet textbooks: **197, 208** and **236.** Recommended modern Western textbooks: **190, 203, 206, 216–217, 223, 229, 232** and **234.** Of the many primers available, **220, 226** and **239–240** are representative. No. **201** (of which 4 volumes have been published to date, 1967) promises to be the most comprehensive and scholarly treatise.

128 FORBES, NEVILL. 'The Composition of the Earlier

Russian Chronicles', *SEER*, vol. 1, 1922–3, pp. 73–85.

129 RUSSIAN PRIMARY CHRONICLE: Laurentian Text. (Povest' Vremennykh Let) (Nachal'naya Letopis') (Nestor's Chronicle) (Tale of Bygone Years.) Translated and Edited by Samuel H. Cross and Olgerd P. Sherbowitz-Wetzor. Cambridge, Mass., 1953. Pp. 313. Bibl.

130 CROSS, SAMUEL H. 'The Russian Primary Chronicle: [Introduction and the Laurentian Text]', *Harvard Studies and Notes in Philology and Literature*, vol. 12, 1930, pp. 75–320.

131 The CHRONICLE OF NOVGOROD, 1016–1471 (Novgorodskaya Letopis'.) Translated from Russian by Robert Michell and Nevill Forbes. (Royal Historical Society Publications. Camden 3rd Series, vol. 25.) L., 1914. Pp. xliii, 237.

132 F., J. A Brief Historical Relation of the Empire of Russia ... L., 1654. Pp. 44. Also in **373** (abridged).

133 MILTON, JOHN. A Brief History of Moscovia, and of other Less-Known Countries Lying Eastward of Russia as Far as Cathay ... L., 1682. Pp. vi, 109. Another Edition, L., 1929. Pp. 120.

   Summarizes information provided by contemporary travellers to Russia.

134 CAWLEY, ROBERT R. Milton's Literary Craftsmanship: a Study of *A Brief History of Moscovia*. With an Edition of the Text. (Princeton Studies in English, vol. 24.) Princeton U.P., O.U.P., 1941. Pp. viii, 105.

135 MOTTLEY, JOHN. The History of the Russian Empire, from its Foundation to the Death of the ... Empress Catherine ... 2 vols. L., 1757–8.

136 LOMONOSOV, MIKHAIL V. A Chronological Abridgement of the Russian History ... (Trans. from Russian.) L., 1767. Pp. vi, 85.

137 WILLIAMS, JOHN. The Rise, Progress and Present State of the Northern Governments, viz. the United Provinces ... Russia, and Poland. 2 vols. L., 1777.

138 GEORGI, JOHANN G. Russia; or, A Compleat Historical Account of all the Nations which Compose that Empire. (Trans. from German by W. Tooke.) 4 vols. L., 1780–83.

D

139   LEVESQUE, PIERRE C. The History of Russia. (Trans. from French by J. Newman.) Vol. 1. Hull, 1789.
Rare work cited in 4.

140   TOOKE, WILLIAM. History of Russia from the Foundation of the Monarchy by Rurik to the Accession of Catharine the Second. 2 vols. L., 1800.

141   CARD, HENRY. The History of the Revolutions of Russia to the Accession of Catharine the First ... L., 1803. Pp. xii, 708. 2nd ed. L., 1804. Pp. xvi, 674.

142   CLAUSEN, HEINRICH. F. C. Characteristic Anecdotes from the History of Russia ... (Trans. from French.) L., 1805. Pp. xv, 207.
The original work was written in German.

143   A NEW HISTORY OF THE RUSSIAN EMPIRE and the Burning of ... Moscow, on the Approach of Bonaparte ... Sept., 1812. Falkirk, 1813. Pp. 24.

144   ANDERSON, WILLIAM. Sketches of the History and Present State of the Russian Empire ... L., 1815. Pp. xii, 439.

145   HUNTER, C. G. Russia : Being a Complete Picture of that Empire ... with the History of Russia ... from the Earliest Period to the Present Time ... L., 1817. Pp. 389.

146   SÉGUR, PHILLIPPE P. de, *Count*. History of Russia and of Peter the Great. L., 1829. Pp. xxxix, 447.

147   WILLCOCKS, T. History of Russia from the Foundation of the Empire by Rurik to the Present Time. Devonport, 1832. Pp. 543.

148   BELL, ROBERT. A History of Russia. 3 vols. (Lardner's Cabinet Cyclopaedia : History.) L., 1836–8.

149   CORNER, JULIA. The History of Poland and Russia from the Earliest Period to the Present Time ... L., c. 1840. Pp. 257.

150   GILBERT, LINNEY. Russia Illustrated : an Historical and Descriptive Account of that Immense Empire. L., 1844.
Rare work cited in 4.

151   FOWLER, GEORGE. Lives of the Sovereigns of Russia. Vol. 1. L., 1852. Vols. 1–2. L., 1858.
No more published. The volume published in 1852 was to be the first of a projected four-volume work. Later withdrawn, it was replaced by two volumes of a projected three-volume work in 1858.

152   KELLY, WALTER K. The History of Russia from the Earliest Period to the Present Time. 2 vols. L., 1854–5.

153 RABBE, ALPHONSE *and* DUNCAN, JONATHAN. History of Russia from the Foundation of the Empire by Rourick to the Close of the Hungarian War. 2 vols. L., 1854.
Translated from the French of A. Rabbe and augmented by J. Duncan.

154 FRISWELL, JAMES H. The Russian Empire: its History and Present Condition of its People. L., 1854. Pp. xii, 266.

155 RUSSIA THE LAND OF THE CZAR: a Sketch ... of the Muscovite Empire from 862 to 1854 ... (Trans. from German.) L., 1854. Pp. 93.

156 MILNER, THOMAS. Russia: its Rise and Progress, Tragedies and Revolutions. L., 1856. Pp. xv, 500.

157 KRASIŃSKI, HENRYK, *Count.* Private Anecdotes of the Late and Present Emperors of Russia ... L., 1858. Another Edition, L., 1874. Pp. viii, 96.

158 GRAHAME, F. R. The Archer and the Steppe; or, The Empires of Scythia: a History of Russia and Tartary from the Earliest Ages till the Fall of the Mongol Power in Europe in the Middle of the Sixteenth Century. L., 1860. Pp. 479.

159 TREVOR, GEORGE. Russia, Ancient and Modern. L., 1862. Pp. xii, 416.

160 ACKLAND, JOSEPH. Russia: a Review of her History and of her Economic Condition. L., 1878. Pp. 63.

161 RAMBAUD, ALFRED N. The History of Russia ... (Trans. from French.) 2 vols. L., 1879, Boston, Mass., 1879–82. Other Editions: 3 vols. L., 1886; 3 vols. N.Y., 1905.

162 LANKENAU, H. VON *and* OELNITZ, L. Russia, Past and Present. Adapted from the German by Henrietta M. Chester. L., 1881. Pp. viii, 434.

163 BENSON, M. E. The Story of Russia. L., 1885. Pp. viii, 268.

164 LITTLE, HENRY W. A Short History of Russia. L., 1885. Pp. 112.

165 SHEARWOOD, JOSEPH A. A Short History of Russia. L., 1888. Pp. 123, iv.

166 EDWARDS, H. S. The Romanoffs: Tsars of Moscow and Emperors of Russia. L., 1890. Pp. iv, 376.

167 MORFILL, WILLIAM R. Russia (The Story of the Nations,

vol. 23.) L., N.Y., 1890. Pp. xxi, 394. 6th ed. L., N.Y., 1904. Pp. xxiii, 416.

168 LEROY-BEAULIEU, ANATOLE. The Empire of the Tsars and the Russians. (Trans. from French.) 3 vols. N.Y., 1893–6. Reprinted 1902–5.

169 STERN, BERNHARD. The Private Life of the Romanoffs. (Trans. from German.) Washington, 1896. Pp. (320).

170 PARMELE, MARY P. A Short History of Russia. Flint, Mich., 1899. Pp. xii, 251.

171 LAWSON, BETTINA L. A Short Outline of the History of Russia. 2 vols. Edinburgh, 1900.
Not inspected personally.

172 MUNRO, HECTOR H. The Rise of the Russian Empire. L., 1900. Pp. xii, 334. Bibl.
Covers the early period to 1618.

173 RAPPOPORT, ANGELO S. Russian History. L., 1905. Pp. 155.

174 DUMAS, ALEXANDRE. Celebrated Crimes of the Russian Court. (Trans. from French.) L., 1906. Pp. xxiv, 321.

175 PARES, *Sir* BERNARD. Russia and Reform. L., 1907. Pp. xiv, 576.
Topical arrangement.

176 GASIOROWSKY, WACŁAW. Tragic Russia. (Trans. from Polish.) L., 1908. Pp. xiv, 288.

177 KLYUCHEVSKI, VASILI O. A History of Russia. (Trans. from Russian by C. J. Hogarth.) 5 vols. L., N.Y., 1911–31. Reprinted N.Y., 1960.
The classic Russian work in a notoriously bad translation. See also **432**.

178 BARING, MAURICE. The Russian People. L., 1911. Pp. xix, 366.

179 WINTER, NEVIN O. The Russian Empire of Today and Yesterday . . . L., 1914. Pp. xvi, 487. Bibl.

180 WALLACE, DONALD M., *and others*. A Short History of Russia and the Balkan States. L., 1914. Pp. (iv, 186).
Reproduced from the 11th ed. of *Encyclopaedia Britannica*.

181 HOWE, SONIA E. A Thousand Years of Russian History. L., 1915. Pp. viii, 432.

182 CAZALET, LUCY. A Short History of Russia. O., 1915. Pp. 88.

183 BEAZLEY, Sir CHARLES R., *and others*. Russia from the

Varangians to the Bolsheviks. O., 1918. Pp. xxiv, 601.

184 MacCabe, Joseph. The Romance of the Romanoffs. N.Y., 1917; L., 1918. Pp. (xiv, 391).

185 Saltus, Edgar E. The Imperial Orgy: an Account of the Tsars . . . N.Y., 1920. Pp. (237).

186 Hewitt, Norah. The Rulers of Russia. L., 1924. Pp. 356.

187 Platonov, Sergey F. A History of Russia. (Trans. from Russian.) L., N.Y., 1925. Pp. vii, 435.
Emphasizes early Russian history.

188 Pares, Sir Bernard. A History of Russia. L., N.Y., 1926. Pp. xxiii, 558. Bibl. Other Editions and Reprints, L., N.Y., 1928, 1937, 1944, 1947, 1949, 1953, 1958 and 1960. Also Pbk. (Methuens Univ. Pbks.)
Standard British textbook with straightforward chronological arrangement. Successive editions have been characterized chiefly by additional text to cover the most recent developments in Soviet history.

189 Mirsky, Dmitry S., Prince. A History of Russia. L., 1927. Pp. 79.

190 Vernadsky, George V. A History of Russia. Yale U.P., 1929. Pp. xix, 397. Bibl. Other Editions: 1930, 1944, 1951, 1954; 5th ed. 1961. Pp. 512. Also Pbk.
Rev.: V. Minorsky in SEER, vol. 23, 1945, pp. 159–161.

191 Bryanchaninov, Aleksandr N. (Brianchaninov). A History of Russia. (Trans. from French by C. J. Hogarth.) L., N.Y., 1930. Pp. viii, 295.

192 Pokrovski, Mikhail N. History of Russia from the Earliest Times to the Rise of Commercial Capitalism. (Trans. from Russian by J. D. Clarkson and M.R.M. Griffiths.) L., N.Y., 1931. Pp. xvi, 383.
An early Marxist work. This English translation is a considerable abridgement of the original which ran to 5 volumes.

193 Eckardt, Hans von (Eckhardt). Russia. (Trans. from German.) L., N.Y., 1932. Pp. xxix, 711, vii.

194 Pokrovski, Mikhail N. Brief History of Russia. (Trans. from Russian.) 2 vols. L., 1933.
cf. 192; volume 1 has been described as a "frankly political tract"— volume 2 is a translation of the 5th volume of the History etc.

195 Box, Pelham H. Russia. L., 1933. Pp. x, 150.

196 Spector, Ivar. Russia: a New History. Seattle, 1934. Pp. (viii, 129). Bibl. Another Edition: Portland, Or., 1935. Pp. xvi, 222.

197 SHESTAKOV, A. V., *ed*. A Short History of the U.S.S.R.: Textbook for 3rd and 4th Classes. Moscow, 1938. Pp. 257.

198 TOMPKINS, STUART R. Russia through the Ages, from the Scythians to the Soviets. N.Y., 1940. Pp. xxi, 799. Bibl.

199 GERHARDI, WILLIAM. The Romanovs ... L., 1940. Pp. 542.

200 KERNER, ROBERT J. The Urge to the Sea: the Course of Russian History: the Role of Rivers, Portages, Ostrogs, Monasteries and Furs. U. of California P., 1942. Pp. xvii, 212.
> Rev.: Stuart R. Tompkins in *Rus R*, vol. 2, no. 1, 1942–43, pp. 119–121.

201 VERNADSKY, GEORGE V. *and* KARPOVICH, M. A History of Russia. Vol. 1– Yale U.P., 1943–
> In progress. When completed will provide the most comprehensive treatment of Russian history in English. 4 volumes, all by Vernadsky, have been written to date (i.e.—1967). These have been given separate entries in the Bibliography but are listed here for convenience, viz.: 1. *Ancient Russia*. 1943. 2. *Kievan Russia*. 1948. 3. *The Mongols and Russia*. 1953. 4. *Russia at the Dawn of the Modern Age*. 1959. For further details, see: **243**, **284**, **322** and **334**. See also **74**.

202 OBOLENSKY, DIMITRI. 'Professor Vernadsky's History of Ancient and Medieval Russia', *OSP*, vol. 5, 1954, pp. 20–31.

203 SUMNER, BENEDICT H. A Short History of Russia. N.Y. 1943. Pp. (469).
> Rev.: Michael Karpovich in *SEER*, vol. 22, no. 3, pp. 135–136.

204 PRICE, MORGAN P. Russia through the Centuries ... L., 1943. Pp. 136.

205 THOMSON, JOAN (*Mrs*. Joan Charnock). The Making of Russia. O.U.P., 1943. Pp. viii, 132.

206 SUMNER, BENEDICT H. Survey of Russian History. L., 1944. 2nd ed. L., 1947. Pp. 506. Bibl. Also Pbk. (Methuen's Univ. Pbks.)
> Topical arrangement.

207 SEGAL, LOUIS. Russia: a Concise History from the Foundation of the State to Hitler's Invasion. L., 1944. Pp. 262.

208 PANKRATOVA, A. M., *ed*. A History of the U.S.S.R.

Compiled by K. V. Bazilevich and Others. (Trans. from Russian.) 3 vols. Moscow, 1947–8.
Soviet textbook.

209 PRATT, HELEN G. *and* MOORE, HARRIET L. Russia: a Short History. N.Y., 1947. Pp. 282; L., 1948. Pp. 224.

210 KIRCHNER, WALTHER. An Outline History of Russia. N.Y., 1948. Pp. viii, 326. Bibl. 2nd ed. N.Y., 1950. Pp. viii, 329. Bibl. Another Edition, Entitled: A History of Russia. N.Y., 1955. Pp. 329. Bibl.
Rev.: D. F. White in *ASEER*, vol. 8, 1949, pp. 65–67.

211 CROWSON, PAUL. A History of the Russian People. L., N.Y., 1948. Pp. xiv, 225. Bibl.

212 THOMSON, JOAN (*Mrs.* Joan Charnock). Russia: the Old and the New. L., 1948. Pp. vii, 195.

213 SPECTOR, IVAR. An Introduction to Russian History and Culture. N.Y., 1949. Pp. xxi, 454. Bibl. 2nd ed. N.Y., 1954. Pp. xxii, 477. Bibl. 3rd ed. Princeton, 1961. Pp. 506. Bibl. 4th ed. Princeton, 1965. Pp. xxviii, 529. Bibl.
Rev.: Valentine T. Bill in *Rus R*, vol. 9, 1950, pp. 161–162.

214 SEEGER, ELIZABETH. Pageant of Russian History. N.Y., 1950. Pp. (x, 433).
Rev.: Donald W. Treadgold in *Rus R*, vol. 10, 1951, pp. 317–319.

215 MAZOUR, ANATOLE G. Russia: Past and Present. N.Y., 1951. Pp. viii, 785.
Rev.: Thomas T. Hammond in *ASEER*, vol. 11, 1952, pp. 312–313; C. E. Black in *Rus R*, vol. 11, 1952, pp. 252–254.

216 HARCAVE, SIDNEY S. Russia: a History. Chicago, 1952. Pp. xiii, 665, xxxiv; L., 1954. Pp. xv, 668, xxiv. Other Editions: Philadelphia, 1953, 1956. 4th ed. Chicago, Philadelphia, 1959. Pp. 701. Bibl.
Rev.: C. E. Black in *ASEER*, vol. 14, 1955, pp. 127–128; Donald W. Treadgold in *Rus R*, vol 12, 1953, pp. 54–56.

217 FLORINSKY, MICHAEL T. Russia: a History and an Interpretation. 2 vols. N.Y., 1953. Bibl.
Rev.: N. Andreyev in *SEER*, vol. 34, 1955–56, pp. 528–532; Anatole G. Mazour in *ASEER*, vol. 13, 1954, pp. 432–435; V. A. Riasanovsky in *Rus R*, vol. 14, 1955, pp. 60–65.

218 MARTOVYCH, OLEH R., *pseud.* Eight Hundred Years of Russia's March to World Conquest. Edinburgh, 1953. Pp. (26).

219 JONES, DORSEY D. Russia: a Concise History. Harrisburg, Pa., 1955. Pp. (377).

220 CHARQUES, RICHARD D. A Short History of Russia. L., 1956. Pp. 232; N.Y., 1956. Pp. 284. 2nd ed. L., 1962, Pp. 232.
Rev.: Ralph T. Fisher in *Rus R*, vol. 16, no. 4, 1957, pp. 76–77; S. J. Zyzniewski in *ASEER*, vol. 17, 1958, pp. 352–353.

221 SETHE, PAUL. A Short History of Russia. (Trans. from German.) N.Y., 1956, Chicago, 1957. Pp. (192).

222 LAWRENCE, JOHN W. Russia in the Making. L., 1957. Pp. 335. Bibl.

223 WREN, MELVIN C. The Course of Russian History. N.Y., 1958. Pp. xiii, 725. 2nd ed. N.Y., 1963. Pp. xvii, 779.
Rev.: J. L. H. Keep in *SEER*, vol. 38, 1959–60, pp. 250–252.

224 KOSLOW, JULES. The Kremlin: Eight Centuries of Tyranny and Terror. N.Y., 1958. Pp. vii, 244. Bibl.
Rev.: R. H. McNeal in *ASEER*, vol. 18, 1959, p. 254.

225 KARAMZIN, NIKOLAY M. Karamzin's Memoir on Ancient and Modern Russia... Translated and Edited by Richard Pipes. Harvard U.P., 1959. Pp. xiv, 266. Bibl. Also Pbk. (Atheneum Pbks. Trans-Atlantic Book Service.)
Rev.: R. E. McGrew in *ASEER*, vol. 19, 1960, pp. 291–293; Donald W. Treadgold in *Rus R*, vol. 19, 1960, pp. 207–209.

226 LAWRENCE, JOHN W. A History of Russia. N.Y., 1960. Pp. 372. Also Pbk ed. N.Y., 1961.

227 KOSLOW, JULES. The Kremlin: Symbol of Russia. L., 1960. Pp. 222. Bibl.
A general history written around the Kremlin and its art treasures.

228 MAZOUR, ANATOLE G. Rise and Fall of the Romanovs. Princeton, N.J., 1960. Pp. 189. Bibl. (Pbk., Anvil Originals.)

229 CLARKSON, JESSE D. A History of Russia from the Ninth Century. N.Y., 1961. Pp. xx, 857. Bibl. L., 1962. Pp. xii, 974. Bibl.
Rev.: A. Lobanov-Rostovsky in *Slavic Rev*, vol. 21, 1962, pp. 343–344; John S. Curtiss in *Rus R*, vol. 21, 1962, pp. 84–85.

230 MAZOUR, ANATOLE G. Russia: Tsarist and Communist. Princeton, 1962. Pp. x, 995. Bibl.
Revised version of **215**. Rev.: Marc Raeff in *Slavic Rev*, vol. 21, 1962, pp. 737–738; J. L. H. Keep in *SEER*, vol. 41, 1962–63, pp. 562–563.

231 KOCHAN, LIONEL. The Making of Modern Russia. L., 1962. Pp. 320. Bibl. Baltimore, 1963. Pp. 335. Also Pbk.
Rev.: Jesse D. Clarkson in *Slavic Rev*, vol. 23, 1964, pp. 579–580.

232 RIASANOVSKY, NICHOLAS V. A History of Russia. N.Y., O.U.P., 1963. Pp. xviii, 711. Bibl.
Rev.: Serge A. Zenkovsky in *Rus R*, vol. 23, 1964, pp. 67–69; Michael T. Florinsky in *Slavic Rev*, vol. 22, 1963, pp. 753–754.

233 ALEXANDROV, VICTOR. The Kremlin: Nerve-Centre of Russian History. (Trans. from French.) L., 1963. Pp. 335.

234 ELLISON, HERBERT J. History of Russia. N.Y., 1964. Pp. x, 644. Bibl.

235 STURLEY, D. M. A Short History of Russia. L., 1964. Pp. ix, 310. Bibl.

236 A SHORT HISTORY OF THE U.S.S.R. (Trans. from Russian.) 2 vols. Moscow, 1965.
Modern Soviet textbook; translation of *Kratkaya istoriya SSSR*.

237 LAWRENCE, JOHN W. Russia. L., 1965. Pp. 88. Bibl. (Pbk. Methuen's Outlines.)

238 ALMEDINGEN, EDITH M. The Romanovs: Three Centuries of an Ill-Fated Dynasty. L., 1966. Pp. 333.

239 JONES, SHEILA. A Student's History of Russia. O., 1966. Pp. xii, 221. Bibl.

240 HOETZSCH, OTTO. The Evolution of Russia. (Trans. from German.) L., 1966. Pp. 214. Bibl. Also Pbk. (Library of Early Civilizations, Thames and Hudson.)

241 BARRAGY, TERENCE J. 'Romanovs or Pseudo-Romanovs?', *Ukr Rev* (L.), vol. 13, no. 3, 1966, pp. 27–39.

B. ANCIENT HISTORY, ORIGINS, EARLY INHABITANTS

Of the general works on ancient Russia, **243–248**, the best modern treatise is undoubtedly **243**; yet the older classics **246** and **250** retain much of their original value. No. **244** is a useful introduction to a complex field of study.

The Scythians are treated in **249–258**; Sarmations, **259–260**; Antae and Avars, **261–262**; Slav origins and early settlements, **263–269**; Khazars, **270–277** (see also **311** and **697**). Pechenegs and Polovtsy, **278–280**.

On the Slavs in general, see: **36, 47, 63, 79–80** and **107–127**. See also the section on archaeology (9).

242 DOMBROVSKY, ALEXANDER. 'Prehistory of Ukraine and

Russian Historiography', *Ukr Qly,* vol. 5, 1949, pp. 356–9.

243 VERNADSKY, GEORGE V. Ancient Russia. Yale U.P., 1943. Pp. xiv, 425. Bibl.
   Vol. 1 of **201**. Rev.: Richard N. Frye in *ASEER*, vol. 5, no. 1, 1946, pp. 212–221; V. Minorsky in *SEER*, vol. 23, 1945, pp. 155–157.

244 WREN, MELVIN C. Ancient Russia. L., 1965. Pp. 128. Bibl.

245 VERNADSKY, GEORGE. The Origins of Russia. O.U.P., 1959. Pp. xi, 354. Bibl.
   To be used with caution. See review of the French translation of this work by D. M. Lang in *SEER*, vol. 38, 1959–60, pp. 564–567. cf. **1519–1521**.

246 ROSTOVTZEFF, MIKHAIL I. (Rostovtsev). Iranians and Greeks in South Russia. O., 1922. Pp. xvi, 260. Bibl.

247 ROSTOVTZEFF, MIKHAIL I. (Rostovtsev). 'South Russia in the Prehistoric and Classical Period', *AHR,* vol. 26, 1920–21, pp. 203–24.

248 KALMYKOW, A. D. 'Iranians and Slavs in South Russia', *JAOS,* vol. 45, 1925, pp. 68–71.

249 RICE, *Mrs.* TAMARA TALBOT (Talbot-Rice). The Scythians. (Ancient Peoples and Places, vol. 2.) L., 1957. Pp. 255. Bibl. 2nd ed. L., N.Y., 1958. 3rd ed. L., N.Y., 1961.

250 MINNS, ELLIS H. Scythians and Greeks: a Survey of Ancient History and Archaeology on the North Coast of the Euxine from the Danube to the Caucasus. C.U.P., 1913. Pp. xl, 720. Bibl.

251 MINNS, ELLIS H. 'The Scythians and Northern Nomads', *CAH,* vol. 3, C.U.P., 1925, chapter 9, pp. 187–205; Bibl.: pp. 718–9.

252 McGOVERN, WILLIAM M. The Early Empires of Central Asia: a Study of the Scythians and the Huns and the Part they Played in World History . . . U. of North Carolina P., 1939. Pp. xiii, 529. Bibl.

253 DOMBROVSKY, ALEXANDER. 'The General Characteristics of the Scythia of Herodotus', *Proceedings of the Shevchenko Scientific Society, Historical-Philosophical Section,* vol. 1, 1951, pp. 48–55.

254 DOMBROVSKY, ALEXANDER. 'The Genesis of the Geographical Notion of Scythia in the Ancient World,' *AUA,* vol. 5, 1956, pp. 1178–87.

255 PINKERTON, JOHN. A Dissertation on the Origin and Progress of the Scythians or Goths ... L., 1787. Pp. xxii, 209.

256 JOHNSON, JAMES W. 'The Scythian: his Rise and Fall', *JHI*, vol. 20, 1959, pp. 250–7.

257 SULIMIRSKI, T. 'Scythian Antiquities in Western Asia', *AA*, vol. 17, 1954, pp. 282–318.

258 DOMBROVSKY, ALEXANDER. 'A Few Examples of Analogy in the Ancient Ukrainian and Judaic Cultures', *AUA*, vol. 7, 1959, pp. 1531–41.

259 HARMATTA, JOHN. Studies on the History of the Sarmatians. Budapest, 1950. Pp. 64.

> Reprinted from: *Études slaves et romaines*, vol. 2, 1949, pp. 13–45, and, *Folia ethnographica*, vol. 1, 1949, pp. 127–154.

260 ROSTOVTZEFF, MIKHAIL I. (Rostovtsev). 'The Sarmatae and Parthians', *CAH*, vol. 11, C.U.P., 1936, chapter 3, pp. 91–130; Bibl.: pp. 874–81.

261 VERNADSKY, GEORGE V, 'On the Origins of the Antae', *JAOS*, vol. 59, 1939, pp. 56–66.

262 BAYNES, NORMAN H. 'The Date of the Avar Surprise: a Chronological Study', *Byz. Zeit*, vol. 21, 1912, pp. 110–28.

263 CHARANIS, PETER. 'The Chronicle of Monemvasia and the Question of the Slavonic Settlements in Greece', *DOP*, no. 5, 1950, pp. 139–66.

264 PEISKER, T. 'The Expansion of the Slavs', *C Med H*, vol. 2, C.U.P., 1913, chapter 14, pp. 418–58; Bibl.: pp. 770–84.

265 ZABOROWSKI-MOINDRON, SIGISIMUND. 'The Origin of the Slavs', *Annual Report of the Smithsonian Institution*, 1906 (Washington, 1907), pp. 399–422.

266 CZEKANOWSKI, JAN. 'The Ancient Home of the Slavs', *SEER*, vol. 25, 1946–7, pp. 356–72.

267 SMAL–STOCKY, ROMAN. 'Vernadsky's Conception of the Origin of the Slavs', *Proceedings of the Shevchenko Scientific Society, Historical-Philosophical Section*, vol. 1, 1951, pp. 56–62.

268 SMAL-STOCKY, ROMAN. Slavs and Teutons: the Oldest Germanic-Slavic Relations. Milwaukee, 1950. Pp. x, 108.

269 RAPOPORT, SEMEN. 'On the Early Slavs: the Narrative of

Ibrahim-Ibn-Yakub. Commentary and Translation by S. Rapoport', *SEER,* vol. 8, 1929–30, pp. 331–41.

270   NEW YORK. *Public Library.* 'The Khazars: a Bibliography', *Bulletin of the New York Public Library,* vol. 42, 1938, pp. 695–710.

271   YARMOLINSKY, A., *comp.* 'Khazars: a Bibliography, 1940–1958', *Bulletin of the New York Public Library,* vol. 63, 1959, pp. (237–41).

272   WEINRYB, BERNARD, D., *comp.* 'The Khazars: an Annotated Bibliography', *Studies in Bibliography and Booklore* (Cincinnati), vol. 6, 1963, pp. (111–29).

273   WEINRYB, BERNARD D. 'Solving the "Khazar Problem": a Study in Soviet Historiography', *Judaism,* vol. 13, 1964, pp. (431–43).

274   DUNLOP, DOUGLAS M. The History of the Jewish Khazars. Princeton U.P., 1954. Pp. xv, 293. Bibl.
     Rev.: S. A. Birnbaum in *SEER,* vol. 35, 1956–57, pp. 340–341; Frederick I. Kaplan in *ASEER,* vol. 14, 1955, pp. 404–405, cf. **311**.

275   FRIEDMAN, PHILIP. 'The First Millenium of Jewish Settlement in the Ukraine and in the Adjacent Areas', *AUA,* vol. 7, 1959, pp. 1483–1516; Bibl.

276   SCHECHTER, S. 'An Unknown Khazar Document', *Jewish Quarterly Review,* New Series, vol. 3, 1912–3, pp. 181–219.

277   KAPLAN, FREDERICK I. 'The Decline of the Khazars and the Rise of the Varangians', *ASEER,* vol. 13, 1954, pp. 1–10.

278   MACARTNEY, C. A. 'The Petchenegs', *SEER,* vol. 8, 1929–30, pp. 342–55.

279   MENGES, K. H. 'Etymological Notes on some Päčänag Names', *Byzantion,* vol. 17, 1944–5, pp. 256–80.

280   BOSWELL, A. BRUCE. 'The Kipchak Turks', *SEER,* vol. 6, 1927–8, pp. 65–85.

C. KIEVAN PERIOD, FOUNDATION OF THE STATE, 864–1238

There is a substantial body of literature, including many scholarly texts, available in English on this period of Russian history. This is no doubt partly due to the controversies and disputes which have long been centred on Kiev Rus'. The two main points at issue concern the significance of the part played by the Vikings or Varangians in the foundation of the state, and secondly the respective claims of Muscovy and Ukraine to be considered its cultural heir. For the historiography of the latter question see **60–63** in the general section on historiography; for the former, **281–283**. General treatises by Western émigré scholars, **284–286**; Soviet scholars, **290–291**. Useful introductions provided by **287**, now available in a 1966 reprint, and a Soviet work, **292**. Foundation of the State, **293–294**; rôle of the Vikings, arranged by date, **299–309**. Special topics in chronological order, **312–317**. Background studies, **318–320**.

On foreign relations, see **537–542** and **692–698**; early military campaigns, **1570–1579**; law, **795–798**; social structure, **823–825**; economics, **853–858**; feudalism and agrarian history of the period, **877** *et seq.*; civilization and culture, **1120–1123**; early Byzantine influence, **1152**; religion, **1212** and **1228–1236**.

281 VUCINICH, ALEXANDER (Vukinich). 'The First Russian State: an Appraisal of the Soviet Theory', *Speculum*, vol. 28, 1953, pp. 324–34.

282 VUCINICH, ALEXANDER (Vukinich). 'The First Russian State' in **37**, chapter 5, pp. 123–42.

283 DERZHAVYN, VOLODYMYR. 'The History of the Rus', *Ukr Rev (L.)*, vol. 4, no. 2, 1957, pp. 24–31.
   A discussion of *Istoriya Rusov*.

284 VERNADSKY, GEORGE V. Kievan Russia, Yale U.P., 1948. Pp. xii, 412. Bibl.
   Vol. 2 of **201**. Rev.: Philip E. Mosely in *ASEER*, vol. 7, 1948, pp. 374–375; Nicholas P. Vakar in *Rus R*, vol. 8, 1949, pp. 168–170.

285 PASZKIEWICZ, HENRYK. The Origin of Russia. L., N.Y., 1954. Pp. xii, 556, Bibl.
   Rev.: C. B. O'Brien in *JCEA*, vol. 16, 1956, pp. 73–74; O. Halecki in *ASEER*, vol. 14, 1955, pp. 403–404; N. V. Riasanovsky in *Rus R*, vol. 15, 1956, pp. 134–136.

286 PASZKIEWICZ, HENRYK. The Making of the Russian Nation. L., 1963. Pp. 509. Bibl.
   Rev.: A. D. Stokes in *SEER*, vol. 43, 1964–65, pp. 446–450; Victor Terras in *Slavic Rev*, vol. 25, 1966, pp. 333–334.

287 CHADWICK, *Mrs. NORAH, née Kershaw*. The Beginnings of Russian History: an Enquiry into Sources. C.U.P., 1946, Pp. xi, 180. Reprinted 1966.

288 CHUBATY, NICHOLAS D. (Czubatyj). 'The Beginnings of Russian History', *Ukr Qly,* vol. 3, 1946–7, pp. (262 et seq.).

289 RALSTON, W. R. S. Early Russian History. (Ilchester Lectures, 1874.) L., 1874. Pp. iii, 236.

290 GREKOV, BORIS D. Kiev Rus. (Trans. from Russian by Y. Sdobnikov.) Moscow, 1959. Pp. 685.
> An important work by a leading Russian mediaevalist in a poor translation.

291 TIKHOMIROV, MIKHAIL N. The Towns of Ancient Rus. (Trans. from 2nd Russian ed. by Y. Sdobnikov.) Moscow, 1959. Pp. 503.
> Rev. (of original Russian work): G. Vernadsky in *ASEER,* vol. 7, 1948, pp. 189-190.

292 RYBAKOV, B. Early Centuries of Russian History. (Trans. from Russian.) Moscow, 1965. Pp. 231. (Pbk.)

293 ROSTOVTZEFF, MIKHAIL I. (Rostovtsev). 'The Origin of the Russian State on the Dnieper', *Annual Report of the American Historical Association,* 1920, pp. 163–71.

294 POLONSKA-WASYLENKO, NATALIA D. 'The Beginnings of the State of Ukraine-Rus' ', *Ukr Rev (L),* vol. 10, no. 2, 1963, pp. 33–58.

295 MINORSKY, VLADIMIR F. 'Rūs' in *Encyclopaedia of Islam,* vol. 3, Leiden, 1936, pp. 1181–3; Bibl.

296 FRYE, RICHARD N. 'Remarks on some New Islamic Sources of the Rūs', *Byzantion,* vol. 18, 1948, pp. 119–25.
> cf. **28**, **82** and **269**.

297 VERNADSKY, GEORGE V. 'The Origin of the Name Rus' ', *Südost-Forschungen,* vol. 15, 1956, pp. 167–79.
> cf. **60–63**.

298 SMAL-STOCKY, ROMAN. The Origin of the Word Rus'. (Slavistica, no. 6.) Winnipeg, 1949. Pp. 24.
> See note above.

299 RIASANOVSKY, NICHOLAS V. 'The Norman Theory of the Origin of the Russian State', *Rus R,* vol. 7, no. 1, 1947–8, pp. 96–110.

300 CLARKE, HYDE. The Warings or Waringhians in Germania, Britain, Russia, Byzantium and the East ... Constantinople, L., 1861. Pp. 147–66.
> Reprinted from the *Levant Quarterly Review.*

301 THOMSEN, VILHELM. The Relations between Ancient Russia and Scandinavia and the Origin of the Russian State ... (Ilchester Lectures, 1876.) O., 1877. Pp. vi, 150.

302 KENDRICK, Sir T. D. A History of the Vikings. L., N.Y., 1930. Pp. xi, 412. Bibl.
Chapter 5, pp. 143–178, discusses Viking activities in Russia.

303 KVÁLEN, EIVIND. The Early Norwegian Settlements on the Volga. Vienna, 1937. Pp. vi, 49.

304 TOMPKINS, STUART R. 'The Varangians in Russian History', in Cate, James L. and Anderson, Eugene N., ed. Medieval and Historiographical Essays in Honor of James Westfall Thompson. U. of Chicago P., 1938, pp. 465–90.

305 RAVNDAL, GABRIEL B. Stories of the East Vikings. Minneapolis, 1938. Pp. (383).

306 CROSS, SAMUEL H. 'The Scandinavian Infiltration into Early Russia', Speculum, vol. 21, 1946, pp. 505–14.

307 BELAIEV, N. T. 'Rorik of Jutland and Rorik of the Russian Chronicles', Saga Book of the Viking Society for Northern Research, vol. 10, 1928–9, pp. 267–97.

308 RIASANOVSKY, ALEXANDER V. 'The Embassy of 838 Revisited: Some Comments in Connection with a Normanist Source on Early Russian History', Jahrbücher für Geschichte Osteuropas, Neue Folge, vol. 10, 1962, pp. 1–12.

309 RIASANOVSKY, ALEXANDER V. ' "Runaway Slaves" and "Swift Danes" in Eleventh-Century Kiev', Speculum, vol. 39, 1964, pp. 288–97.

310 CLARKE, HYDE. 'On the Settlement of Britain and Russia by the English Races', Trans RHS, vol. 7, 1878, pp. 249–308.

311 BRUTZKUS, J. 'The Khazar Origin of Ancient Kiev', SEER, vol. 22, no. 1, 1944, pp. 108–24.
See also: 270–277.

312 ANDRUSIAK, MYKOLA. 'Kings of Kiev and Galicia ...', SEER, vol. 33, 1954–5, pp. 342–9.

313 POLONSKA-WASYLENKO, NATALIA D. 'The Princess Olha—First Christian Ruler of Ukraine, c. 945–c. 964', Ukr Rev (L.), vol. 2, no. 4, 1955, pp. 3–11.

314 The GREAT PRINCESS ST. OLGA: Thousandth Anniversary of Christianity in Ukraine. N.Y., 1955.

315 CROSS, SAMUEL H. 'Yaroslav the Wise in Norse Tradition', *Speculum,* vol. 4, 1929, pp. 177–97.

316 WRATISLAW, ALBERT H. 'Vladimir Monomachus: Grand Prince of Kyjev', *Trans RHS,* vol. 8, 1880, pp. 12–19.

317 NAZARKO, IRÉNÉE. 'Dobroniha: Daughter of St. Volodymyr the Great', *Études Slaves et Est-Européenes,* vol. 2, 1957, pp. 138–44.

318 VERNADSKY, GEORGE V. 'Lebedia: Studies on the Magyar Background of Kievan Russia', *Byzantion,* vol. 14, 1939, pp. 179–203.

319 RAST, N. A. 'Russians in the Medieval Iranian Epos', *ASEER,* vol. 14, 1955, pp. 260–4.

320 LANTZEFF, GEORGE V. 'Russian Eastward Expansion before the Mongol Invasion', *ASEER,* vol. 6, no. 2, 1947, pp. 1–10.
Advances into European Russia chiefly by the principalities of Novgorod and Rostov-Suzdal. On Russian expansion, see also **483, 1161, 1816, 1821** and **1829–1840.**

D. THE MONGOL INVASION AND THE RISE OF MUSCOVY, 1238–1598

Logically this class should be divided into two separate sections: the Mongol Period, 1238–1462 and the Rise of Muscovy, 1462–1598. However the scarcity of works in English on the Mongol period has called for the present marriage of convenience. Of the works which have been written, **321–329,** many are now outdated, and the only modern general work of importance, **322,** emphasizes Mongol history rather than Russian history in the Mongol period. Interesting sidelights on the relationships existing between conquerors and conquered are provided by **326** and **328.** Mongol history proper is classed in section 19E q.v.

The Rise of Muscovy, **330–362,** has received much fuller treatment. Historiography of the period, **330–331** and **343.** General works, **332–334**; of these, **333** is an excellent introduction to the subject, whilst **334** has been described as the most thorough study available in the English language. Of the biographies of Ivan the Great, **399** is a useful primer and **338** is especially strong on diplomacy and expansion. Ivan the Dread has attracted the attention of numerous biographers, whose zeal in some cases might have been better applied to the cause of literature. Of the more commendable works, **348** illustrates the sympathetic attitude to the subject which prevails in modern Soviet historiography, (see **343**); **351** and especially **352** are thoughtful and well balanced studies; **354** is a contemporary treatise written for political motives by an opponent of the Tsar, cf. **357–358**. Particular events, chiefly eye-witness accounts, arranged chronologically, **359–362**. For more general descriptive accounts written by contemporaries, see: **1908–1978**.

321 CURTIN, JEREMIAH. The Mongols in Russia. L., 1908. Pp. xx, 481.

322 VERNADSKY, GEORGE V. The Mongols and Russia. Yale U.P., 1953. Pp. xi, 462. Bibl.
> Vol. 3 of **201**. Rev.: Harold H. Fisher in *ASEER*, vol. 13, 1954, pp. 606–608; Marc Szeftel in *Rus R*, vol. 14, 1955, pp. 65–67.

323 MIRSKY, DMITRI S., *Prince*. 'Russia, 1015–1462', *C Med H*, vol. 7, C.U.P., 1932, chapter 21, pp. 599–631; Bibl.: pp. 932–6.

324 CHESHIRE, HAROLD T. 'The Great Tartar Invasion of Europe', *SEER*, vol. 5, 1926–7, pp. 89–105.

325 LAMB, HAROLD. The March of the Barbarians. L., 1941. Pp. 347. Bibl.

326 VOEGELIN, ERIC. 'The Mongol Orders of Submission to European Powers, 1245–1255', *Byzantion*, vol. 15, 1940–1, pp. 378–413.

327 FENNELL, JOHN L. I. 'The Tver Uprising of 1327: a Study of the Sources', *Jahrbücher für Geschichte Osteuropas*, Neue Folge, vol. 15, 1967, pp. (161–79).

328 ZDAN, MICHAEL B. 'The Dependence of the Halych-Volyn' Rus' on the Golden Horde', *SEER*, vol. 35, 1956–7, pp. 505–22.

329 ALEXANDER NEVSKY. Moscow, 1943. Pp. (14).

330 YARESH, LEO A., *pseud*. [A. Moskalenko]. 'The Formation of the Great Russian State' in **37**, chapter 7, pp. 198–223.

C

331 BACKUS, OSWALD P. 'Muscovite History in Recent Soviet Publications', *Slavic Rev,* vol. 20, 1961, pp. 517–22.

332 BURY, J. B. 'Russia, 1462–1682', *C Mod H,* vol. 5, C.U.P., 1908, chapter 16, pp. 477–517; Bibl.: pp. 861–71.

333 FENNELL, JOHN L. I. 'Russia, 1462–1583', *New C Mod H,* vol. 2, C.U.P., 1958, chapter 18, pp. 534–61.

334 VERNADSKY, GEORGE V. Russia at the Dawn of the Modern Age. Yale U.P., 1959; O.U.P., 1960. Pp. xii, 347. Bibl.
> Vol. 4 of **201**. Rev.: N. Andreyev in *SEER,* vol. 39, 1960–61, pp. 247–250; Oswald P. Backus in *Rus R,* vol. 19, 1960, pp. 289–290.

335 BILL, VALENTINE T. (Tschebotarioff-Bill). 'The Circular Frontier of Muscovy', *Rus R,* vol. 9, 1950, pp. 45–52.

336 FENNELL, JOHN L. I. 'The Dynastic Crisis, 1497–1502', *SEER,* vol. 39, 1960–1, pp. 1–23.

337 ANDREYEV, NIKOLAY. 'Interpolations in the 16th-Century Muscovite Chronicles', *SEER,* vol. 35, 1956–7, pp. 95–115.

338 FENNELL, JOHN L. I. Ivan the Great of Moscow. L., N.Y., 1961. Pp. xiv, 386. Bibl.
> Rev.: Gustave Alef in *Slavic Rev,* vol. 22, 1963, pp. 139–140; Nikolay Andreyev in *SEER,* vol. 41, 1962–63, pp. 556–558.

339 GREY, IAN. Ivan III and the Unification of Russia. (Teach Yourself History Library.) L., 1964. Pp. ix, 182.

340 ALEF, GUSTAVE. 'Reflections on the Boyar Duma in the Reign of Ivan III', *SEER,* vol. 45, 1967, pp. 76–123.

341 VERNADSKY, GEORGE V. 'The Heresy of the Judaisers and the Policies of Ivan III of Moscow', *Speculum,* vol. 8, 1933, pp. 436–54.

342 RABA, JOEL. 'The Fate of the Novgorodian Republic', *SEER,* vol. 45, 1967, pp. 307–23.

343 BOLSOVER, G. H. 'Ivan the Terrible in Russian Historiography', *Trans RHS,* series 5, vol. 7, 1957, pp. 71–89.

344 'A Briefe Treatise of the Great Duke of Moscovia, his Genealogie: Being Taken out of the Moscovites Manuscript Chronicles. Written by a Polacke' in **1872b**, vol. 2, pp. 182–94.

345 PEMBER, AUSTEN. Ivan the Terrible, his Life and Times. L., 1895. Pp. xii, 262.

346 WALISZEWSKI, KAZIMIERZ. Ivan the Terrible. (Trans. from French by Lady Mary Loyd.) Philadelphia, L., 1904. Pp. xiv, 431.

347 GRAHAM, STEPHEN. Ivan the Terrible: Life of Ivan IV of Russia . . . L., 1932. Pp. 319; Yale U.P., 1933. Pp. 335.

348 VIPPER, ROBERT YUR'EVICH. (Wipper). Ivan Grozny. (Trans. from Russian by J. Fineberg.) Moscow, 1947. Pp. 254. Bibl.
Sympathetic treatment by a modern Soviet historian.

349 LAMB, HAROLD. The March of Muscovy: Ivan the Terrible and the Growth of the Russian Empire, 1400–1648. N.Y., 1948. Pp. (vi, 309).

350 ECKHARDT, HANS VON (Eckhardt). Ivan the Terrible. (Trans. from German.) N.Y., 1949. Pp. (421, xi).
Rev.: Walther Kirchner in *Rus R*, vol. 9, 1950, pp. 162–165.

351 KOSLOW, JULES. Ivan the Terrible. L., 1961. Pp. 285; N.Y., 1962. Pp. 271.

352 GREY, IAN. Ivan the Terrible. L., 1964. Pp. xiii, 256. Bibl.
Rev.: William H. Chamberlin in *Rus R*, vol. 24, 1965, pp. 302–303.

353 NØRRETRANDERS, BJARNE. The Shaping of Tsardom under Ivan Groznyj. Copenhagen, 1964. Pp. (192).

354 KURBSKI, ANDREY M., *Prince*. Prince A. M. Kurbsky's History of Ivan IV. Edited [and Translated] by J. L. I. Fennell. C.U.P., 1965. Pp. xi, 314. Bibl.
Parallel Russian and English texts. Contemporary treatise biased against the Tsar. cf. **357**. Rev.: Walther Kirchner in *Slavic Rev*, vol. 25, 1966, pp. 691–692.

355 NØRRETRANDERS, BJARNE. 'Ivan Groznyj's Conception of Tsarist Authority', *Scandoslavica*, vol. 9, 1963, pp. 238–48.

356 YARESH, LEO A., *pseud*. [A. Moskalenko]. 'Ivan the Terrible and the Oprichnina' in **37**, chapter 8, pp. 224–41.

357 KURBSKI, ANDREY M., *Prince and* Ivan IV, *Emperor of Russia*. The Correspondence between Prince A. M. Kurbsky and Tsar Ivan IV of Russia. Edited and Translated from Russian by J. L. I. Fennell. C.U.P., 1955. Pp. xi, 275.
Parallel Russian and English texts. See also **354**. Rev.: C. E.

Black in *ASEER*, vol. 16, 1957, pp. 415–417; N. Andreyev in *SEER*, vol. 35, 1956–57, pp. 304–306.

358 ANDREYEV, NIKOLAY. 'Kurbsky's Letters to Vas'yan Muromtsev', *SEER*, vol. 33, 1954–5, pp. 414–36.

359 USCOMBE, RICHARD. 'A Letter . . . to M. Henrie Lane, Touching the Burning of the Citie of Mosco by the Crimme Tartar, Written . . . the 5. Day of August, 1571' in 1872b, vol. 3, pp. 169–70.

360 CULPEPPER, JACK M. 'The Kremlin Executions of 1575 and the Enthronement of Simeon Bakbulatovich', *Slavic Rev*, vol. 24, 1965, pp. 503–6.

361 HORSEY, JEROME. 'The Most Solemne and Magnificent Coronation of Pheodor Ivanowich, Emperour of Russia etc. the 10th of June in the Yere 1584, Seene and Observed by Master Jerom Horsey . . .' in 1872b, vol. 3, pp. 336–47. Also in 1873, vol. 14, pp. 114–25.

362 MERRICK, JOHN (Merick). 'A Branch of a Letter . . . Closed up in the Mosco the 14. of March Anno 1597 [i.e. 1598], Touching the Death of Pheodor Ivanowich Late Emperour of all Russia etc.' in 1872b, vol. 3, pp. 448–9.
cf. 577.

E. THE TIME OF TROUBLES, 1598–1613

This interesting and significant period of Russian history has excited curiously little response from modern Western historians. Of the few general treatises available, only 372 merits close attention. For a discussion of the circumstances surrounding the tsarevich's death, see 367–368. Amongst the relative wealth of source material available in English, 370 and 373 deserve special mention. For contemporary travel accounts relating to the period, see 1979–1988.

363 MANLEY, *Sir* ROGER. The Russian Impostor; or, The History of Muskovie under the Usurpation of Boris and The Imposture of Demetrius, Late Emperors of Muskovy. L., 1674. Pp. viii, 250.

364 LOEWENSON, LEO. 'Sir Roger Manley's History of

Muscovy: *The Russian Impostor,* 1647', *SEER,* vol. 31, 1952–3, pp. 232–40.

365 SAPIEHA, LEO. 'Leo Sapieha, Chancellor of Lithuania, on the Events of the Time of Troubles. [Three Speeches Edited by Professor Lyubavsky]', *Rus R (Liverpool),* vol. 3, no. 2, 1914, pp. 47–59.

366 GRAHAM, STEPHEN. Boris Godunov. L., Yale U.P., 1933. Pp. 269.

367 VERNADSKY, GEORGE V. 'The Death of the Tsarevich Dimitry: a Reconsideration of the Case', *OSP,* vol. 5, 1954, pp. 1–19.

368 NIKOLAIEFF, A. M. (Nikolaev). 'Boris Godunov and the Ouglich Tragedy', *Rus R,* vol. 9, 1950, pp. 275–85.

369 AFANASYEV, GEORGE. 'Boris Godunov and the First Pretender', *Rus R (Liverpool),* vol. 2, no. 4, 1913, pp. 31–53.

370 DMITRY THE PRETENDER (Yuri Otrepev). 'Letters and Documents' in **1873,** vol. 14, pp. 157–83.

371 MÉRIMÉE, PROSPER. Demetrius the Impostor: an Episode in Russian History. (Trans. from French by A. R. Scoble.) L., 1853. Pp. viii, 312. Bibl.
     Straightforward historical account.

372 BARBOUR, PHILIP L. Dimitry, Called the Pretender: Tsar and Great Prince of all Russia, 1605–1606. Boston, Mass., 1966, L., 1967. Pp. xxvii, 387. Bibl.
     Rev.: Gustave Alef in *Rus R,* vol. 26, 1967, pp. 303–305.

373 HOWE, SONIA E., *ed.* The False Dmitri: a Russian Romance and Tragedy, Described by British Eye Witnesses, 1604–1612. L., 1916. Pp. xvi, 239.
     A valuable work, containing: 1. Russell's *Reporte of a Bloudie and Terrible Massacre* . . . pp. 27–62; 2. *The Report of Capt. Gilbert of Dmitry's Bodyguard,* pp. 63–68; 3. Brereton's *Newes of the Present Miseries of Rushia* . . . pp. 69–150; 4. *Narrative of an Englishman Serving against Poland for Sweden,* pp. 151–183; and, 5. J.F.: *A Brief Historical Relation* . . . 1654, pp. 184–220. The full references for items 1, 3 and 5 may be found at **374, 1988** and **132.** Item 5 is abridged.

374 The REPORTE OF A BLOUDIE AND TERRIBLE MASSACRE IN THE CITTY OF MOSCO, with the Fearefull and Tragicall End of Demetrius the Last Duke before Him Raigning at this Present. (Trans. from Dutch by William Russell.) L.,

1607. Pp. 26. Also in **373**. Facsimile reprints: L., Berlin, 1854.

Report of a Dutch factor in Moscow translated by William Russell and frequently listed under his name in catalogues etc.

375 ŻÓŁKIEWSKI, STANISLAS. Expedition to Moscow: a Memoir. (Trans. from Polish.) L., 1959. Pp. ix, 167. Bibl.

A description of the invasion of Russia in 1610 by the commander of the Polish forces. Rev.: Oswald P. Backus in *Slavic Rev*, vol. 22, 1963, pp. 763–764.

F. SEVENTEENTH CENTURY, 1613–1689

General works on the period, **376–378**. Special topics and events, arranged chronologically, **379–389**. The rebellion of Sten'ka Razin, **383–386**. For an account of his life, see **1728**.

The latter part of the period is well covered by **387–389**. Relevant contemporary accounts, **1989–2013**.

376 BAIN, ROBERT N. The First Romanovs, 1613–1725: a History of Moscovite Civilisation and the Rise of Modern Russia under Peter the Great and his Forerunners. L., 1905. Pp. xii, 413.

377 PHILIPP, WERNER. 'Russia: the Beginning of Westernisation', *New C Mod H*, vol. 5, C.U.P., 1961, chapter 25, pp. 571–91.

378 MAZOUR, ANATOLE G. 'Curtains in the Past', *JMH*, vol. 20, 1948, pp. 212–22.

Russia's policy of self-isolation in the 17th century.

379 LYUBAVSKY, M. 'The Accession of the Romanovs: March 3, 1613 in the History of Russia', *Rus R (Liverpool)*, vol. 2, no. 1, 1913, pp. 11–31.

380 ALEXEYEV, BASIL. 'The Restoration of Order and the First Romanovs', *Rus R (Liverpool)*, vol. 2, no. 2, 1913, pp. 14–50.

381 KEEP, JOHN L. H. 'The Régime of Filaret, 1619–1633', *SEER*, vol. 38, 1959–60, pp. 334–60.

382 LOEWENSON, LEO. 'The Moscow Rising of 1648', *SEER*, vol. 27, 1948–9, pp. 146–56.

383 KONOVALOV, SERGEY. 'Razin's Execution: Two Contemporary Documents', *OSP*, vol. 12, 1965, pp. 94–8.

384 A NARRATIVE OF THE GREATEST VICTORY KNOWN IN THE MEMORY OF MAN: Being the Total Overthrow of the Great Rebel, Stepan Radzin. Written by an English Factor from the Port of Moscow. L., 1671.
   Rare work cited in **4**.

385 A RELATION CONCERNING THE PARTICULARS OF THE REBELLION LATELY RAISED IN MUSCOVY BY STEN'KA RAZIN ... L., 1672.

386 KONOVALOV, SERGEY. 'Ludwig Fabritius' Account of the Razin Rebellion', *OSP*, vol. 6, 1955, pp. 72–101.

387 SCHAKOVSKOY, ZINAIDA. Precursors of Peter the Great: the Reign of Tsar Alexis, Peter the Great's Father and the Young Peter's Struggle against the Regent Sophia for the Mastery of Russia. (Trans. from French.) L., 1964. Pp. 320. Bibl.
   Rev.: C. Bickford O'Brien in *Rus R*, vol. 24, 1965, pp. 189–190.

388 O'BRIEN, C. BICKFORD (Bickford O'Brien). Russia under Two Tsars, 1682–1689: the Regency of Sophia Alekseevna. (Univ. of California Publications in History, vol. 42.) U. of California P., 1952. Pp. xii, 178. Bibl.
   Rev.: David M. Lang in *ASEER*, vol. 12, 1953, pp. 263–266.

389 HAYES, *Mrs.* ALICE M. 'The Regent Sophia and the Tzarina Eudoxia', *Proceedings of the Anglo-Russian Literary Society*, no. 27, Feb.-Apr., 1900, pp. 41–55.

G. PETER THE GREAT, PERIOD OF REFORMS, 1689–1725

General surveys of the period aranged by date of publication, **390–396**; the best general introduction, **396**. Bibliography of Peter the Great, **398**. Historiography of the tsar and his reign, **399–400**.

The literature of the period is dominated by biographies of Peter, arranged by date, **401–434**. Of the older works, **403–404**, **418** and **422** are the most informative; the best recent studies are undoubtedly **430–431** and **433**, whilst **432** is a new and excellent translation from Klyuchevsky's classic work.

On the tsarevich Aleksey, **437–439**; Prince Menshikov, **440–441**.

For the economic aspects of the reign, see **867–868**; foreign relations, **546**—Peter's 'will', **533–536**; relations with England, **585–595** and **631**; with Poland, **707–710**; military campaigns, **1585–1591**; the emergent navy, **1610–1613**; the tsar's attitude to the Church, **1250** and **1282**. For relevant contemporary accounts, see: **2001–2002** and **2013–2032**.

390 VOLTAIRE, FRANÇOIS M. A. DE. The History of the Russian Empire under Peter the Great. (Trans. from French.) 2 vols. L., 1763. And other Editions, e.g. 2 vols. Berwick, [17—].

391 RAUMER, FRIEDRICK L. G. VON. 'Russia from 1704 to 1740. (Trans. from German)' in his *Contributions to Modern History*...L., 1837, pp. 421–68.

392 BANTYSH-KAMENSKI, DMITRI N. (Bantisch-Kamenski). Kamenski's Age of Peter the Great. (Trans. from Russian by I. Golovin.) L., 1851. Pp. viii, 272.

Collective biography of people living at the Court of Peter I.

393 BAIN, ROBERT N. The Pupils of Peter the Great: a History of the Russian Court and Empire from 1697 to 1740. L., 1897. Pp. xxiv, 318. Bibl.

394 BAIN, ROBERT N. 'Peter the Great and his Pupils, 1689–1730', *C Mod H*, vol. 5, C.U.P., 1908, chapter 17, pp. 518–57; Bibl.: pp. 872–5.

395 LAMB, HAROLD. The City and the Tsar: Peter the Great and the Move to the West, 1648–1762. N.Y., 1948. Pp. (x, 368). Reprinted 1954.

396 YOUNG, IAN. 'Russia [in the First Half of the Eighteenth Century]', *New C Mod H*, vol. 7, C.U.P., 1957, chapter 14, pp. 318–38.

397 ŠERECH, JURIJ. 'Stefan Yavorsky and the Conflict of Ideologies in the Age of Peter I', *SEER*, vol. 30, 1951–2, pp. 40–62.

cf. **1173**.

398 MINTSLOF, R., *comp.* (Mintzloff). Podrobny katalog inostrannykh sochineni o Rossii...v Imperatorskoy Publichnoy Biblioteke v S.–Peterburge. Tom 1: Petr Veliki v inostrannoy literature. St. Petersburg, 1872. Pp. x, 691.

Annotated catalogue of foreign works on Russia in the St. Petersburg Imperial Public Library. Vol. 1: Peter the Great in foreign literature.

399 BLACK, CYRIL E. 'The Reforms of Peter the Great' in 37, chapter 9, pp. 242–70.

400 McNALLY, RAYMOND T. 'Chaadaev's Evaluation of Peter the Great', *Slavic Rev.*, vol. 23, 1964, pp. 31–44.

401 DEFOE, DANIEL. An Impartial History of the Life and Actions of Peter Alexowitz, the Present Czar of Muscovy ... Written by a British Officer in the Service of the Czar. L., 1723. Pp. 420. 2nd ed., Entitled: A True, Authentick and Impartial History etc., L., 1725. Pp. 429.

402 THE NORTHERN WORTHIES; or, The Lives of Peter the Great ... and of his Illustrious Consort Catherine, the Late Czarina. (Trans. from French.) 2 pts. (in 1.) L., 1728. Pp. viii, 74, ii; 94, ii. 2nd ed. To which is Added an Account of the Short Reign and Death of Peter II and the Succession of the New Czarina. 2 pts. L., 1730.
Pt. 1 is entitled: *Memoirs of Peter I, Emperor of Russia.* By Bernard Le Bovier de Fontenelle. Pt. 2 entitled: *Memoirs of the Reign of Catherine.* By Jean Rousset.

403 MOTTLEY, JOHN. The History of the Life of Peter the First, Emperor of Russia ... L., 1739. Pp. 389. Also 3 vols. L., 1739; 3 vols. Dublin, 1740. 2nd ed. 3 vols. L., 1740.

404 BANKS, JOHN (Bancks). The History of the Life and Reign of the Czar Peter the Great ... L., 1740. Pp. 346, xiv. 2nd ed., Entitled: A New History of the Life etc. L., 1740. Pp. 354. 3rd ed. ditto, L., 1755. Pp. 354. Another ed. Montpelier, Vt., 1811. Pp. 316.

405 GORDON, ALEXANDER. The History of Peter the Great, Emperor of Russia. 2 vols. Aberdeen, 1755.

406 DILWORTH, W. H. The Father of his Country; or, The History of the Life and Glorious Exploits of Peter the Great, Czar of Muscovy ... L., 1758. Pp. 155. Another ed. L., 1760. Pp. 135.

407 STAEHLIN-STORCKSBURG, JAC. VON. Original Anecdotes of Peter the Great ... (Trans. from German.) L., 1788. Pp. ix, 448.

408 VOLTAIRE, FRANÇOIS M. A. DE. The History of Charles XII. To which are Prefixed Anecdotes of Peter the Great.

(Trans. from French by John J. Stockdale.) L., 1807. Pp. (522).

For a translation by Tobias Smollett, see **412–413**.

409 PILKINGTON, *Mrs.* MARY. Parental Care Producing Practical Virtue . . . With a Description of the Inhabitants of Russia and a Variety of Interesting Anecdotes of Peter the Great. L., 1810.

Rare work cited in **4**.

410 EVSTAFIEV, ALEKSEY G. (Alexis Eustaphieve). Reflections, Notes and Original Anecdotes Illustrating the Character of Peter the Great . . . Boston, Mass., 1812. Pp. 215. 2nd ed. 1814. Pp. 272.

411 ESCHERNY, FRANÇOIS L. d', *Count*. Anecdotes Hitherto Unpublished of the Private Life of Peter the Great. (Trans. from French.) L., 1813. Pp. 170.

412 VOLTAIRE, FRANÇOIS M. A. DE. The History of Charles the Twelfth and Peter the Great. (Trans. from French by Tobias Smollett.) L., 1817. Pp. xii, 632.

413 VOLTAIRE, FRANÇOIS M. A. DE. The History of Peter the Great, Emperor of Russia. (Trans. from French by Tobias Smollett.) L., 1836. Pp. 408. And other Editions.

For an earlier translation by J. J. Stockdale, see **408**.

414 BARROW, *Sir* JOHN. A Memoir of the Life of Peter the Great. L., 1832. Pp. xvi, 366. Other Editions: L. and N.Y., 1834, 1839 and 1845.

See also **418**.

415 BUNBURY, SELINA. Anecdotes of Peter the Great . . . L., 1843. Pp. 187.

416 BRADFORD, *Mrs.* SARAH E., *née Hopkins*. The History of Peter the Great, Czar of Russia. N.Y., 1858. Pp. (233).

417 ABBOTT, JACOB. History of Peter the Great, Emperor of Russia. L., 1860. Pp. iv, 232.

418 BARROW, *Sir* JOHN. The Life of Peter the Great. L., 1874. Pp. xvi, 414. Reprinted Edinburgh, 1883. Another Edition: N.Y., 1903. Pp. xv, 405.

See also **414**.

419 COBB, JAMES F. The Story of the Great Czar: a Sketch of the Life of Peter of Russia. L., c. 1875. Pp. 127.

420 MOTLEY, JOHN L. Peter the Great. L., N.Y., 1877. Pp. 106. Other Editions: L., 1887. Pp. 128; N.Y., 1893. Pp. 70.

421 SCHUYLER, EUGENE. Passages from the Life of Peter the Great. L., 1881. Pp. 128.

422 SCHUYLER, EUGENE. Peter the Great, Emperor of Russia : a Study of Historical Biography. 2 vols. L., N.Y., 1884.

423 WALISZEWSKI, KASIMIR. Peter the Great. (Trans. from French.) N.Y., 1897. Pp. x, 562. Also 2 vols., L., 1897. 2nd ed. L., 1898.

424 BROWNING, OSCAR. Peter the Great. L., 1898. Pp. viii, 347.

425 BIRKHEAD, ALICE. Peter the Great. L., 1915. Pp. 188.

426 GRAHAM, STEPHEN. Peter the Great: a Life of Peter I of Russia. L., 1929. Pp. xi, 376; N.Y., 1929. Pp. 339. 2nd ed. L., 1950. Pp. xi, 376.

427 OUDARD, GEORGES. Peter the Great. (Trans. from French.) N.Y., 1929. Pp. 386. Bibl.; L., 1930. Pp. 384. Bibl.

428 SHIRLEY, RALPH. 'Peter the Great', *Contemporary Review,* vol. 161, 1942, pp. 229–34.

429 BAKER, NINA B. Peter the Great. L., 1945. Pp. 272.

430 SUMNER, BENEDICT H. Peter the Great and the Emergence of Russia. L., 1950, N.Y., 1951. Pp. viii. 216.
Rev.: C. E. Black in *ASEER,* vol. 12, 1953, pp. 144–145.

431 GRUNWALD, CONSTANTIN DE. Peter the Great. (Trans. from French.) L., N.Y., 1956. Pp. 224.
Rev.: C. B. O'Brien in *ASEER,* vol. 16, 1957, pp. 91–92; Warren B. Walsh in *Rus R,* vol. 16, 1957, pp. 75-76.

432 KLYUCHEVSKI, VASILI O. Peter the Great. (Trans. from Russian by L. Archibald.) L., 1958, N.Y., 1959. Pp. vii, 282. (Pbk.)
An excellent translation from the 4th volume of his *Course of Russian History* (177), 1937 edition. Rev.: Albert Parry in *Slavic Rev,* vol. 22, 1963, pp. 140-141; J. L. H. Keep in *SEER,* vol. 38, 1959–60, pp. 254–255.

433 GREY, IAN. Peter the Great, Emperor of all Russia. Philadelphia, 1960, L., 1962. Pp. 505. Bibl.
Rev.: John S. Curtiss in *Rus R,* vol. 20, no. 2, 1961, pp. 157–158.

434 RAEFF, MARC, *ed.* Peter the Great: Reformer or Revolutionary? Boston, Mass., 1963. Pp. xviii, 109. Bibl. (Pbk.)
Selections from the writings of Russian historians in translation.

435 LE BOVIER DE FONTENELLE, BERNARD (Fontenelle). The Elogium of His Imperial Majesty, Peter I, Czar of Muscovy. (Trans. from French.) L., 1728. Pp. 46.

436   PLATON, *Metropolitan of Moscow* (Petr G. Levshin). A
      Sermon Preached by Order of Her Imperial Majesty
      on the Tomb of Peter the Great in the Cathedral
      Church of St. Petersbourg. (Trans. from Russian.) L.,
      1770. Another Edition, Entitled: An Oration etc. O.,
      1771.

437   VOGÜÉ, EUGÈNE M. DE, *Viscount*. A Czarevitch of the
      Eighteenth Century [i.e. Alexis, Son of Peter], and
      other Studies in Russian History. (Trans. from French.)
      L., 1913. Pp. 306.

438   MANIFESTO OF THE CRIMINAL PROCESS OF THE
      CZAREWITZ ALEXEI PETROWITZ . . . (Trans. from the
      French Translation of the Russian Original Printed by
      Order of the Czar at the Hague, 1718) in **2028**, vol. 2,
      pp. 93–206.

439   The TRYAL OF THE CZAREWITZ, ALEXIS PETROWITZ,
      Who Was Condemned at Petersburg on the 25th June,
      1718 . . . (Trans. from Russian.) L., 1725. Pp. 110.
        Collection of documents relating to his son's trial, published on
        the Tsar's instructions.

440   MEMOIRS OF THE LIFE OF PRINCE MENZIKOFF . . . in a
      Letter from a Foreign Minister at the Court of Russia.
      Dublin, 1727.

441   NIERITZ, KARL G. Alexander Menschikoff, the Founder
      of a Family. (Trans. from German.) Edinburgh, 1855.
      Pp. 126. Many other Editions under Various Titles, e.g.
      1865, 1894, and 1902.

H. EIGHTEENTH CENTURY, 1725–1800

None of the general works on the period, **442–445**, is satisfactory. The best introduction is a background study, **1129**.
Rulers of the first half of the 18th century, **446–454**. Recommended as an introduction to the second half, **455**. Memoirs
and writings of Catherine II, **459–463**; the best translations
of her *Memoirs* being **461–462**. Biographies of the empress,
464–489. Of these, particularly recommended are **477, 483,
486** and **489**. Contemporaries of Catherine, **491–501**. Works
on Radishchev, **504–524**. The closing years of the 18th century
are well covered in **525**. On Paul I, **526–529**.

Relevant material on the economic aspects of the period may be found at **869** and **873**. On foreign relations, arranged chronologically, **548–559**; Anglo-Russian relations, **596–612, 631–633** and **672–678**. Wars and campaigns, **1592–1603**; the Russian fleet, **1613–1617**. Contemporary accounts of 18th century travellers, **2022–2081**.

442 MORFILL, WILLIAM R. A History of Russia from the Birth of Peter the Great to the Death of Alexander II. L., 1902. Pp. viii, 486.

443 MOLLOY, JOSEPH F. The Russian Court in the Eighteenth Century. 2 vols. L., 1905.

444 POLYAKOV, V. (Poliakoff). When Lovers Ruled Russia. N.Y., L., 1928. Pp. 284.

445 HEARD, JAMES A. The Life and Times of Nathalia Borissovna, Princess Dolgorookov. L., 1857. Pp. xxiv, 260.

446 The NORTHERN HEROINE: Being Authentick Memoirs of the Late Czarina, Empress of Russia [i.e. Catherine I] ... L., 1727. Pp. 28.

447 ROUSSET, JEAN [Baron Ivan Nestesuranoi, *pseud.*] Memoirs of the Reign of Catherine, Empress of all Russia (=**402**, pt. 2). L., 1728. 2nd ed. L., 1730.

448 MOTTLEY, JOHN. The History of the Life and Reign of the Empress Catherine ... 2 vols. L., 1744.

449 KIRCHNER, WALTHER. 'The Death of Catherine I of Russia', *AHR*, vol. 51, 1945–6, pp. 254–61.

450 LIPSKI, ALEXANDER. 'A Re-examination of the "Dark Era" of Anna Ioannovna', *ASEER*, vol. 15, 1956, pp. 477–88.

451 LIPSKI, ALEXANDER. 'Some Aspects of Russia's Westernization during the Reign of Anna Ioannovna, 1730–1740', *ASEER*, vol. 18, 1959, pp. 1–11.

452 BAIN, ROBERT N. 'Russia under Anne and Elizabeth', *C Mod H*, vol. 6, C.U.P., 1909, chapter 10, pp. 301–28; Bibl.: pp. 889–91.

453 BAIN, ROBERT N. The Daughter of Peter the Great: a History of Russian Diplomacy and of the Russian Court under the Empress Elizabeth Petrovna, 1741–1762. L., 1899. Pp. xviii, 328. Bibl.

454 BAIN, ROBERT N. Peter III, Emperor of Russia. L., 1902. Pp. xvi, 208.

455 YOUNG, IAN. 'Russia [in the Second Half of the 18th Century]', *New C Mod H*, vol. 8, C.U.P., 1965, chapter 11, pp. 306–32.

456 TOOKE, WILLIAM. View of the Russian Empire during the Reign of Catherine the Second to the Close of the Present Century. 3 vols. L., 1799. 2nd ed. 3 vols. L., 1800. 3rd ed. 3 vols. Dublin, 1801.

457 TOOKE, WILLIAM. 'View of the Russian Empire' in **1878**, vol. 2, pp. 146–94.

458 RULHIÈRE, C. C. de. The History; or, Anecdotes of the Revolution in Russia in the Year 1762. (Trans. from French.) L., 1797. Pp. viii, 178.

459 CATHERINE II, *Empress of Russia*. Documents of Catherine the Great : the Correspondence with Voltaire and the Instruction of 1767 in the English Text of 1768. Edited by W. F. Reddaway. C.U.P., 1931. Pp. xxxii, 349.

460 CATHERINE II, *Empress of Russia*. Memoirs of the Empress Catherine II . . . (Trans. from French.) With a Preface by A. Herzen. L., 1859. Pp. xvi, 352.

461 CATHERINE II, *Empress of Russia*. Memoirs of Catherine the Great. Edited and Translated from French by K. Anthony. L., N.Y., 1927. Pp. ix, 337.

462 CATHERINE II, *Empress of Russia*. The Memoirs of Catherine the Great. Edited by D. Maroger. (Trans. from French by M. Budberg.) L., N.Y., 1955. Pp. 400.

463 CATHERINE II, *Empress of Russia*. The Memoirs of Catherine the Great. (Trans. from French by L. Bair.) With the Preface to the Edition of 1859 by A. Herzen. N.Y., 1957. Pp. x, 305. (Pbk.)

464 AUTHENTIC MEMOIRS OF THE LIFE AND REIGN OF CATHERINE II, Empress of all the Russias . . . L., 1797. Pp. 291.

465 CASTÉRA, JEAN H. The History of the Reigns of Peter III and Catharine II of Russia. (Trans. from French.) 2 vols. L., 1798.

466 CASTÉRA, JEAN H. The Life of Catherine II, Empress of Russia. (Trans. from French by W. Tooke.) 3 vols. L.,

1798. New Edition by W. W. Dakins. 2 vols. L., 1799. 3rd ed. 3 vols. L., 1799. 4th ed. 3 vols. L., 1800. 5th ed. by W. Tooke. 3 vols. Dublin, 1800.

467 CASTÉRA, JEAN H. History of Catherine II, Empress of Russia. (Trans. from French by H. Hunter.) L., 1800. Pp. 579.

468 SCHMUCKER, SAMUEL M. (Smucker). Memoirs of the Court and Reign of Catherine the Second, Empress of Russia . . . N.Y., 1855. Pp. (xiv, 338).

469 WALISZEWSKI, KASIMIR. The Romance of an Empress: Catherine II of Russia. (Trans. from French.) 2 vols. L., 1894–5.

470 WALISZEWSKI, KASIMIR. The Story of a Throne: Catherine II of Russia. (Trans. from French.) 2 vols. L., 1895.

471 MASSON, CHARLES F. P. Secret Memoirs of the Court of Petersburg, Particularly towards the End of the Reign of Catherine II and the Commencement of that of Paul I . . . (Trans. from French.) 2 vols. L., 1800. 2nd ed. 3 vols. (in 2.) L., 1801–2. Another Edition L., 1895. Pp. xv, 390.

472 MASSON, CHARLES F. P. Memoirs of Catherine II and the Court of St. Petersburg during her Reign and that of Paul I . . . (Trans. from French.) L., 1904. Pp. 353.

473 SERGEANT, PHILIP W. The Courtships of Catherine the Great. L., Philadelphia, 1905. Pp. x, 337. Reprinted L., 1910 and 1925.

474 HOETZSCH, OTTO. 'Catharine II', C Mod H, vol. 6, C.U.P., 1909, chapter 19, pp. 657–701; Bibl.: pp. 949–53.

475 GRIBBLE, FRANCIS H. The Comedy of Catherine the Great. L., N.Y., 1912. Pp. xix, 368.

476 HODGETTS, EDWARD A. B. The Life of Catherine the Great of Russia. L., 1914. Pp. ix, 335.

477 ANTHONY, KATHARINE S. Catherine the Great. N.Y., 1925. Pp. 331; L., 1926. Pp. 317. Reprinted N.Y., 1927.

478 MURAT, MARIE, Princess. The Private Life of Catherine the Great of Russia. (Trans. from French.) N.Y., 1928. Pp. 212.

479 QUIBERON, PAUL. Catherine the Great. L., 1934. Pp. 180.

480 KAUS, GINA. Catherine the Great. (Trans. from German.) L., 1935. Pp. 434. Another Edition, Entitled: Catherine: the Portrait of an Empress. N.Y., 1935. Pp. 384.

481 HYDE, HARFORD M. The Empress Catherine and Princess Dashkov. L., 1935. Pp. xi, 282.

482 DREIFUSS, JEROME. The Romance of Catherine and Potemkin. L., 1938. Pp. 256. Bibl.

483 THOMSON, GLADYS S. Catherine the Great and the Expansion of Russia. L., 1947. Pp. x, 294; N.Y., 1950. Pp. x, 294.
    Rev.: Leo Loewenson in SEER, vol. 27, 1948–49, pp. 618–622.

484 ARETZ, GERTRUDE K. The Empress Catherine. (Trans. from German.) L., 1947. Pp. 244.

485 GOOCH, GEORGE P. Catharine the Great and other Studies. L., N.Y., 1954. Pp. xi, 292.

486 GREY, IAN. Catherine the Great, Autocrat and Empress of all Russia. L., 1961, Philadelphia, 1962. Pp. 254. Bibl.
    Rev.: Hans Rogger in Slavic Rev, vol. 22, 1963, pp. 141–142; Allen McConnell in Rus R, vol. 21, 1962, pp. 385–386.

487 ALMEDINGEN, EDITH M. Catherine, Empress of Russia. N.Y., 1961. Pp. (312).

488 ALMEDINGEN, EDITH M. Catherine the Great: a Portrait. L., 1963. Pp. 240. Bibl.

489 OLDENBOURG, ZOÉ. Catherine the Great. (Trans. from French.) N.Y., 1965. Pp. xvii, 378. Bibl.
    Rev.: William H. Chamberlin in Rus R, vol. 24, 1965, pp. 418–419.

490 ODE TO HER IMPERIAL MAJESTY CATHERINE THE GREAT. Presented by the Chief National School at St. Petersburgh, on the Day of her ... Visit, January the 21st, 1785. (Trans. from Russian.) L., 1815. Pp. 27.

491 POLOVTSOFF, ALEXANDER. The Favourites of Catherine the Great. L., 1940. Pp. 288.

492 SOLOVEYTCHIK, GEORGE. Potemkin: a Picture of Catherine's Russia. L., 1938. Pp. 349. 2nd ed. L., 1949. Pp. 227. Another Edition, Entitled: Potemkin: Soldier, States-

man, Lover and Consort of Catherine of Russia. N.Y., 1947. Pp. 346.

Rev.: Robert V. Allan in *ASEER*, vol. 7, 1948, pp. 190–191.

493 MEMOIRS OF THE LIFE OF PRINCE POTEMKIN, Comprehending Original Anecdotes of Catherine the Second and of the Russian Court. (Trans. from German.) L., 1812. Pp. viii, 256. 2nd ed., Entitled: Memoirs of Prince Potemkin ... L., 1813. Pp. 270.

494 DASHKOVA, *Princess* EKATERINA R. Memoirs of the Princess Daschkaw, Lady of Honour to Catherine II ... (Trans. from French.) 2 vols. L., 1840.

495 DASHKOVA, *Princess* EKATERINA R. The Memoirs of Princess Dashkov. Translated and Edited by K. Fitzlyon. L., 1958. Pp. 322. Also Pbk. (Calder and Boyars Ltd.)

496 GOLOVINA, VARVARA N., *Countess*. Memoirs of Countess Golovine: a Lady at the Court of Catherine II. (Trans. from French.) L., 1910. Pp. xliii, 390.

497 LIGNE, CHARLES J., *Prince de*. The Prince de Ligne, his Memoirs, Letters and Miscellaneous Papers. (Trans. from French.) 2 vols. L., 1899.

The Prince de Ligne accompanied Catherine on her journey to the Crimea in 1787.

498 LIGNE, CHARLES J., *Prince de*. Letters and Memoirs ... (Trans. from French.) L., 1927. Pp. viii, 194.

Selected extracts.

499 BISCHOFF, ILSE. 'Madame Vigée Le Brun at the Court of Catherine the Great', *Rus R*, vol. 24, 1965, pp. 30–45.

500 HANS, NICHOLAS. 'François Pierre Pictet: Secretary to Catherine II', *SEER*, vol. 36, 1957–8, pp. 481–91.

Pictet was a friend of Voltaire.

501 CRESSON, WILLIAM P. Francis Dana: a Puritan Diplomat at the Court of Catherine the Great. N.Y., 1930. Pp. (397).

502 SUMNER, BENEDICT H. 'New Material on the Revolt of Pugachev. 2 pts.', *SEER*, vol. 7, 1928–9, pp. 113–27 and 338–48.

503 PETROVICH, MICHAEL B. 'Catherine II and a False Peter III in Montenegro', *ASEER*, vol. 14, 1955, pp. 169–94.

504 SHMURLO, E. 'Catherine II and Radishchev', *SEER,* vol. 17, 1938–9, pp. 618–22.

505 THALER, RODERICK P. 'Catherine II's Reaction to Radishchev', *Études Slaves et Est-Européenes,* vol. 2, 1957, pp. 154–60.

506 LANG, DAVID M. 'Radishchev and Catherine II: New Gleanings from Old Archives' in Curtiss, John S., *ed. Essays in Russian and Soviet History in Honor of G. T. Robinson,* Leiden, 1963, pp. 20–33.

507 MCCONNELL, ALLEN. 'The Empress and her Protégé: Catherine II and Radishchev', *JMH,* vol. 36, 1964, pp. 14–27.
Attacks Catherine's treatment of Radishchev. For a defence of her position, see **504**.

508 RADISHCHEV, ALEKSANDR N. A Journey from St. Petersburg to Moscow. (Trans. from Russian by L. Wiener. Edited by R. P. Thaler.) Harvard U.P., O.U.P., 1958. Pp. xiv, 286. Bibl.
Rev.: Allen McConnell in *ASEER,* vol. 19, 1960, pp. 108–109; David M. Lang in *SEER,* vol. 37, 1958–59, pp. 516–518.

509 MCCONNELL, ALLEN. 'Soviet Images of Radiščev's Journey from St. Petersburg to Moscow', *SEEJ,* vol. 7, 1963, pp. 9–17; Bibl.

510 EVGENIEV, BORIS. Alexander Radishchev: a Russian Humanist of the Eighteenth Century. L., 1946. Pp. 52.

511 LANG, DAVID M. The First Russian Radical: Alexander Radishchev, 1749–1802. L., 1959, N.Y., 1960. Pp. 298. Bibl.
Rev.: Roderick P. Thaler in *Slavic Rev,* vol. 22, 1963, pp. 561–562; R. Hare in *SEER,* vol. 38, 1959–60, pp. 592–593.

512 MCCONNELL, ALLEN. A Russian Philosophe: Alexander Radischchev, 1749–1802. The Hague, 1964. Pp. xii, 228. Bibl.
Rev.: Roderick P. Thaler in *Slavic Rev,* vol. 24, 1965, pp. 724–725; Louis J. Shein in *Rus R,* vol. 24, 1965, pp. 416–417.

513 CLARDY, JESSE V. The Philosophical Ideas of Alexander Radishchev. L., N.Y., 1964. Pp. 155. Bibl.

514 HECHT, DAVID. 'Alexander Radishchev: Pioneer Russian Abolitionist', *American Review on the Soviet Union,* vol. 7, no. 4, 1946, pp. 45–50.

515 LASERSON, MAX M. 'Alexander Radishchev—an Early

Admirer of America', *Rus R*, vol. 9, 1950, pp. 179–86.

516 CLARDY, JESSE V. 'Radishchev's Notes on the Geography of Siberia', *Rus R*, vol. 21, 1962, pp. 362–9.

517 McCONNELL, ALLEN. 'Radishchev's Political Thought', *ASEER*, vol. 17, 1958, pp. 439–53.

518 LANG, DAVID M. 'Some Western Sources of Radiščev's Political Thought', *Revue des Études Slaves*, vol. 25, 1949, pp. 73–86.

519 LANG, DAVID M. 'Sterne and Radishchev: an Episode in Russian Sentimentalism', *Revue de Littérature Comparée*, vol. 21, 1947, pp. 254–60.

520 BECK, L. N. 'Pennsylvania and an Early Russian Radical [Aleksandr Radishchev]', *Pennsylvania Magazine of History and Biography*, vol. 75, 1951, pp. 193–6.

521 McCONNELL, ALLEN. 'Rousseau and Radiščev', *SEEJ*, vol. 8, 1964, pp. 253–72; Bibl.

522 McCONNELL, ALLEN. 'Abbé Raynal and a Russian Philosophe [i.e. Radishchev]', *Jahrbücher für Geschichte Osteuropas*, Neue Folge, vol. 12, 1964, pp. 499–512.

523 THALER, RODERICK P. 'Radiščev, Britain and America', *HSS*, vol. 4, 1957, pp. 59–75.

524 LANG, DAVID M. 'Radishchev and the Legislative Commission of Alexander I', *ASEER*, vol. 6, no. 2, 1947, pp. 11–24.

525 VYVYAN, J. M. K. 'Russia, 1789–1825', *New C Mod H*, vol. 9, C.U.P., 1965, chapter 18, pp. 495–524.

526 RAPPOPORT, ANGELO S. The Curse of the Romanovs: a Study of the Lives and the Reigns of Two Tsars, Paul I and Alexander I of Russia, 1754–1825. L., 1907. Pp. xxiv, 424. Bibl.

527 WALISZEWSKI, KASIMIR. Paul the First of Russia: the Son of Catherine the Great. (Trans. from French.) L., 1913. Pp. 496.

528 ALMEDINGEN, EDITH M. So Dark a Stream: a Study of the Emperor Paul I of Russia, 1754–1801. L., 1959. Pp. 240.

529 GRANT, *Mrs.* COLQUHOUN. A Mother of Czars: a Sketch of the Life of Marie Fedorowna, Wife of Paul I and Mother of Alexander I and Nicholas I. L., 1905. Pp. xii, 292.

6

DIPLOMATIC AND FOREIGN
RELATIONS

General surveys, **530–532**; of these, **530**, though somewhat dated, is the most thorough study of the subject. Peter the Great's supposed will, **533–536**.

Foreign relations of Kiev Rus', **537–542**; Muscovy, **543–545** (see also **335** and **338–339**); 18th century relations, **546–559** (cf. **430** and **483**). On the partitions of Poland, **551–558** (see also **601–602**).

Related material is contained in the sections on economic history (8B) and military history (17), q.v. For works on the eastward expansion of Russia, see **320**, **483**, **1161** and **1829–1840**; on the question of Russian imperialism, **1158–1160**.

530 VERNADSKY, GEORGE V. Political and Diplomatic History of Russia. Boston, Mass., 1936, L., 1937. Pp. ix, 499. Bibl.

531 SETON–WATSON, ROBERT W. 'Main Currents in Russian Foreign Policy', *Trans RHS*, 4th Series, vol. 29, 1947, pp. 167–86.

532 SENN, ALFRED E., *comp.* Readings in Russian Political and Diplomatic History. 2 vols. Homewood, Ill., 1966.

533 PETER I, *the Great, supposed author.* Peter the Great's Last Will and Testament ... Southsea, 1876. Pp. 17. Other Editions with Varying Titles, e.g. L., 1896, 1920. Also in **152**.

> Ascribed to Peter the Great, and purporting to list the aims of Russian foreign policy which he recommended to his heirs. Almost certainly a forgery, see **535–536**.

534 NELL, LOUIS. Peter's Will: a Pamphlet ... Colombo, 1856. Pp. viii, 68.

> Text and commentary.

535 LOCKHART, LAURENCE. 'The "Political Testament" of Peter the Great', *SEER*, vol. 14, 1935–6, pp. 438–41.

536 LEHOVICH, DIMITRY V. 'The Testament of Peter the Great', *ASEER*, vol. 7, 1948, pp. 111–24.

537 DOMBROWSKY, ALEXANDER. 'The Economic Relations of Ukraine and the Ancient World', *Ukr Qly*, vol. 6, 1950, pp. 352–8.
  cf. **856**.

538 CROSS, SAMUEL H. 'Mediaeval Russian Contacts with the West', *Speculum*, vol. 10, 1935, pp. 137–44.

539 DVORNIK, FRANCIS. 'The Kiev State and its Relations with Western Europe', *Trans RHS*, 4th Series, vol. 29, 1947, pp. 27–46.

540 HALICH, VASYL. 'Ukraine and Medieval Trade', *Ukr Qly*, vol. 3, 1946–7, pp. 377–84.
  cf. **856**.

541 POLONSKA–WASYLENKO, NATALIA D. Ukraine-Rus' and Western Europe in 10th–13th Centuries. L., 1964. Pp. 47.

542 KIPARSKY, VALENTIN. 'The Earliest Contacts of the Russians with the Finns and Balts', *OSP*, vol. 3, 1952, pp. 57–79.

543 WESTERGAARD, WALDEMAR. 'Denmark, Russia, and the Swedish Revolution, 1480–1503', *SEER*, vol. 16, 1937–8, pp. 129–40.

544 KIRCHNER, WALTHER. 'Russia and Europe in the Age of the Reformation', *Archiv für Reformationsgeschichte*, vol. 43, 1952, pp. 172–86.

545 LEWITTER, L. R. 'Poland, the Ukraine and Russia in the 17th Century. 2 pts.', *SEER*, vol. 27, 1948–9, pp. 157–71 and 414–29.

546 The NORTHERN CRISIS; or, Reflections on the Policies of the Czar . . . L., 1716. Pp. 28. 2nd ed., Entitled: The Northern Crisis; or, Impartial Reflections etc. L., 1716. Pp. 28.
  Ascribed to Count Carl Gyllenborg.

547 A SHORT NARRATIVE OF THE LIFE AND DEATH OF JOHN RHINHOLDT, COUNT PATKUL . . . (Trans. from German by L[ord] M[olesworth.]) L., 1717. Pp. 59. 2nd ed. L., 1717. Pp. 59. 3rd ed. L., 1738. Pp. 46. Another Edition, Entitled: Anecdotes Concerning the Famous John Reinhold Patkul . . . L., 1761. Pp. 48.

548 PIERCE, RICHARD A. 'Source Materials on a Project for Russian Colonization in South America, 1735–1737', *CSS,* vol. 1, 1960, pp. 182–96.

549 LODGE, *Sir* RICHARD. 'Russia, Prussia and Great Britain, 1742–4', *EHR,* vol. 45, 1930, pp. 579–611.

550 SCHMIDT, KNUD R. 'Problems Connected with the Last Polish Royal Election: a Study in the Development of Count Panin's Northern System', *Scandoslavica,* vol. 2, 1956, pp. 134–48.

551 EVERSLEY, GEORGE J. SHAW-LEFEVRE, *1st baron.* The Partitions of Poland. L., 1915. Pp. 328.

552 HALECKI, OSCAR. 'Why was Poland Partitioned?', *Slavic Rev.,* vol. 22, 1963, pp. 432–41.

553 LEWITTER, L. R. 'The Partitions of Poland', *New C Mod H,* vol. 8, C.U.P., 1965, chapter 12, pp. 333–59.

554 KAPLAN, HERBERT H. The First Partition of Poland. Columbia U.P., L., 1962. Pp. xvi, 215. Bibl.
    Rev.: Oswald P. Backus in *Slavic Rev,* vol. 22, 1963, pp. 764–765; P. Skwarczyński in *SEER,* vol. 42, 1963–64, pp. 221–225.

555 PADOVER, S. K. 'Prince Kaunitz and the First Partition of Poland', *SEER,* vol. 13, 1934–5, pp. 384–98.

556 LORD, ROBERT H. The Second Partition of Poland: a Study in Diplomatic History. (Harvard Historical Studies, vol. 23.) Harvard U.P., 1915. Pp. xxx, 586. Bibl.

557 An AUTHENTIC NARRATIVE OF FACTS RELATIVE TO THE LATE DISMEMBERMENT OF POLAND. L., 1794. Pp. ii, 42.

558 LORD, ROBERT H. 'The Third Partition of Poland', *SEER,* vol. 3, 1924–5, pp. 481–98.

559 ANDERSON, MATTHEW S. 'The Great Powers and the Russian Annexation of the Crimea, 1783–4', *SEER,* vol. 37, 1958–9, pp. 17–41.

B. ANGLO-RUSSIAN RELATIONS

(i) General and Chronological

The English were particularly active in Russia in the latter half of the 16th century, following the landing of Richard Chancellor in 1553. The new alliance was welcomed by the sovereigns of both countries; to the one it offered a new and extensive market with the prospect of a trade route to the

East, whilst to Ivan IV it seemed to offer important political advantages. Communication between the two countries was mainly by the North Cape route until the opening of Narva and St. Petersburg in the early 18th century. The 17th century was marked by a decline in the activities of the English merchants in Russia, who were largely replaced by the Dutch. Close contact was resumed in the following century but was not confined as previously to England and Russia alone.

There is a wealth of material, including many primary sources, available in English on Anglo-Russian relations. Outstanding work in this field has been done by Lubimenko, Loewenson, Anderson and Konovalov. Of the general works, **561–565,** the best introduction to the subject is **561,** which is both readable and scholarly. On the activities of the English in Russia in the 16th century, **566–573;** the 17th century, **574–583.** From the reign of Peter the Great to the end of the period, **584–612.** Peter's reign itself, **585–595;** his visit to England, **587–590.** Anglo-Ukrainian relations, **1730–1733.** See also section 20B for contemporary accounts of English travellers and residents in Russia. On Britain and the Russian Navy, see **1605, 1613– 1614** and **1616–1617.** See also **1303** on English physicians at the Court of Moscow.

560 HARVEY, ELIZABETH A. 'The Norman Conquest of England and its Connections with Old Ukraine', *Ukr Rev* (L.), vol. 13, no. 4, 1966, pp. 33–53.

561 ANDERSON, MATTHEW S. Britain's Discovery of Russia, 1553–1815. L., N.Y., 1958. Pp. viii, 245.
   Rev.: G. H. N. Seton-Watson in *SEER*, vol. 38, 1959–60, pp. 252–253; Andrew Lossky in *Rus R*, vol. 19, 1960, pp. 78–80.

562 GREAT BRITAIN—U.S.S.R.: an Historical Exhibition Organized by the British Foreign Office and the Soviet Ministry of Foreign Affairs ... Victoria and Albert Museum, February 9 to April 2, 1967. L., 1967. Pp. 32.

563 LOBANOV-ROSTOVSKY, A. 'Anglo-Russian Relations through the Centuries', *Rus R,* vol. 7, no. 2, 1947–8, pp. 41–52.

564 WEINER, ABRAHAM, *comp.* Select Passages Illustrating Commercial and Diplomatic Relations between England and Russia. L., 1920. Pp. 76. Bibl.

565 MILYUKOV, PAUL N. 'The Influence of English Political Thought in Russia', *SEER*, vol. 5, 1926–7, pp. 258–70.

566 TOLSTOY, YURI V., *comp.* (George Tolstoy). The First Forty Years of Intercourse between England and Russia, 1553–1593 : Documents ... St. Petersburg, 1875. Pp. 441, xv.
> Texts in English and Russian.

567 LUBIMENKO, INNA. 'The First Relations of England with Russia', *Rus R (Liverpool)*, vol. 3, no. 1, 1914, pp. 54–73.

568 LUBIMENKO, INNA. 'England's Part in the Discovery of Russia', *SEER*, vol. 6, 1927–8, pp. 104–18.

569 YAKOBSON, S. 'Early Anglo-Russian Relations, 1553–1613', *SEER*, vol. 13, 1934–5, pp. 597–610.

570 BOGUSHEV-BOGUSHEVSKI, NIKOLAY K., *baron* (Bogoushevsky) (Nicholas Casimir). 'The English in Muscovy during the 16th Century', *Trans RHS*, vol. 7, 1878, pp. 58–129.

571 WRETTS-SMITH, MILDRED. 'The English in Russia during the Second Half of the Sixteenth Century', *Trans RHS*, 4th Series, vol. 3, 1920, pp. 72–102.

572 'A Discourse of the Honourable Receiving into England of the First Ambassador [Ossip Nepea] from the Emperor of Russia in the Yeere ... 1556 ...', in **1872b**, vol. 2, pp. 350–62.

573 LANE, HENRY. 'A Letter ... Concerning the First Ambassage to our Most Gracious Queene Elizabeth from the Russian Emperour, Anno 1567 ...' in **1872b**, vol. 3, pp. 98–100.

574 ANDERSON, MATTHEW S. 'English Views of Russia in the 17th Century', *SEER*, vol. 33, 1954–5, pp. 140–60.

575 LOEWENSON, LEO. 'Escaped Russian Slaves in England in the 17th Century', *SEER*, vol. 42, 1963–4, pp 427–9.
> cf. **845**.

576 LUBIMENKO, INNA. A Project for the Acquisition of Russia by James I', *EHR*, vol. 29, 1914, pp. 246–56.

577 GEBLER, B. A. 'John Merrick in Russia', *Proceedings of the Anglo-Russian Literary Society*, no. 28, May-Jul., 1900, pp. 103–13.
> cf. **362**.

578 KONOVALOV, SERGEY. 'Anglo-Russian Relations, 1617–18', *OSP,* vol. 1, 1950, pp. 64–103.

579 KONOVALOV, SERGEY. 'Anglo-Russian Relations, 1620–4', *OSP,* vol. 4, 1953, pp. 71–131.

580 LUBIMENKO, INNA. 'Anglo-Russian Relations during the First English Revolution', *Trans RHS,* 4th Series, vol. 11, 1928, pp. 39–60.

581 LOEWENSON, LEO. 'Did Russia Intervene after the Execution of Charles I...?', *Bulletin of the Institute of Historical Research,* vol. 18, 1940–1, pp. 13–20.

582 KONOVALOV, SERGEY. 'England and Russia: Three Embassies, 1662–5', *OSP,* vol. 10, 1962, pp. 60–104.

583 KONOVALOV, SERGEY. 'Patrick Gordon's Dispatches from Russia, 1667', *OSP,* vol. 11, 1964, pp. 8–16.
Includes the texts of 7 letters. See also: 2001–2002.

584 MARRIOTT, *Sir* John A. R. Anglo-Russian Relations, 1689–1943. L., 1944. Pp. viii, 227.

585 ANDERSON, MATTHEW S. 'English Views of Russia in the Age of Peter the Great', *ASEER,* vol. 13, 1954, pp. 200–14.

586 LOEWENSON, LEO. 'The First Interviews between Peter I and William III in 1697: some Neglected English Material', *SEER,* vol. 36, 1957–8, pp. 189–94.

587 LOEWENSON, LEO. 'Some Details of Peter the Great's Stay in England in 1698: Neglected English Material', *SEER,* vol. 40, 1961–2, pp. 431–43.

588 GREY, IAN. 'Peter the Great in England', *History Today,* vol. 6, 1956, pp. 225–34.

589 LOEWENSON, LEO. 'People Peter the Great Met in England: Moses Stringer, Chymist and Physician', *SEER,* vol. 37, 1958–9, pp. 459–68.

590 A CONGRATULATORY POEM TO THE CZAR OF MUSCOVY ON HIS ARRIVAL IN ENGLAND. L., 1698.
Perhaps by Moses Stringer, see **589** above.

591 BRUCE, MAURICE. 'Jacobite Relations with Peter the Great', *SEER,* vol. 14, 1935–6, pp. 343–62.

592 CHANCE, J. F. 'George I and Peter the Great after the Peace of Nystad', *EHR,* vol. 26, 1911, pp. 278–309.

593 TRUTH IS BUT TRUTH AS IT IS TIMED; or, Our Ministry's Present Measures against the Muscovite Vindicated

by Plain and Obvious Reasons ... From a Representation ... by N. N. on his Return ... from the Court of Muscovy in August 1715. L., 1719. Pp. 9. Also in: Boyer, A. *The Political State of Great Britain,* vol. 18, 1719, pp. 160–75.

594 A MEMORIAL PRESENTED TO THE KING OF GREAT-BRITAIN BY M. WESSELOFSKI, the Czar's Resident at London, on the 14th of December, 1719. L., 1720. Pp. 51.

595 The MEMORIAL OF M. BESTUCHEV, His Czarish Majesties Resident in London, Presented Oct. 17, 1720 to the Court of Great Britain ... L., 1721. Pp. 43.

596 LODGE, *Sir* RICHARD. 'The First Anglo-Russian Treaty, 1739–42', *EHR,* vol. 43, 1928, pp. 354–75.

597 LODGE, *Sir* RICHARD. 'Lord Hyndford's Embassy to Russia, 1744–9. 2 pts.', *EHR,* vol. 46, 1931, pp. 48–76 and 389–422.

598 LODGE, *Sir* RICHARD. 'An Episode in Anglo-Russian Relations during the War of the Austrian Succession', *Trans RHS,* 4th Series, vol. 9, 1926, pp. 63–83.

599 REDDAWAY, W. F. 'Macartney in Russia, 1765–67', *CHJ,* vol. 3, 1929–31, pp. 260–94.
    cf. **2051**.

600 ANDERSON, MATTHEW S. 'Great Britain and the Russo-Turkish War of 1768–1774', *EHR,* vol. 69, 1954, pp. 39–58.

601 HORN, D. B. British Public Opinion and the First Partition of Poland. Edinburgh, L., 1945. Pp. viii, 98.
    Rev.: Oscar Halecki in *ASEER,* vol. 4, nos. 3–4, 1945, pp. 205–207.

602 KONOPCZYNSKI, W. 'England and the First Partition of Poland', *JCEA,* vol. 8, 1948–9, pp. 1–23.

603 BLUE, GEORGE V. 'A Rumor of an Anglo-Russian Raid on Japan, 1776', *Pacific Historical Review,* vol. 8, 1939, pp. 453–63.

604 MADARIAGA, ISABEL DE (De Madariaga) (*Mrs. I.* Schapiro). 'The Use of British Secret Funds at St. Petersburg, 1777–1782', *SEER,* vol. 32, 1953–4, pp. 464–74.

605 MADARIAGA, ISABEL DE (De Madariaga) (*Mrs. I.* Schapiro). Britain, Russia and the Armed Neutrality of 1780: Sir James Harris's Mission to St. Petersburg dur-

ing the American Revolution. L., Yale U.P., 1962. Pp.
xiv, 496. Bibl.

Rev.: Robert P. Browder in *Rus R*, vol. 22, 1963, pp. 318–319;
Andrew Lossky in *Slavic Rev*, vol. 22, 1963, pp. 142–144. See
also **2062**.

606 HUMPHREYS, R. A. 'Richard Oswald's Plan for an
English and Russian Attack on Spanish America',
Hispanic American Historical Review, vol. 18, 1938, pp.
95–101.

607 STRUVE, GLEB. 'John Paradise—Friend of Doctor Johnson, American Citizen and Russian Agent . . .', *Virginia
Magazine of History and Biography*, vol. 57, 1949,
pp. 355–75.

608 An ADDRESS TO THE PEOPLE OF ENGLAND upon the
Subject of the Intended War with Russia. L., 1791.
Pp. 55.

609 SERIOUS ENQUIRIES INTO THE MOTIVES AND CONSE-
QUENCES OF OUR PRESENT ARMAMENT AGAINST RUSSIA.
L., 1791. Pp. 60.

See **711**, p. 65 on the authorship of this work.

610 FOX, CHARLES J. 'Speech on Mr. Whitbread's Motions
on the Russian Armament, March 1, 1792', in his:
Speeches in the House of Commons, L., 1848, pp. 428–
56.

611 PIECHOWIAK, A. B. 'The Anglo-Russian Expedition to
Holland in 1799', *SEER*, vol. 41, 1962–3, pp. 182–95.

612 BRIDGE, W. CYPRIAN. 'Our Russian Guests in 1799–
1800', *Proceedings of the Anglo-Russian Literary Society*,
no. 29, Oct.—Dec., 1900, pp. 102–8.

(ii) Diplomatic Correspondence

Entries are arranged chronologically. Much of the earlier
material in this section is to be found in Richard Hakluyt's
collection of voyages and travels. Letters of the 16th century,
613–626; 17th century, **627–630**; 18th century, **631–633**. See
also **566**.

613 IVAN IV, *the Dread, Emperor of Russia*. 'The Copie of
the Duke of Muscovie and Emperour of Russia his Letters
Sent to King Edward the Sixt, by the Hands of Richard

Chancelour', in **1872b**, vol. 2, pp. 271–2. Also in **1873**, vol. 11, pp. 621–3.

614 MARY I, *Queen of England*. 'The Letters of King Philip and Queene Marie to Ivan Vasilivich the Emperour of Russia, Written the 1st of April, 1555 and in the Second Voyage', in **1872b**, vol. 2, pp. 278–81.

615 LUBIMENKO, INNA. 'The Correspondence of Queen Elizabeth with the Russian Czars', *AHR*, vol. 19, 1913–4, pp. 525–42.

616 LUBIMENKO, INNA. 'A Suggestion for the Publication of the Correspondence of Queen Elizabeth with the Russian Czars', *Trans RHS*, 3rd Series, vol. 9, 1915, pp. 111–22.

617 ELIZABETH I, *Queen of England*. 'A Letter Sent . . . to the Sayd Great Duke of Russia [i.e. Ivan IV] . . . 19. June 1583', in **1872b**, vol. 3, pp. 312–4.

618 ELIZABETH I, *Queen of England*. 'A Copie of the Commission given to Sir Jerome Bowes, Authorizing him Her Majesties Ambassadour unto the Emperor of Russia, Anno 1583', in **1872b**, vol. 3, pp. 308–11.

619 GODUNOV, BORIS. 'The Lord Boris Pheodorowich his Letter to the Rt. Hon. William Burghley Lord High Treasurer of England etc. [1590]', in **1872b**, vol. 3, pp. 419–22.

620 ELIZABETH I, *Queen of England*. 'The Queenes Majesties Letter to Theodore Ivanovich, Emperour of Russia, 1591', in **1872b**, vol. 3, pp. 422–7.

621 ELIZABETH I, *Queen of England*. 'The Queenes Majesties Letters to the Lord Boris Pheodorowich [1591]', in **1872b**, vol. 3, pp. 428–30.

622 BURGHLEY, WILLIAM CECIL, *Lord*. '[Letter] to the Right Honourable . . . the Lord Boris Pheodorowich . . . [1591]', in **1872b**, vol. 3, pp. 430–2.

623 FEDOR I, *Emperor of Russia* (Theodore I). 'A Letter from the Emperour of Russia, Theodore Ivanovich to the Queenes Majestie [1592]', in **1872b**, vol. 3, pp. 432–4.

624 GODUNOV, BORIS. '[Letter] to the Queenes Most Excellent Majestie from the Lord Boris Pheodorovich Godonova [1592]', in **1872b**, vol. 3, pp. 434–6.

625 GODUNOV, BORIS. 'A Letter . . . to the Right Honourable

Lord William Burghley, Lord High Treasurer of England [1592]', in **1872b**, vol. 3, pp. 436–8.

626 EVANS, NORMAN, *comp.* 'Queen Elizabeth I and Tsar Boris: Five Letters, 1597–1603', *OSP,* vol. 12, 1965, pp. 49–68.

627 LUBIMENKO, INNA. 'Letters Illustrating the Relations of England and Russia in the Seventeenth Century', *EHR,* vol. 32, 1917, pp. 92–103.

628 LUBIMENKO, INNA. 'The Correspondence of the First Stuarts with the First Romanovs', *Trans RHS,* 4th Series, vol. 1, 1918, pp. 77–91.

629 KONOVALOV, SERGEY. 'Two Documents Concerning Anglo-Russian Relations in the Early Seventeenth Century: *a.* John Tradescant's Diary of a Voyage to Russia in 1618, *b.* Letter of Tsar Mikhail to King James I, 17 June 1621', *OSP,* vol. 2, 1951, pp. 128–44.
See also **1990**.

630 KONOVALOV, SERGEY. 'Seven Letters of Tsar Mikhail to King Charles I, 1634–8', *OSP,* vol. 9, 1960, pp. 32–63.

631 D'ARCY COLLYER, *Mrs.* ADELAIDE. 'Notes on the Diplomatic Correspondence between England and Russia in the First Half of the Eighteenth Century', *Trans RHS,* New Series, vol. 14, 1900, pp. 143–74.

632 CATHERINE II, *Empress of Russia.* Correspondence of Catherine the Great ... with Sir Charles Hanbury-Williams, and Letters from Count Poniatowski. Edited and Translated by the Earl of Ilchester and Mrs. Langford-Brooke. L., 1928. Pp. 288.

633 BUCKINGHAMSHIRE, JOHN HOBART, *2nd Earl.* The Despatches and Correspondence of John, Second Earl of Buckinghamshire, Ambassador to the Court of Catherine II of Russia, 1762–1765. Edited by Adelaide D'Arcy Collyer. (Royal Historical Society Publications. Camden 3rd Series, vols. 2–3.) 2 vols. L., 1900–2.

(iii) Commercial, the Russia Company

None of the general works listed here, **634–638**, adequately covers the whole period. The best general introduction is **561**. Works on the Russia Company, including source material, **639–**

658, 669 and **671–672.** Of these **639** is the standard work on the subject. On 17th–century trade relations, **660–671**; of these **660** is a useful introduction, the remainder are chiefly in the form of contemporary commercial tracts. On the 18th century, **672–679.** See also **2044.**

634 VENEVITINOFF, N. N. (Venevitinov). 'The Development of Russia's Commercial Relations with Western Europe and Especially with Great Britain', *Proceedings of the Anglo-Russian Literary Society,* no. 19, Oct.–Dec., 1897, pp. 5–24.

635 SHIPPARD, *Sir* SIDNEY. 'Anglo-Russian Commerce', *Proceedings of the Anglo-Russian Literary Society,* no. 25, May-July, 1899, pp. 64–87.

636 MEYENDORFF, A. F. 'Anglo-Russian Trade in the 16th Century', *SEER,* vol. 25, 1946–7, pp. 109–21.

637 WILLAN, THOMAS S. 'Trade between England and Russia in the Second Half of the Sixteenth Century', *EHR,* vol. 63, 1948, pp. 307–21.

638 STUDIES IN THE HISTORY OF ENGLISH COMMERCE IN THE TUDOR PERIOD. N.Y., 1912. Pp. xi, 344. Bibl.

639 WILLAN, THOMAS S. The Early History of the Russia Company, 1553–1603. Manchester U.P., 1956. Pp. ix, 295.

640 PAGE, WILLIAM S. The Russia Company from 1553 to 1660. Hull, L., 1912. Pp. 196.

641 GERSON, ARMAND J. 'The Organization and Early History of the Muscovy Company' in **638**, pp. 1–122.

642 CAWSTON, GEORGE *and* KEANE, A. H. The Early Chartered Companies, A.D. 1296–1858. L., N.Y., 1896. Pp. xi, 329.
Russia Company, chapter 4, pp. 32–59.

643 WILLAN, THOMAS S. The Muscovy Merchants of 1555. Manchester U.P., 1953. Pp. viii, 141.

644 'The Charter of the Marchants of Russia, Graunted by King Philipe and Queen Marie [1555]', in **1872b,** vol. 2, pp. 304–16.

645 'The Commission Given to the Merchants Agents Resiant in Russia [1555]', in **1872b,** vol. 2, pp. 281–9.

646 IVAN IV, *the Dread, Emperor of Russia.* 'A Copie of

the First Privileges Graunted . . . to the English Marchants in the Yeere 1555', in **1872b,** vol. 2, pp. 297–303.

647 KILLINGWORTH, GEORGE. 'The Letter of . . . the Companies First Agent . . . 1555, the 27 of Nov. in Mosco', in **1872b,** vol. 2, pp. 291–7.

648 RUSSIA COMPANY. 'A Letter of the Company of the Marchants Adventurers to Russia unto George Killingworth, Richard Gray and Henry Lane, their Agents Here', in **1872b,** vol. 2, pp. 379–92.

649 WILLAN, THOMAS S. 'The Russia Company and Narva, 1558–81', *SEER,* vol. 31, 1952–3, pp. 405–19.

650 RUSSIA COMPANY. 'A Letter . . . to their Agents in Russia, Master Henrie Lane, Christopher Hudson and Thomas Glover . . . the Fifth of May, 1560', in **1872b,** vol. 2, pp. 401–10.

651 ENGLAND. *Laws, Statutes etc. (Elizabeth I).* 'An Act for the Corporation of Merchants Adventurers for the Discovering of New Trades . . . Anno 1566', in **1872b,** vol. 3, pp. 83–91.

652 IVAN IV, *the Dread, Emperor of Russia.* 'The Priviledges Graunted by the Emperour of Russia to the English Merchants of that Company. Obtained the 22. of Sept., Anno 1567 by M. Anthony Jenkinson', in **1872b,** vol. 3, pp. 92–7.

653 IVAN IV, *the Dread, Emperor of Russia.* 'A Copie of the Priviledges Granted . . . unto the . . . English Merchants for the Discoverie of New Trades . . . in the Yere . . . 1569', in **1872b,** vol. 3, pp. 108–19.

654 HUDSON, CHRISTOPHER *and* BURROUGH, WILLIAM. 'The Copy of a Letter Sent to the Emperour of Moscovie . . . Anno 1570', in **1872b,** vol. 3, pp. 167–9.

655 BURROUGH, WILLIAM. 'The Deposition . . . Concerning the Narve, Kegor etc, to what King or Prince they do Appertaine and are Subject . . . 23 of June, 1576', in **1872b,** vol. 3, pp. 203–6.

656 FEDOR I, *Emperor of Russia* (Theodore I). 'Pheodor Ivanowich the New Emperors Gracious Letter of Privilege to the English Merchants . . . 1586', in **1872b,** vol. 3, pp. 347–53.

657 FEDOR I, *Emperor of Russia* (Theodore I). 'A Most Gracious Letter Given to the English Merchants, Sir John Hart and his Company... [1596]', in **1872b,** vol. 3, pp. 439–45.

658 READ, JOHN M. A Historical Inquiry Concerning Henry Hudson... his Connection with the Muscovy Company ... Albany, 1866. Pp. vi, 209. Another (Abridged) Edition, Edinburgh, 1883, Pp. 88.

659 'The Maner of the Preferring of Sutes in Russia, by the Example of our English Merchants Bill, Exhibited to the Emperour', in **1872b,** vol. 3, pp. 329–30.

660 LUBIMENKO, INNA. 'The Struggle of the Dutch with the English for the Russian Market in the Seventeenth Century', *Trans RHS,* 4th Series, vol. 7, 1924, pp. 27–51.

661 PRICE, JACOB M. The Tobacco Adventure to Russia: Enterprise, Politics and Diplomacy in the Quest for a Northern Market for English Colonial Tobacco, 1676–1722. (Transactions of the American Philosophical Society. New Series, vol. 51, pt. 1, 1961.) Philadelphia, 1961, Pp. 120.

> Rev.: J. L. H. Keep in *SEER,* vol. 40, 1961–62, pp. 543-545; Walther Kirchner in *Slavic Rev,* vol. 21, 1962, pp. 346–347.

662 FREDERIKSEN, O. J. 'Virginia Tobacco in Russia under Peter the Great', *SEER,* vol. 21, no. 1, 1943, pp. 40–56.

663 HEATHCOTE, SAMUEL. The Case of the Contractors with the Czar of Muscovy for the Sole Importation of Tobacco into his Dominions. L., 1698. Pp. 2.

664 HEATHCOTE, SAMUEL. Heads of Some of those Advantages this Nation might Enjoy, by Encouraging the Tobacco Trade to Russia... L., 1698. Pp. 1.

665 HEATHCOTE, SAMUEL. Some Considerations Relating to the Enlarging the Russia Trade, and the Contract for Importing Tobacco into that Country... L., 1698.

666 An ANSWER to the Reasons Alleged against the Repealing a Clause in the Act of Navigation in the Favour of the Russia Company. L., [16—].

667 A REPLY TO THE ANSWER to the Reasons Alledged against the Repealing a Clause in the Act of Navigation in Favour of the Russia-Company. L., [16—]. Pp. 3.

668 REASONS Humbly Offered for Passing the Bill for Enlarging the Trade to Russia. L., [1695]?

669 REASONS Humbly Offered for an Easie Admission into the Russia Company. L., [1695]?

670 REASONS for Englarging and Regulating the Trade to Russia and the Narve. L., [1695]?

671 An ANSWER TO SOME MISTAKES Offered to the House of Commons by way of Objection against the Continuance of the Russia Company. L., 1697.

672 HUNT, N. C. 'The Russia Company and the Government, 1730–1742', *OSP*, vol. 7, 1957, pp. 27–65.

673 READING, DOUGLAS K. The Anglo-Russian Commercial Treaty of 1734. Yale U.P., L., O.U.P., 1938. Pp. ix, 337.

674 STRUVE, PETER. 'The Anglo-Russian Trade Treaty of 1734', *Rus R (Liverpool)*, vol. 1, no. 2, 1912, pp. 20–6.

675 A LETTER TO A MEMBER OF PARLIAMENT, Relating to the Bill for the Opening of a Trade to and from Persia through Russia. L., 1741. Pp. (67).

676 SCHMIDT, KNUD R. 'The Treaty of Commerce between Great Britain and Russia, 1766: a Study on the Development of Count Panin's Northern System', *Scandoslavica*, vol. 1, 1954, pp. 115–34.

677 BROUGH, ANTHONY. A View of the Importance of the Trade between Great Britain and Russia. L., 1789. Pp. 51.

678 A COMPARATIVE ESTIMATE of the Advantages Great Britain would Derive from a Commercial Alliance with the Ottoman in Preference to the Russian Empire. L., 1791.

679 STRUVE, PETER. 'English Tissue-Printing in Russia: an Episode in Russian Economic History', *SEER*, vol. 19, 1939–40, pp. 303–10.

(iv) *Cultural and Literary*

680 SIMMONS, ERNEST J. English Literature and Culture in Russia, 1553–1840. Harvard U.P., 1935. Pp. xi, 357.

681 DRAPER, J. W. 'Shakespeare and Muscovy', *SEER*, vol. 33, 1954–5, pp. 217–21.

E

682   Vočadlo, O. 'Shakespeare and the Slavs', *SEER*, vol. 44, 1966, pp. 36–50.

683   Anderson, Matthew S. 'Some British Influences on Russian Intellectual Life and Society in the 18th Century', *SEER*, vol. 39, 1960–1, pp. 148–63.

684   Simmons, John S. G. 'Samuel Johnson on the Banks of the Wolga', *OSP*, vol. 11, 1964, pp. 28–37.

685   Cross, Anthony G. 'Karamzin and England', *SEER*, vol. 43, 1964–5, pp. 91–114.

686   Berkov, P. N. 'English Plays in St. Petersburg in the 1760's and 1770's', *OSP*, vol. 8, 1958, pp. 90–7.

687   McLean, Hugh. 'The Adventures of an English Comedy in Eighteenth-Century Russia : Dodsley's *Toy Shop* and Lukin's *Ščepetiľnik*', in *American Contributions to the 5th International Congress of Slavists*, 1963, Sofia, vol. 2, The Hague, 1963, pp. 201–12.

688   Phelps, Gilbert. 'The Early Phases of British Interest in Russian Literature. 2 pts.', *SEER*, vol. 36, 1957–8, pp. 418–33 and vol. 38, 1959–60, pp. 415–30.

689   Konovalov, Sergey. Oxford and Russia : an Inaugural Lecture Delivered before the University of Oxford on 26 Nov., 1946. O., 1947. Pp. 24.

690   Simmons, John S. G. 'H. W. Ludolf and the Printing of his "*Grammatica Russica*" at Oxford in 1696', *OSP*, vol. 1, 1950, pp. 104–29.

691   Oman, Charles C. The English Silver in the Kremlin, 1557–1663. L., 1961. Pp. xviii, 94. Bibl.

C. RELATIONS WITH OTHER EUROPEAN COUNTRIES

Relations with Byzantium, **692–698.** For works on the early campaigns against Constantinople, see **1570–1577**; on Russia's Byzantine cultural inheritance, **1147–1157.** Relations with Livonia, **699**; Sweden, **700**; Denmark, **701**; Poland, **702–711**; Germany, **712–713**; Austria, **714**; Holland, **715**; France, **716–721**; Ukraine, **722–744**; the Caucasus, **745**; Georgia, **746–749**; Turkey, **750–756.**

692   Kadlec, Charles. 'The Empire [i.e. Byzantium]

and its Northern Neighbours', *C Med H,* vol. 4, C.U.P., 1923, chapter 7A, pp. 183–215; Bibl.: pp. 819–21.

693 OBOLENSKY, DMITRI. 'The Empire [i.e. Byzantium] and its Northern Neighbours, 568–1018', *C Med H,* 2nd ed., vol. 4, pt. 1, C.U.P., 1966, chapter 11, pp. 473–518; Bibl.: pp. 952–65.

694 VASILIEV, A. A. 'Was Old Russia a Vassal State of Byzantium?', *Speculum,* vol. 7, 1932, pp. 350–60.

695 VASILIEV, A. A. 'Economic Relations between Byzantium and Old Russia', *JEBH,* vol. 4, 1931–2, pp. 314–34.

696 OSTROGORSKY, G. 'Byzantium and the South Slavs', *SEER,* vol. 42, 1963–4, pp. 1–14.

697 VERNADSKY, GEORGE V. 'Byzantium and Southern Russia, Two Notes: 1. The Eparchy of Gotha, 2. The Date of the Conversion of the Khazars to Judaism', *Byzantion,* vol. 15, 1940–1, pp. 65–76; 76–86.

698 VERNADSKY, GEORGE V. 'The Rus in the Crimea and the Russo-Byzantine Treaty of 945', *Byz-Met,* vol. 1, no. 1, 1946, pp. (249-59).

699 KIRCHNER, WALTHER. 'The Russo-Livonian Crisis, 1555: Extracts from Joachim Burwitz' Report of February 19, 1555', *JMH,* vol. 19, 1947, pp. 142–51.

700 WESTERGAARD, WALDEMAR. 'Gustavus Vasa and Russia, 1555–1557', *PHR,* vol. 2, 1933, pp. 158–69.

701 KIRCHNER, WALTHER. 'A Milestone in European History: the Danish-Russian Treaty of 1562', *SEER,* vol. 22, no. 2, 1944, pp. 39–48.

702 BAIN, ROBERT N. Slavonic Europe: a Political History of Poland and Russia from 1447 to 1796. C.U.P., 1908. Pp. viii, 452. Bibl.

703 HALECKI, OSKAR. 'Polish-Russian Relations, Past and Present', *Review of Politics,* vol. 5, 1943, pp. 322–38.

704 KONOVALOV, SERGEY, *ed.* Russo-Polish Relations: an Historical Survey. L., 1945. Pp. 90. Princeton U.P., 1945. Pp. viii, 102.
    Rev.: W. Lednicki in *ASEER,* vol. 4, nos. 3–4, 1945, pp. 207–210.

705 COATES, WILLIAM P. *and* COATES, ZELDA K. Six Centuries of Russo-Polish Relations. L., 1948. Pp. ix, 235.

706 HALECKI, OSKAR. 'Possevino's Last Statement on Polish-

Russian Relations', *OCP,* vol. 19, 1953, pp. 261–302.

707 ROBERTS, LOUISE B. 'Peter the Great in Poland', *SEER,* vol. 5, 1926–7, pp. 537–51.

708 LEWITTER, L. R. 'Peter the Great, Poland and the Westernization of Russia', *JHI,* vol. 19, 1958, pp. 493–506.

709 LEWITTER, L. R. 'Peter the Great and the Polish Dissenters', *SEER,* vol. 33, 1954–5, pp. 75–101.

710 LEWITTER, L. R. 'Peter the Great and the Polish Election of 1697', *CHJ,* vol. 12, 1956, pp. 126–43.

711 STRUVE, GLEB. 'A Chapter in Russo-Polish Relations', *Rus R,* vol. 6, no. 1, 1946–7, pp. 56–68.
Covers the period from 1785–1793.

712 LOBANOV-ROSTOVSKY, A. 'Russia and Germany: an Historical Survey of Russo-German Relations', *Rus R,* vol. 2, no. 2, 1942–3, pp. 27–44.

713 DODGSON, CAMPBELL. 'A German-Russian Alliance in 1514', *Burlington Magazine,* vol. 76, 1940, pp. 139–44.

714 MADARIAGA, ISABEL de (De Madariaga) (*Mrs.* I. Schapiro). 'The Secret Austro-Russian Treaty in 1781', *SEER,* vol. 38, 1959–60, pp. 114–45.

715 BALBIAN VERSTER, J. F. L. DE. Peter the Great of Russia at Zaandam and Amsterdam, 1697–1698. Amsterdam, 1924. Pp. 14.

716 KALMYKOW, ALEXANDRA. 'A Sixteenth-Century Russian Envoy to France', *Slavic Rev,* vol. 23, 1964, pp. 701–5.

717 LOSSKY, ANDREW. 'La Piquetière's Projected Mission to Moscow in 1682 and the Swedish Policy of Louis XIV', in **83**, pp. 69–106.

718 MOHRENSCHILDT, DIMITRI S. VON. Russia in the Intellectual Life of Eighteenth Century France. Columbia U.P., 1936. Pp. x, 325. Bibl.

719 HOROWITZ, SIDNEY. 'Albert Vandal and Franco-Russian Relations, 1740–1746', *JCEA,* vol. 14, 1954, pp. 123–42.

720 OLIVA, L. J. Misalliance: a Study of French Policy in Russia during the Seven Years War. N.Y.U.P., 1964. Pp. xi, 218. Bibl.
Rev.: Herbert H. Kaplan in *Slavic Rev,* vol. 24, 1965, pp. 127–128.

721 MAZOUR, ANATOLE G. 'The Russian Ambassador in France, 1789–1792', *Rus R,* vol. 1, no. 2, 1941–2, pp. 86–93.

722 O'BRIEN, CARL B. (C. Bickford O'Brien). Muscovy and the Ukraine, from the Pereiaslavl Agreement to the Truce of Andrusovo, 1654–1667. (Univ. of California Publications in History, vol. 74.) U. of California P., 1963. Pp. 138. Bibl.

> Rev.: Horst Jablonowski in *Slavic Rev*, vol. 23, 1964, pp. 744–746; J. L. H. Keep in *SEER*, vol. 42, 1963–64, pp. 219–221; Arthur E. Adams in *Rus R*, vol. 22, 1963, pp. 430–431.

723 PYRCHODKO, NICHOLAS. 'Three Hundred Years of Russian Dealings with Ukraine', *Ukr Qly*, vol. 10, 1954, pp. 93–9.

724 KONONENKO, KONSTANTYN S. Ukraine and Russia: a History of the Economic Relations between Ukraine and Russia, 1654–1917. (Marquette Slavic Studies, vol. 4.) Marquette U.P., 1958. Pp. xvi, 257. Bibl.

> Emphasis on the 19th century. Rev.: Edward Ames in *ASEER*, vol. 18, 1959, pp. 258–260; Olga Crisp in *SEER*, vol. 38, 1959–60, pp. 255–258.

725 TIMOSHENKO, VLADIMIR P. Ukraine and Russia: a Survey of their Economic Relations. Washington, 1919. Pp. (15).

726 HORDYNSKY, SVIATOSLAV. 'Three Hundred Years of Moscow's Cultural Policy in Ukraine', *Ukr Qly*, vol. 10, 1954, pp. 71–84.

727 MANNING, CLARENCE A. 'The Theses of the Treaty of Pereyaslav', *Ukr Rev (L.)*, vol. 2, no. 2, 1955, pp. 41–5.

728 FEDENKO, PANAS. '*Istoriya Russov* and the Treaty of Pereyaslav', *Ukr Rev (Munich)*, vol. 7, 1959, pp. 37–44.

729 OHLOBLYN, ALEKSANDR. Treaty of Pereyaslav, 1654. (Trans. from Ukrainian.) Toronto, N.Y., 1954. Pp. 104.

> Rev.: N. Polons'ka-Vasylenko in *AUA*, vol. 5, 1956, pp. 1224–1226.

730 THREE CENTURIES OF STRUGGLE: Addresses on the Occasion of the 300th Anniversary of the Treaty of Pereyaslav between Ukraine and Russia, 1654–1954. Winnipeg, 1954. Pp. 48.

731 YAKOVLIV, ANDRIY. 'Bohdan Khmelnyts'ky's Treaty with the Tsar of Muscovy in 1654', *AUA*, vol. 4, no. 3, 1955, pp. 904–16.

732 POLONSKA-WASYLENKO, NATALIA. '1654: the Pereyaslav

Treaty in the Light of Contemporary Evidence', *Ukr Rev (L.)*, vol. 2, no. 2, 1955, pp. 45–54.

733 KRUPNYTSKY, BORYS. 'Treaty of Pereyaslav and the Political Orientation of Bohdan Khmelnytsky', *Ukr Qly*, vol. 10, 1954, pp. 32–40.

734 IVANYTSKY, SOKRAT. 'Did the Treaty of Pereyaslav Include a Protectorate?', *Ukr Qly*, vol. 10, 1954, pp. 176–82.

735 GOLDMAN, ILYA J. 'West-East Antagonism in the Pereyaslav', *Ukr Qly*, vol. 10, 1954, pp. 13–21.

736 OHLOBLYN, ALEKSANDR. 'The Pereyaslav Treaty and Eastern Europe', *Ukr Qly*, vol. 10, 1954, pp. 41–50.

737 IVANYTSKY, SOKRAT. 'The Juridical Aspect of the Treaty of Pereyaslav, Concluded in 1654 between Russia and Ukraine', *Proceedings of the Shevchenko Scientific Society, Historical-Philosophical Section*, vol. 1, 1951, pp. 106–8.

738 YAKOVLIV, ANDRIY. 'The Juridical Character of the Pereyaslav Treaty and its Fate', *Ukr Qly*, vol. 10, 1954, pp. 51–9.

739 HALAYCHUK, BOHDAN. 'The Treaty of Pereyaslav in the Light of International Law', *Proceedings of the Shevchenko Scientific Society, Historical-Philosophical Section*, vol. 1, 1951, pp. 102–5.

740 PROKOPOVYCH, VYACHESLAV. 'The Problem of the Juridical Nature of the Ukraine's Union with Muscovy', *AUA*, vol. 4, no. 3, 1955, pp. 917–80.

741 CZYROWSKI, NICHOLAS. 'Economic Aspects of the Ukrainian Moscovite Treaty of 1654', *Ukr Qly*, vol. 10, 1954, pp. 85–92.

742 CHUBATY, NICHOLAS D. (Czubatyj). 'Moscow and the Ukrainian Church after 1654', *Ukr Qly*, vol. 10, 1954, pp. 60–70.

743 ORELETSKY, VASYL. 'Ukraine's Relations with Russia in the Middle of the 17th Century', *Ukr Rev (L.)*, vol. 6, no. 3, 1959, pp. 30–3.

744 WYNAR, L. 'The Abduction of Andriy Voynarovsky by Tsar Peter I, Hamburg, 1716', *Ukr Rev (L.)*, vol. 10, no. 4, 1963, pp. 46–59.

745 ALLEN, W. E. D. 'The Volga-Terek Route in Russo-

Caucasian Relations', *BK*, New Series, vols. 15–6, 1963, pp. 158–66.

746 POLYEVKTOV, M. 'The Ways of Communication between Russia and Georgia in the Sixteenth and Seventeenth Centuries', *JMH*, vol. 2, 1930, pp. 367–77.

747 ALLEN, W. E. D. 'The Georgian Marriage Projects of Boris Godunov', *OSP*, vol. 12, 1965, pp. 69–79.

748 LANG, DAVID M. 'Count Todtleben's Expedition to Georgia, 1769–1771, According to a French Eyewitness', *BSOAS*, vol. 13, 1949–50, pp. 878–907.

749 RUSSO-GEORGIAN TREATY Concluded in 1783 between Catherine II, Empress of Russia, and Irakly II, King of Georgia ... L., 1919. Pp. 20.

750 İNALCIK, HALIL. 'The Origin of the Ottoman-Russian Rivalry and the Don-Volga Canal (1569)', *Annales de l'Université d'Ankara*, vol. 1, 1946–7, pp. 47–110.

751 KURAT, A. N. 'The Turkish Expedition to Astrakhan in 1569 and the Problem of the Don-Volga Canal', *SEER*, vol. 40, 1961–2, pp. 7–23.

752 VERNADSKY, GEORGE V. 'Russia, Turkey, and Circassia in the 1640's', *Südost-Forschungen*, vol. 19, 1960, pp. 134–45.

753 O'BRIEN, CARL B. (C. Bickford O'Brien). 'Russia and Turkey, 1677–1681 : the Treaty of Bakhchisarai', *Rus R*, vol. 12, 1953, pp. 259–68.

754 SUMNER, BENEDICT H. Peter the Great and the Ottoman Empire. O., 1949. Pp. 80.
   Rev.: Victor S. Mamatey in *ASEER*, vol. 10, 1951, pp. 76–78.

755 LAUGIER, MARC A. The History of the Negociations for the Peace Concluded at Belgrade, September 18, 1739 between the Emperor, Russia, and the Ottoman Porte ... (Trans. from French.) L., 1770. Pp. xx, 534.

756 HOLLAND, THOMAS E. A Lecture on the Treaty Relations of Russia and Turkey from 1774 to 1853. L., 1877. Pp. 72.

D. ASIA AND AMERICA

General works on relations with Asia, **757–758**. For related material, see also sections 19E and 19F on Central Asia and Siberia. Relations with China, **759–768**; Japan, **769–772**;

India, **773–775**; Africa, **776;** America, **777–782**. On Russo-Turkish relations, see **750–756**.

757   LOBANOV-ROSTOVSKY, *Prince* ANDREY. Russia and Asia. N.Y., 1933. Pp. viii, 334. Bibl. Another Edition: Ann Arbor, 1951. Pp. 342.
      Rev.: B. Goldman in *SEER*, vol. 12, 1933–34, pp. 226–229.

758   BEAZLEY, *Sir* RAYMOND. 'Early Russian Embassies and Treaties in Asia', *Contemporary Review*, vol. 166, 1944, pp. 32–7.

759   HSÜAN-MIN LIN. 'Russo-Chinese Relations up to the Treaty of Nerchinsk', *Chinese Social and Political Science Review*, vol. 23, 1939–40, pp. 391–440.

760   PAVLOVSKY, MICHEL N. Chinese-Russian Relations. N.Y., 1949. Pp. 194.
      Rev.: Allen S. Whiting in *ASEER*, vol. 9, 1950, pp. 222–224; Albert Parry in *Rus R*, vol. 9, 1950, pp. 330–333.

761   CHENG, TIEN-FANG. A History of Sino-Russian Relations. Washington, 1957. Pp. (viii, 389). Bibl.
      Rev.: Charles B. McLane in *Rus R*, vol. 18, 1959, pp. 72-73.

762   SCHWARTZ, HARRY. Tsars, Mandarins and Commissars: a History of Chinese-Russian Relations. L., Philadelphia, 1964. Pp. 252.
      Rev.: George A. Lensen in *Rus R*, vol. 24, 1965, pp. 65–66.

763   BADDELEY, JOHN F. Russia, Mongolia and China: Being some Record of the Relations between Them . . . A.D. 1602–1676 . . . 2 vols. L., 1919. Bibl.

764   CHEN, VINCENT. Sino-Russian Relations in the Seventeenth Century. The Hague, 1966. Pp. x, 147. Bibl. (Pbk.)

765   HSÜ, IMMANUEL C. Y. 'Russia's Special Position in China during the Early Ch'ing Period', *Slavic Rev*, vol. 23, 1964, pp. 688–700.

766   MISH, JOHN L. 'Russia Meets China Three Centuries Ago', *Bulletin of the New York Public Library*, vol. 65, 1961, pp. 435–41.

767   TU-LI-SHIN. Narrative of the Chinese Embassy to the Khan of the Tourgouth Tartars in the Years 1712, 13, 14 and 15 by the Chinese Ambassador . . . (Trans. from Chinese by *Sir* George T. Staunton.) L., 1821. Pp. xxxix, 330.

768   BALL, J. DYER. 'The Intercourse between Russia and

China after the Reign of Peter the Great', *Proceedings of the Anglo-Russian Literary Society*, no. 75, Feb.-Apr., 1916, pp. 32–40.

769 WILDES, HARRY E. 'Russia Meets the Japanese', *Rus R*, vol. 3, no. 1, 1943–4, pp. 55–63.

770 WILDES, HARRY E. 'Russia's Attempts to Open Japan', *Rus R*, vol. 5, no. 1, 1945–6, pp. 70–9.

771 LENSEN, GEORGE A. 'Early Russo-Japanese Relations', *Far Eastern Quarterly*, vol. 10, 1950–1, pp. 3–37.

772 LENSEN, GEORGE A. The Russian Push toward Japan: Russo-Japanese Relations, 1697–1875. Princeton U.P., O.U.P., 1959. Pp. xv, 554. Bibl.

> Rev.: D. W. Treadgold in *ASEER*, vol. 20, 1961, pp. 320–321; Hugh Seton-Watson in *SEER*, vol. 39, 1960–61, pp. 545–547.

773 ZEINE, A. N. 'Russia in the Near East from 1453 to the Present Day', *Middle East Forum*, vol. 33, 1958, pp. (11–4).

774 KEMP, P. M. Bharat-Rus: an Introduction to Indo-Russian Contacts and Travels from Mediaeval Times . . . Delhi, 1958. Pp. 288. Bibl.

775 EDWARDS, HENRY S. Russian Projects against India from the Czar Peter to General Skobeleff. L., 1885. Pp. 295.

> Emphasis on the 19th century.

776 YAKOBSON, SERGIUS. 'Russia and Africa', *SEER*, vol. 17, 1938–9, pp. 623–37.

777 CROSBY, ALFRED W. 'The Beginnings of Trade between the United States and Russia', *American Neptune*, vol. 21, 1961, pp. (207–15).

778 RICH, E. E. 'Russia and the Colonial Fur Trade', *Econ HR*, Series 2 vol. 7, 1954–5, pp. 307–28.

779 MILLER, DAVID E. 'Maritime Fur Trade Rivalry in the Pacific Northwest', *The Historian*, vol. 21, 1959, pp. 392–408.

780 GOLDER, FRANK A. 'Catherine II and the American Revolution', *AHR*, vol. 21, 1915–16, pp. 92–6.

781 HILDT, JOHN C. Early Diplomatic Negotiations of the United States with Russia. Baltimore, 1906. Pp. 196.

782 PHILLIPS, JAMES D. 'Salem Opens American Trade with Russia', *New England Quarterly*, vol. 14, 1941, pp. 685–9.

7

INSTITUTIONS, ADMINISTRATION
AND THE LAW

Constitutional and administrative law, **783–792**. General works on Russian law, **793–794**; law of Kiev Rus', **795-798**; Muscovite law, **799–810**; 18th century law, **811–812** (cf. **790–792**). Lithuanian law, **813–815**; Ukraine, **816–817**.

783 KOVALEVSKY, MAKSIM M. Russian Political Institutions from the Beginnings to the Present Time. U. of Chicago P., 1902. Pp. 299.

784 LEE, FRANCIS. 'Proposals Given to Peter the Great, Czar of Muscovy, Anno 1698, for the Right Framing of his Government', in his: *Apoleipomena; or, Dissertations, Theological, Mathematical and Physical* ... vol. 1, L., 1752, pp. 1–12.

785 DEWEY, HORACE W. 'The White Lake Charter: a Mediaeval Russian Administrative Statute', *Speculum,* vol. 32, 1957, pp. 74–83.
    Statute of 1488.

786 DEWEY, HORACE W. 'Charters of Local Government under Tsar Ivan IV', *Jahrbücher für Geschichte Osteuropas,* Neue Folge, vol. 14, 1966, pp. 10–20.

787 DEWEY, HORACE W. 'The Decline of the Moscovite "Namestnik" ', *OSP,* vol. 12, 1965, pp. 21–39.

788 HULBERT, ELLERD. 'The Zemskii Sobor of 1575: a Mistake in Translation', *Slavic Rev,* vol. 25, 1966, pp. 320–2.

789 KEEP, JOHN L. H. 'The Decline of the Zemsky Sobor', *SEER,* vol. 36, 1957–8, pp. 100–22.

790 CATHERINE II, *Empress of Russia.* The Grand Instructions to the Commissioners Appointed to Frame a New Code of Laws ... (Trans. from Russian by M. Tatishchev. L., 1768. Also in **459**.
    cf. **873** for the economic aspects.

791 A DESCRIPTION OF THE MANNER IN WHICH THE

COMMISSION FOR ESTABLISHING A NEW CODE OF LAWS WAS OPENED at Moscow on Friday the 3rd Day of August, 1767. Translated from the Russian Language by Michael Tatischeff ... n.p., n.d. Pp. (27).

792 PAPMEHL K. A. 'The Problem of Civil Liberties in the Records of the "Great Commission" ', *SEER*, vol. 42, 1963–4, pp. 274–91.

793 A SUMMARY OF HISTORICAL SKETCHES on the Formation of the Body of the Russian Laws. (Trans. from Russian.) St. Petersburg, 1841.
Rare work cited in **4**.

794 SIGEL, FEODOR F. Lectures on Slavonic Law. (Ilchester Lectures for 1900). L., N.Y., 1902. Pp. vi, 152.

795 PADOKH, YAROSLAV. 'The Democratic Character of the Criminal Law of Ukraine in the Period of the Princes', *Proceedings of the Shevchenko Scientific Society, Historical-Philosophical Section,* vol. 1, 1951, pp. 97–8.

796 PADOKH, YAROSLAV. 'The Humaneness of the Criminal Code of Ukraine in the Times of the Princes, 11–13 Centuries', *Proceedings of the Shevchenko Scientific Society, Historical-Philosophical Section,* vol. 1, 1951, pp. 99–101.

797 RUSSIA. *Laws, Statutes, etc.* Medieval Russian Laws. Translated by George V. Vernadsky. Columbia U.P., 1947. Pp. 106. Bibl.
Includes a translation of the *Russkaya Pravda*. Rev.: Vladimir V. Gsovski in *ASEER*, vol. 6, no. 2, 1947, pp. 152–158.

798 BIRNBAUM, HENRIK. 'On Old Russian and Old Scandinavian Legal Thought : some Comparative Notes on Style and Syntax', *Scandoslavica*, vol. 8, 1962, pp. 115–40.
A discussion of the *Russkaya Pravda*.

799 DEWEY, HORACE W., *ed.* Muscovite Judicial Texts, 1488–1556. (Trans. from Russian.) (Michigan Slavic Materials, 7.) Ann Arbor, 1966. Pp. ([vi], 94).

800 DEWEY, HORACE W. 'The 1497 Sudebnik—Muscovite Russia's First National Law Code', *ASEER*, vol. 15, 1956, pp. 325–38.

801 DEWEY, HORACE W. 'The 1550 Sudebnik as an Instrument of Reform', *Jahrbücher für Geschichte Osteuropas,* Neue Folge, vol. 10, 1962, pp. 161–80.

802   DEWEY, HORACE W. 'Judges and the Evidence in Muscovite Law', *SEER*, vol. 36, 1957–8, pp. 189–94.

803   DEWEY, HORACE W. 'Immunities in Old Russia', *Slavic Rev*, vol. 23, 1964, pp. 643–59.

804   LANE, HENRY. 'The Manner of Justice by Lots in Russia . . .', in **1872b**, vol. 2, pp. 411–2.
      Contemporary account of a trial by lot in 1560 between the author and a Russian native.

805   DEWEY, HORACE W. 'Trial by Combat in Muscovite Russia', *OSP*, vol. 9, 1960, pp. 21–31.

806   BACKUS, OSWALD P. 'Muscovite Legal Thought, the Law of Theft, and the Problem of Centralization, 1497–1589', in **83**, pp. 33–68; Bibl.

807   KEEP, JOHN L. H. 'Bandits and the Law in Muscovy', *SEER*, vol. 35, 1956–7, pp. 201–22.

808   DEWEY, HORACE W. 'Historical Drama in Muscovite Justice: the Case of the Extorted Deed', *Canadian Slavonic Papers*, vol. 2, 1957, pp. 38–46.

809   VERNADSKY, GEORGE V. 'Studies in the History of Moscovian Private Law of the 16th and the 17th Centuries; Inheritance, the Case of the Childless Wife', *Studi in Memoria di Aldo Albertoni*, vol. 3, Padova, 1938, pp. 433–54.

810   GSOVSKI, V. I. 'Roman Private Law in Russia', *Bulletino dell' Istituto di Diritto Romano*, vol. 46, 1939, pp. 363–75.
      Covers the period up to the 17th century.

811   HAMMER, DARRELL P. 'Russia and the Roman Law', *ASEER*, vol. 16, 1957, pp. 1–13.
      Defends the thesis that Roman Law was received into Russia from West European sources in the 18th century.

812   CIZOVA, T. 'Beccaria in Russia', *SEER*, vol. 40, 1961–2, pp. 384–408.
      A study of the 18th-century Italian criminal law theorist, said to have influenced Catherine II.

813   OKINSHEVYCH, LEV. The Law of the Grand Duchy of Lithuania: Background and Bibliography. N.Y., 1953. Pp. (53).

814   PLATERIS, ALEKSANDRAS. 'Codification of the Law in the Grand Duchy of Lithuania', *Lituanus*, vol. 11, no. 2, 1965, pp. 28–44.

815   SRUOGA, VANDA. 'The Lithuanian Statute: a Progres-
      sive 16th Century Legislative Document', *Lituanus,*
      vol. 5, 1959, pp. 121–2.
816   ORELETSKY, VASYL. 'The Leading Feature of Ukrainian
      Law', *Ukr Rev (L.),* vol. 4, no. 3, 1957, pp. 48–52.
817   NOL'DE, BORIS. 'Essays in Russian State Law', *AUA,*
      vol. 4, no. 3, 1955, pp. 873–903.
          Ukrainian law and the Russian administration of Ukraine.

8

SOCIAL AND ECONOMIC HISTORY

A. SOCIAL HISTORY

Early social history in Soviet historiography, **818.** General works, **819–822**; of these **821** is the standard introduction to the subject, whilst **820** is a relatively forgotten work which deserves to be more widely known. Kiev Rus', **823–824** (see also section 8C; Novgorod, **825**; 18th century, **826** *et seq.* The nobility of the 18th century, **827–832**; the Russian bourgeoisie, **834**; the Jews in Russia, **835–837**. Women in Russian society, **838–839** (cf. **1284**). Other special topics, **840–845.**

818 VUCINICH, ALEXANDER (Vukinich). 'The Soviet Theory of Social Development in the Early Middle Ages', *Speculum,* vol. 26, 1951, pp. 243–54.

819 KOVALEVSKY, MAXIME M. Modern Customs and Ancient Laws of Russia. (Ilchester Lectures for 1889–90.) L., 1891. Pp. x, 260.

820 ELNETT, *Mrs.* ELAINE. Historic Origin and Social Development of Family Life in Russia. Columbia U.P., 1926. Pp. xi, 151. Bibl.

821 MIRSKY, DMITRY S., *Prince.* Russia: a Social History. L., 1931. Pp. xix, 312, xxi. Reprinted 1942, 1952.
    Rev.: E. H. Minns in *SEER,* vol. 9, 1930–31, pp. 751–752.

822 PLEKHANOV, GEORGI V. History of Russian Social Thought. (Trans. from Russian.) N.Y., 1938. Pp. (224).

823 SCHMIDT, KNUD R. 'The Social Structure of Russia in the Early Middle Ages', *Congrès International des Sciences Historiques, 11, 1960, Stockholm. Rapports,* no. 3, Göteborg, 1960, pp. 22–33.

824 VERNADSKY, GEORGE V. 'Three Notes on the Social History of Kievan Russia: [*1.* Slave and Grantee: Kholop and Vdach, *2.* Peasant and Herdsman: Smerd and Khop, *3.* Freedmen and Aliens: Izgoi]', *SEER,* vol. 22, no. 4, 1944, pp. 81–92.

825 OBOLENSKY, DMITRI. 'The Society of Novgorod in the

Early Middle Ages', *Congrès International des Sciences Historiques, 11, 1960, Stockholm. Résumés des Communications,* Göteborg, 1960, p. 92.

826 BLACK, CYRIL E. 'The Nature of Imperial Russian Society', *ASEER,* vol. 20, 1961, pp. 565–82.
18th–19th centuries.

827 GOODWIN, A. *ed.* The European Nobility in the Eighteenth Century. L., 1953. Pp. vii. 201. Bibl. 2nd ed. L., 1967. Pp. x, 204. Bibl.
Chapter 10 by Max Beloff is on the Russian nobility.

828 RAEFF, MARC. Origins of the Russian Intelligentsia: the Eighteenth Century Nobility. N.Y., 1966.
Rev.: Edward C. Thaden in *Rus R,* vol. 26, 1967, pp. 300–301.

829 McCONNELL, ALLEN. 'The Origin of the Russian Intelligentsia', *SEEJ,* vol. 8, 1964, pp. 1–16; Bibl.

830 RAEFF, MARC. 'Home, School and Service in the Life of the 18th Century Russian Nobleman', *SEER,* vol. 40, 1961–2, pp. 297–307.

831 TATISHCHEV, BASIL. The Testament of Basil Tatistchef. (Trans. from Russian). Paris, 1860. Pp. xv, 46.

832 ESPER, THOMAS. 'The Odnovortsy and the Russian Nobility', *SEER,* vol. 45, 1967, pp. 124–34.

833 BECKER, CHRISTOPHER. ' "Raznochintsy": the Development of the Word and the Concept', *ASEER,* vol. 18, 1959, pp. 63–74.

834 BILL, *Mrs.* VALENTINE T. (Tschebotarioff-Bill). The Forgotten Class: the Russian Bourgeoisie from the Earliest Beginnings to 1900. N.Y., 1959. Pp. 229. Bibl.
Rev.: Miriam H. Berlin in *ASEER,* vol. 19, 1960, pp. 111–113.

835 DUBNOV, SEMEN M. (Simon Dubnow). History of the Jews in Russia and Poland from the Earliest Times ... (Trans. from Russian.) 3 vols. Philadelphia, 1916–20.

836 BARON, SALO W. The Russian Jew under Tsars and Soviets. N.Y., 1964. Pp. xv, 427.
Rev.: Samuel Kucherov in *Rus R,* vol. 24, 1965, pp. 190–193.

837 LEVITATS, ISAAC. The Jewish Community in Russia, 1772–1844. N.Y., Columbia U.P., 1943. Pp. (300). Bibl.

838 HOWE, SONIA E. 'The Evolution of Russian Women', *Proceedings of the Anglo-Russian Literary Society,* no. 75, Feb.-Apr., 1916, pp. 41–63.
cf. **1284**.

839   CURTOIS, M. A. 'Russian Women in the Time of Peter the Great', *Proceedings of the Anglo-Russian Literary Society,* no. 26, Oct.-Dec., 1899, pp. 5–12.
cf. **1284.**

840   UNBEGAUN, B. O. 'Cards and Card-Playing in Muscovite Russia', *SEER,* vol. 41, 1962–3, pp. 25–30.

841   BURGESS, MALCOLM. 'Fairs and Entertainers in 18th Century Russia', *SEER,* vol. 38, 1959–60, pp. 95–113.
cf. **907.**

842   COXE, WILLIAM. Account of the Prisons and Hospitals in Russia, Sweden and Denmark. L., 1781. Pp. viii, 55.
cf. **1295–1304.**

843   GUTHRIE, MATTHEW. 'Part of a Letter . . . to Dr. Priestley on the Antiseptic Regimen of the Natives of Russia', *Philosophical Transactions of the Royal Society of London,* vol. 68, 1778, pp. 622–36.
cf. **1295–1304** and **1866.**

844   GUTHRIE, MATTHEW. 'Account of the Manner in which the Russians Treat Persons Affected by the Fumes of Burning Charcoal in a Letter . . . to Joseph Priestley', *Philosophical Transactions of the Royal Society of London,* vol. 69, 1779, pp. 325–31.

845   SEELEY, FRANK F. 'Russia and the Slave Trade', *SEER,* vol. 23, 1945, pp. 126–36.
cf. **575.**

B. ECONOMIC HISTORY

General works on Russian economic history, written from widely differing viewpoints, **846–850.** Foreign commerce, **851–852.** (Trade relations of Russia with individual countries classed in section 6.) On the early period, **853–858**; of these, **855** is the best general introduction. Muscovy from the 15th to the 17th centuries inclusive, **859–866**; the 18th century, **867–873.** Special topics, **874–876.**

846   MAVOR, JAMES. An Economic History of Russia. 2 vols. L., 1914. 2nd ed. 2 vols. L., N.Y., 1925.

847   LYASHCHENKO, PETR I. History of the National Economy of Russia to the 1917 Revolution. (Trans. from Russian.) N.Y., 1949. Pp. xiii, 880. Bibl.

Orthodox Marxist treatment. Rev.: Michael T. Florinsky in *ASEER*, vol. 10, 1951, pp. 226–227; Warren B. Walsh in *Rus R*, vol. 9, 1950, pp. 157–160.

848 GERSCHENKRON, ALEXANDER. 'An Economic History of Russia', *JEH*, vol. 12, 1952, pp. 146–59.

A discussion of **847**.

849 CZYROWSKI, NICHOLAS L. (Chirovsky) (Freishin-Chirovsky). The Economic Factors in the Growth of Russia : an Economic-Historical Analysis. N.Y., 1957. Pp. 178.

Anti-Russian bias. Rev.: H. S. Levine in *ASEER*, vol. 17, 1958, pp. 128–129.

850 PASHKOV, ANATOLI I., *ed*. A History of Russian Economic Thought, Ninth through Eighteenth Centuries. Translation Edited by John M. Letiche. U. of California P., 1964. Pp. xvi, 690. Bibl.

851 LEWIS, ARCHIBALD R. Northern Seas, Shipping and Commerce in Northern Europe, A.D. 300–1100. Princeton U.P., 1958. Pp. xi, 498.

852 KIRCHNER, WALTHER. Commercial Relations between Russia and Europe, 1400 to 1800 : Collected Essays. Indiana U.P., 1966. Pp. x, 332. Bibl.

853 DAVIES, ROBERT W. 'Russia in the Early Middle Ages', *Econ HR*, Series 2, vol. 5, 1952–3, pp. 116–27.

854 STRUVE, PETER. 'Russia', *CEH*, vol. 1, C.U.P., 1941, chapter 7, section 6, pp. 418–37; Bibl.: pp. 601–5.

855 SMITH, ROBERT E. F. 'Russia', *CEH*, 2nd ed., vol. 1, C.U.P., 1966, chapter 7, section 6, pp. 505–47; Bibl.: pp. 818–23.

856 LEWIS, ARCHIBALD R. 'Was Eastern Europe European in the High Middle Ages?', *Pol R*, vol. 2, no. 1, 1957, pp. 18–26.

Economic trade routes in the Kiev period. cf. **537–541**.

857 BOLIN, STURE. 'Mohammed, Charlemagne and Ruric', *Scandinavian Economic History Review*, vol. 1, 1953, pp. 5–39.

Rôle of Kiev in European/Arab trade.

858 WARD, GRACE F. 'The English Danegeld and the Russian Dan', *ASEER*, vol. 13, 1954, pp. 299–318.

859 VERNADSKY, GEORGE V. 'The Baltic Commerce of the West Russian and Lithuanian Cities during the Middle

Ages', *Baltic and Scandinavian Countries,* vol. 3, 1937, pp. 399–409.

860   MAŁOWIST, M. 'Poland, Russia and Western Trade in the 15th and 16th Centuries', *Past and Present,* no. 13, 1958, pp. 26–41.

861   ESPER, THOMAS. 'Russia and the Baltic, 1494–1558', *Slavic Rev,* vol. 25, 1966, pp. 458–74.

862   EATON, HENRY L. 'Cadasters and Censuses of Muscovy', *Slavic Rev,* vol. 26, 1967, pp. 54–69.

863   BLUM, JEROME. 'Prices in Russia in the Sixteenth Century', *JEH,* vol. 16, 1956, pp. 182–99.
> A review article of Arkadi G. Mankov's *Le mouvement des prix dans l'état russe du 16e siècle,* Paris, 1957.

864   KIRCHNER, WALTHER. 'Entrepreneurial Activity in Russian-Western Trade Relations during the Sixteenth Century', *Explorations in Entrepreneurial History,* vol. 8, 1956, pp. 245–52; Bibl.

865   LUDOLF, HEINRICH W. 'Some Curious Observations Concerning the Products of Russia. (Trans. from Latin.)', in **2014,** pp. 119–34.

866   CHEREPNIN, L. V. 'Russian 17th-Century Baltic Trade in Soviet Historiography', *SEER,* vol. 43, 1964–5, pp. 1–22.

867   O'BRIEN, CARL B. (C. Bickford O'Brien). 'Ivan Pososh-kov: Russian Critic of Mercantilist Principles', *ASEER,* vol. 14, 1955, pp. 503–11.
> Pososhkov was an early 18th century economic theorist.

868   KAHAN, ARCADIUS. 'The Costs of Westernization in Russia: the Gentry and the Economy in the Eighteenth Century', *Slavic Rev,* vol. 25, 1966, pp. 40–66.

869   KAHAN, ARCADIUS. 'Continuity in Economic Activity and Policy during the Post–Petrine Period in Russia', *JEH,* vol. 25, 1965, pp. 61–85.

870   STRUVE, PETR B. 'Past and Present of Russian Economics', in Duff, J. D., *ed. Russian Realities and Problems,* Cambridge, 1917, pp. 47–82.

871   RONIMOIS, H. E. Russia's Foreign Trade and the Baltic Sea. L., 1946. Pp. 51.
> Emphasizes 19th–20th century period.

872   BAYKOV, ALEXANDER. 'The Economic Development of

Russia', *Econ HR*, Series 2, vol. 7, 1954–5, pp. 137–49.
Mid.-18th century onwards.

873 DMYTRYSHYN, BASIL. 'The Economic Content of the 1767 Nakaz of Catherine II', *ASEER*, vol. 19, 1960, pp. 1–9.
cf. **790–792** and **459**.

874 VERNADSKY, GEORGE V. 'Iron Mining and Iron Industries in Medieval Russia', *Études Dédiées à la Mémoire d'André M. Andréadès, Edited by K. Varvaressos*, Athens, 1940, pp. 361–6.

875 GOLDMAN, MARSHALL. 'The Relocation and Growth of the Pre-Revolutionary Russian Ferrous Metal Industry', *Explorations in Entrepreneurial History*, vol. 9, 1956, pp. 19–36.
17th century onwards.

876 TURIN, SERGE P. From Peter the Great to Lenin: a History of the Russian Labour Movement... L., 1935. Pp. xii, 217. Bibl.

C. AGRARIAN HISTORY, FEUDALISM, AGRICULTURE

Of the general works on the development of agrarian relations, **877–878**, the former is recognized as the classic work on the subject. General works on feudalism and the Russian peasantry, arranged by date of publication, **879–889**; more specialized works on this topic, **890–894**. On agriculture, **895–901**.

877 ROBINSON, GEROID T. Rural Russia under the Old Regime. L., N.Y., 1932. Reprinted 1949, 1957. Pp. x, 342. Bibl.

878 BLUM, JEROME. Lord and Peasant in Russia from the Ninth to the Nineteenth Century. Princeton U.P., 1961. Pp. x, 656. Bibl. Also Pbk. (Atheneum Pbks. Trans.-Atlantic Bk. Services.)
Rev.: Alexander Gerschenkron in *JEH*, vol. 24, 1964, pp. 53–59; Henryk Łowmianski in *Past and Present*, no. 26, 1963, pp. 102–109; Marc Szeftel in *Slavic Rev*, vol. 21, 1962, pp. 527–529.

879 VERNADSKY, GEORGE V. 'Feudalism in Russia', *Speculum*, vol. 14, 1939, pp. 300–23.

880 VOLIN, LAZAR. 'The Russian Peasant and Serfdom', *Agricultural History*, vol. 17, 1944, pp. 41–61.

881 VERNADSKY, GEORGE V. 'On Feudalism in Kievan Russia', *ASEER*, vol. 7, 1948, pp. 3–14.

882 BLUM, JEROME. 'The Early History of the Russian Peasantry', *JEH*, vol. 11, 1951, pp. 153–8.

A discussion of B. D. Grekov's *Krest'yane na Rusi* . . . Moscow, 1946.

883 BLUM, JEROME. 'The Smerd in Kievan Russia', *ASEER*, vol. 12, 1953, pp. 122–30.

884 BLUM, JEROME. 'The Beginnings of Large-Scale Private Landownership in Russia', *Speculum*, vol. 28, 1953, pp. 776–90.

885 WARRINER, DOREEN. 'Some Controversial Issues in the History of Agrarian Europe', *SEER*, vol. 32, 1953–4, pp. 168–86.

886 VERNADSKY, GEORGE V. 'Serfdom in Russia', in *Congresso Internazionale di Scienze Storiche, 10, 1955, Rome. Relazioni*, vol. 3, Firenze, 1955, pp. 247–72.

887 SZEFTEL, MARC. 'Aspects of Feudalism in Russian History', in Coulborn, R. *ed.*, *Feudalism in History*, Princeton U.P., 1956, pp. 167–82; Bibl.: pp. 413–9.

888 BLUM, JEROME. 'The Rise of Serfdom in Eastern Europe', *AHR*, vol. 62, 1956–7, pp. 807–36.

889 SMITH, ROBERT E. F., *comp*. Documents Relating to the Enserfment of the Peasants in Russia. (Trans. from Russian.) (Univ. of Birmingham. Centre for Russian and East European Studies. Discussion Papers, Series RC/D, no. 4.) Birmingham, 1966. Pp. vi, 83.

890 BILL, *Mrs*. VALENTINE T. (Tschebotarioff-Bill). 'National Feudalism in Muscovy', *Rus R*, vol. 9, 1950, pp. 209–18.

Late 15th to early 16th centuries.

891 THOMAS, COLIN. The Romanov Estates in Moscow Krai, 1627–1685. (Univ. of Birmingham. Centre for Russian and East European Studies. Discussion Papers, Series RC/D, no. 5.) Birmingham, 1966. Pp. 19.

892 VERNADSKY, GEORGE V. 'The Royal Serfs (Servi Regales) of the "Ruthenian Law" and their Origin', *Speculum*, vol. 26, 1951, pp. 255–64.

893 IGNATIEFF, LEONID. 'Rights and Obligations in Russia

and the West', *Canadian Slavonic Papers,* vol. 2, 1957, pp. 26–37.

894 MILLER, A. 'Feudalism in England and Russia ...', *SEER,* vol. 14, 1935–6, pp. 585–600.

895 TOKAREV, S. A. 'The Study of the Early History of Agriculture in the Territory of the U.S.S.R. in 1945–1955', in **1025,** pp. 356–8.

896 SMITH, ROBERT E. F. The Origins of Farming in Russia. Paris, The Hague, 1959. Pp. 198. Bibl.

Rev.: Olga Crisp in *SEER,* vol. 39, 1960–61, pp. 245–247.

897 SMITH, ROBERT E. F. A Model of Production and Consumption on the Russian Farm, 15th–17th Centuries. (Univ. of Birmingham. Centre for Russian and East European Studies. Discussion Papers, Series RC/D, no. 1.) Birmingham, 1964. Pp. 13, iii.

898 O'BRIEN, CARL B. (C. Bickford O'Brien). 'Agriculture in Russian War Economy in the Later Seventeenth Century', *ASEER,* vol. 8, 1949, pp. 167–74.

899 BLUM, JEROME. 'Russian Agriculture in the Last 150 Years of Serfdom', *Agricultural History,* vol. 34, 1960, pp. 3–12.

900 BRATANIĆ, BRANIMIR. 'On the Antiquity of the One-Sided Plough in Europe, Especially among Slavic Peoples', *Laos* (Stockholm), 1952, pp. 51–61.

901 BRATANIĆ, BRANIMIR. 'Some Similarities between Ards of the Balkans, Scandinavia and Anterior Asia and their Methodological Significance', in **1025,** pp. 221–8; Bibl.

D. SOCIAL AND ECONOMIC HISTORY OF THE BORDERLANDS

902 KARYS, JONAS K. 'Amber and Furs : Means of Exchange in Ancient Lithuania', *Lituanus,* vol. 5, 1959, pp. 73–7.

cf. **1621.**

903 BACKUS, OSWALD P. 'The Problem of Feudalism in Lithuania, 1506–1548', *Slavic Rev,* vol. 21, 1962, pp. 639–59.

904 GIMBUTAS, JURGIS. 'The Outline of Rural Settlements from the 16th Century to the Present', *Lituanus,* vol. 5, 1959, pp. 114–7.

905 CZYROWSKI, NICHOLAS L. (Chirovsky) (Freishin-Chirovsky). Old Ukraine: its Socio-Economic History prior to 1781. Madison, N.J., 1963. Pp. (xiv, 432).

906 KRADER, LAWRENCE. 'Feudalism and the Tatar Polity of the Middle Ages', *Comparative Studies in Society and History*, vol. 1, 1958–9, pp. 76–99.

907 DREW, RONALD F. 'The Siberian Fair, 1600–1750', *SEER*, vol. 39, 1960–1, pp. 423–39.
    cf. **841**.

908 DREW, RONALD F. 'The Emergence of an Agricultural Policy for Siberia in the 17th and 18th Centuries', *Agricultural History*, vol. 33, 1959, pp. 29–39.

9

ARCHAEOLOGY

A. GENERAL

Bibliography, **909–910**. General works on archaeology in the U.S.S.R., **911–913**. Of these, the best general account is **912**; the Penguin translation, **913**, though more readily available is an abridgement of the original work. General surveys of current archaeological work, arranged by date, **914–925**. Archaeology of special eras and cultures, **926–933**. Particularly recommended for their thorough treatment, **929–931**. Special topics, **934–935**. See also section 5B for related material. On ancient art styles, see **1323–1329** and **1399–1405**.

909 FIELD, HENRY, *comp.* List of Publications on Soviet Archaeology. Miami, 1952. Pp. 8.

910 FIELD, HENRY, *comp.* Bibliography [of Soviet Archaeology], 1926–1964. Ann Arbor, 1964. Pp. vii, 112. (Pbk.)

911 MILLER, MIKHAIL O. Archaeology in the U.S.S.R. Trans. from Russian.) L., N.Y., 1956. Pp. 232. Bibl.
    Rev.: M. Gimbutas in *ASEER*, vol. 17, 1958, pp. 140–141; Marc Szeftel in *Rus R*, vol. 16, no. 4, 1957, pp. 74–76.

912 MONGAYT, ALEKSANDR L. Archaeology in the U.S.S.R. (Trans. from Russian.) Moscow, 1959. Pp. 429. Bibl.

913 MONGAYT, ALEKSANDR L. Archaeology in the U.S.S.R. Translated from Russian and Adapted by M. W. Thomson. (Penguin Books.) Harmondsworth, Baltimore, 1961. Pp. 320. Bibl. (Pbk.)
    Rev.: D. B. Shimkin in *Slavic Rev*, vol. 21, 1962, pp. 529–531.

914 TALLGREN, A. M. 'Archaeological Studies in Soviet Russia', *ESA,* vol. 10, 1936, pp. 129–70.

915 FIELD, HENRY *and* PROSTOV, EUGENE. 'Recent Archaeological Investigations in the Soviet Union', *Am Anthrop,* New Series, vol. 38, 1936, pp. 260–90.

916 FIELD, HENRY *and* PROSTOV, EUGENE. 'Archaeology in the Soviet Union', *Am Anthrop,* New Series, vol. 39, 1937, pp. 457–90.

917 FIELD, HENRY *and* PROSTOV, EUGENE. 'Archaeology in the Soviet Union', *Antiquity,* vol. 14, 1940, pp. 404–26.

918 KISELEV, S. V. 'Soviet Archaeology in the War Years', *AJA,* vol. 49, 1945, pp. 178–9.
Abstract of Russian report.

919 FIELD, HENRY. 'Recent Archaeological Discoveries in the Soviet Union', *American Review on the Soviet Union,* vol. 7, no. 4, 1946, pp. 67–75.

920 CHILDE, V. GORDON. 'Archaeological Organisation in the U.S.S.R.', *Anglo-Soviet Journal,* vol. 13, no. 3, 1952, pp. 23–6.

921 FRYE, RICHARD N. 'A Decade of Discovery, 1948–1957', *Archaeology,* vol. 10, 1957, pp. 238–9.

922 PHILLIPS, E. D. 'New Light on the Ancient History of the Eurasian Steppe', *AJA,* vol. 61, 1957, pp. 269–80; Bibl.

923 COUNCIL FOR OLD WORLD ARCHAEOLOGY. Cowa Survey. Area 8: European Russia. Editor: Paul Tolstoy. No. 1, 1958. N.Y., 1958. Pp. 14.

924 RYBAKOV, B. A. *and* KRUPNOV, F. I. 'Basic Trends in Soviet Archaeology', *University of Toronto Quarterly,* vol. 28, 1958–9, pp. 29–36.

925 SHELOV, DMITRY *and* MERPERT, NIKOLAY. 'Soviet Archaeological Expeditions in 1961', *Archaeology,* vol. 14, 1961, pp. 166–70.

926 CHILDE, V. GORDON. 'Recent Excavations on Prehistoric Sites in Soviet Russia', *Man,* vol. 44, 1944, pp. 41–3.

927 CHILDE, V. GORDON. 'Archaeology in the U.S.S.R.: the Forest Zone', *Man,* vol. 43, 1943, pp. 4–9.

928 CHILDE, V. GORDON. 'Prehistory in the U.S.S.R.: *1.* Palaeolithic and Mesolithic, *A.* Caucasus and Crimea, *B.* the Russian Plain, *2.* The Copper Age', *Man,* vol. 42, 1942, pp. 98–103 and 130–6.

929 GOLOMSHTOK, EUGENE A. 'The Old Stone Age in European Russia', *Trans APS,* New Series, vol. 29, pt. 2, 1938, pp. ix, 191–468; Bibl.

930 GIMBUTAS, MARIJA. The Prehistory of Eastern Europe. Pt. 1. Mesolithic, Neolithic and Copper Age Cultures in Russia and the Baltic Area. (American School of Prehistoric Research, Peabody Museum, Harvard Univer-

sity. Bulletin no. 20.) Cambridge, Mass., 1956. Pp. ix, 241.

Rev.: B. P. Lozinski in *ASEER*, vol. 17, 1958, pp. 141–143.

931 GIMBUTAS, MARIJA. Bronze Age Cultures in Central and Eastern Europe. The Hague, 1965. Pp. 681.

932 TALLGREN, A. M. 'The Arctic Bronze Age in Europe', *ESA*, vol. 11, 1937, pp. 1–46.

933 TALLGREN, A. M. 'Problems Concerning the Central-Russian Gorodishche Civilisation', *ESA*, vol. 10, 1936, pp. 171–85.

934 CHILDE, V. GORDON. 'The Socketed Celt in Upper Eurasia', *Annual Report of the University of London Institute of Archaeology*, no. 10, 1952–3, pp. (11–25).

935 TALLGREN, A. M. 'Portable Altars', *ESA*, vol. 11, 1937, pp. 47–68.

B. REGIONAL ARCHAEOLOGY

(i) *European Russia and Borderlands*

Novgorod, **936–939**; Perm and the Desna Valley, **940–941**; Baltic lands, **942–944**; Ukraine, **945–953**; South Russia, **954–958**; the Caucasus, Armenia and Georgia, **959–968**; Crimea, **969.**

936 SMITH, ROBERT E. F. 'Some Recent Discoveries in Novgorod', *Past and Present*, no. 5, 1954, pp. 1–10.

937 YANIN, VALENTIN L. 'Modern Methods in Archaeology: the Novgorod Excavations. (Trans. from Russian.)', *Diogenes*, no. 29, 1960, pp. 82–101.

938 YANIN, VALENTIN L. 'The Dig at Novgorod', *Midway*, no. 5, 1961, pp. 2–25.

939 THOMPSON, M. W., *comp.* Novgorod the Great: Excavations at the Medieval City Directed by A. V. Artsikhovsky and B. A. Kolchin. L., 1967. Pp. xvii, 104.

940 TALLGREN, A. M. 'Permian Studies', *ESA*, vol. 3, 1928, pp. 63–92.

941 TALLGREN, A. M. 'Enamelled Ornaments in the Valley of the Desna', *ESA*, vol. 11, 1937, pp. 147–56.

942 GIMBUTAS, MARIJA. The Balts. (Ancient Peoples and Places, vol. 33.) L., N.Y., 1963. Pp. 286. Bibl.

Rev.: Konstantinas Avižonis in *Slavic Rev*, vol. 24, 1965, pp. 131–132.

943 GIMBUTAS, MARIJA. 'Ancient Baltic Lands: a Resume of Linguistic and Archeological Data', *IJSLP,* vol. 6, 1963, pp. 65–102.

944 TALLGREN, A. M. 'The Prehistory of Ingria', *ESA,* vol. 12, 1938, pp. 79–108.

945 MAKHIV, GREGORY. 'The Nature of Ukraine and its Influence on the Material Culture of the Ukrainian People in Prehistoric Times', *Proceedings of the Shevchenko Scientific Society, Historical-Philosophical Section,* vol. 1, 1951, pp. 26–47.

946 BURKITT, M. C. 'Archaeological Work in Ukrain by Professor Ščerbakivskyj', *Antiquaries Journal,* vol. 5, no. 3, 1925, pp. 273–7.

947 PASTERNAK, YAROSLAV. 'The Trypillyan Culture in Ukraine', *Ukr Qly,* vol. 6, 1950, pp. 122–33.

948 KORDYSH, NEONILA. 'Settlement Plans of the Trypillyan Culture', *AUA,* vol. 3, no. 1, 1953, pp. 535–52.

949 GIMBUTAS, MARIJA. 'From the Neolithic to the Iron Age in the Region between the Upper Vistula and Middle Dnieper Rivers: a Survey...', *IJSLP,* vol. 3, 1960, pp. 1–12.

950 ZAKHAROV, ALEXIS A. 'I. A. Zaretsky's Excavations in the Government of Kharkov', *ESA,* vol. 7, 1932, pp. 59–81.

951 GIMBUTAS, MARIJA. 'The Treasure of Michalkov', *Archaeology,* vol. 12, 1959, pp. 84–7.

952 CHILDE, V. GORDON. 'Kostienki: "East Gravettian" or "Solutrean"?', *Annual Report of the University of London Institute of Archaeology,* no. 12, 1954–5, pp. 8–19.

953 CHIKALENKO, LEVKO. 'The Origin of the Paleolithic Meander', *AUA,* vol. 3, no. 1, 1953, pp. 518–34.
     A discussion of the dig at Mezine in north Ukraine.

954 PHILLIPS, E. D. The Royal Hordes: Nomad Peoples of the Steppes. L., 1965. Pp. 144. Bibl. (Pbk.)
     Archaeology of South Russia to 500 A.D.

955 TALLGREN, A. M. 'Studies of the Pontic Bronze Age', *ESA,* vol. 11, 1937, pp. 103–21.

956 SALMONY, ALFRED. 'An Unknown Scythian Find in Novocherkassk', *ESA,* vol. 10, 1936, pp. 54–60.

957 KAPOSHINA, S. I. 'A Sarmatian Royal Burial at Novo-cherkassk', *Antiquity,* vol. 37, 1963, pp. 256–8.

958 ROSTOVTZEFF, MIKHAIL I. (Rostovtsev). 'A Gold Necklace and a Gold Armlet from S. Russia', *ESA,* vol. 9, 1934, pp. 214–20.

959 KUSHNAREVA, K. Kh. *and* CHUBINISHVILI, T. N. 'The Historical Significance of the Southern Caucasus in the Third Millenium, B.C. (Trans. from Russian.)', *Soviet Anthropology and Archaeology,* vol. 2, no. 3, 1963–4, pp. 3–16.

960 MILLER, M. A. 'The Balkars: some Archaeological Notes', *CR,* vol. 6, 1958, pp. 30–6.

961 TALLGREN, A. M. 'Caucasian Monuments: the Kazbek Treasure', *ESA,* vol. 5, 1930, pp. 109–82.

962 SELIMKHANOV, I. R. 'Spectral Analysis of Metal Objects from Archaeological Monuments of the Caucasus', *Prehistoric Society Proceedings,* vol. 28, 1962, pp. (68–79).

963 ZAKHAROV, A. A. 'Contributions to Caucasian Archaeology: a Large Barrow in Daghestan', *ESA,* vol. 5, 1930, pp. 183–216.

964 ZAKHAROV, A. A. 'Contributions to the Archaeology of Daghestan, II: Kozubki's Excavations in Northern Daghestan', *ESA,* vol. 6, 1931, pp. 159–70.

965 KHOSHTARIA, N. 'Archaeological Excavations at Vani', *BK,* New Series, vol. 15–16, 1963, pp. 167–9.

966 PIOTROVSKI, B. B. Urartu: the Kingdom of Van and its Art. (Trans. from Russian and Edited by Peter S. Gelling.) L., 1967. Pp. viii, 111.

967 TAQAISHVILI, E. 'Antiquities of Georgia', *Georgica,* vol. 1, nos. 4–5, 1937, pp. 96–116.

968 KUFTIN, B. A. 'Prehistoric Culture Sequence in Transcaucasia. Edited by Henry Field', *Southwestern Journal of Anthropology,* vol. 2, 1946, pp. 340–60.

969 FIELD, HENRY. 'Excavations at Olbia, Crimea', *Antiquity,* vol. 21, 1947, pp. 42–5.

(ii) Central Asia

General works, **970–975.** Special areas, arranged alphabetically, **976–988.** (Khorezm and Kizil Kum are listed with Uzbekistan, **984–988**).

970 FRUMKIN, GRÉGOIRE. 'Archaeology in Soviet Central Asia and its Ideological Background', *CAR*, vol. 10, 1962, pp. 334–42.

971 CHARD, CHESTER S. 'Soviet Scholarship on the Prehistory of Asiatic Russia', *Slavic Rev*, vol. 22, 1963, pp. 538–46.

972 WRIGHT, GEORGE F. 'Archaeological Interests in Asiatic Russia', *Records of the Past*, vol. 1, 1902, pp. 1–14.

973 CHARD, CHESTER S. 'Archaeology in Soviet Asia, 1950–1951', *Kroeber Anthropological Society Papers*, no. 16, 1957, pp. (29–43).

974 LARICHEV, V. E. 'The Microlithic Character of Neolithic Cultures in Central Asia, Trans-Baikal and Manchuria. (Trans. from Russian.)', *American Antiquity*, vol. 27, 1961–2, pp. 315–22.

975 FORMOZOV, A. A. 'Microlithic Sites in the Asiatic U.S.S.R. (Trans. from Russian.)', *American Antiquity*, vol. 27, 1961–2, pp. 82–92; Bibl.

976 JETTMAR, KARL. 'The Karasuk Culture and its South-Eastern Affinities', *Bulletin of the Museum of Far Eastern Antiquities*, *(Stockholm)*, vol. 22, 1950, pp. 83–126; Bibl.

977 FRUMKIN, GRÉGOIRE. 'Archaeology in Soviet Central Asia, II : Kazakhstan', *CAR*, vol. 11, 1963, pp. 13–29; Bibl.

978 FRUMKIN, GRÉGOIRE. 'Archaeology in Soviet Central Asia, III : Kirgiziya and the Fergana Valley', *CAR*, vol. 12, 1964, pp. 16–29; Bibl.

979 BERNSHTAM, A. N. 'Archaeological Investigations in Kirghiziya. (Trans. from Russian.)', *Gazette des Beaux Arts*, 1946, pp. 65–74.
    An abridged translation.

980 BERNSHTAM, A. N. 'Kirghizia', *AJA*, vol. 47, 1943, pp. 245–7.
    Abstract of Russian report.

981 FRUMKIN, GRÉGOIRE. 'Archaeology in Soviet Central Asia, IV : Tadzhikistan', *CAR*, vol. 12, 1964, pp. 170–84; Bibl.

982 FRUMKIN, GRÉGOIRE. 'Archaeology in Soviet Central Asia, VII : Turkmenistan', *CAR*, vol. 14, 1966, pp. 71–89; Bibl.

983 BOROZDIN, ILYA. 'Turkmenia at the Dawn of History',
Asiatic Review, vol. 43, 1947, pp. 91–3.

984 FRUMKIN, GRÉGOIRE. 'Archaeology in Soviet Central
Asia, VI : Uzbekistan, Excluding Khorezm', CAR, vol.
13, 1965, pp. 239–57.

985 FRUMKIN, GRÉGOIRE. 'Archaeology in Soviet Central
Asia, V : the Deltas of the Oxus and Jaxartes; Khorezm
and its Borderlands', CAR, vol. 13, 1965, pp. 69–86;
Bibl.

986 TOLSTOV, S. P. 'The Prehistoric Cultures and Primitive
Irrigation Systems of Ancient Chorasmia', Annual Report
of the University of London Institute of Archaeology,
no. 13, 1955–6, pp. 8–36.

987 WATSON, WILLIAM. 'Ancient Khorezm : S. P. Tolstov's
Archaeological Expeditions in the Oxus Basin', Anglo-
Soviet Journal, vol. 12, no. 2, 1951, pp. 4–13.

988 FIELD, HENRY. 'Neolithic Station in Kizil-Kum Desert,
Soviet Central Asia', Southwestern Journal of Anthropology, vol. 2, 1946, p. 239.

(iii) North-East Asia. Siberia

989 ZOLOTAREV, ALEKSANDR M. 'The Ancient Culture of
North Asia', Am Anthrop, New Series, vol. 40, 1938,
pp. 13–23.

990 COUNCIL FOR OLD WORLD ARCHAEOLOGY. Cowa Survey. Area 18 : Northern Asia. Editor : Chester S. Chard.
No. 1, 1957. Cambridge, Mass., 1957, Pp. 7.

991 CHARD, CHESTER S. 'Northeast Asia', in Asian Perspectives, vol. 1— Annual survey of archaeological field work,
published as follows :— vol. 1, 1957, pp. 15–23; vol. 2,
1958, pp. 13–21; vol. 3, 1959, pp. 5–9; vol. 4, 1960,
pp. 7–16; vol. 5, 1961, pp. 16–20; vol. 6, 1962, pp. 8–
18; vol. 7, 1963, pp. 8–15; vol. 8, 1964, pp. 10–20,
et seq.

992 SHIMKIN, DEMITRI B. 'Western Siberian Archaeology :
an Interpretation Summary', in 1025, pp. 648–61;
Bibl.

993 CHARD, CHESTER S. 'An Outline of the Pre-History of
Siberia. Pt. 1 : the Pre-Metal Periods', Southwestern
Journal of Anthropology, vol. 14, 1958, pp. 1–33; Bibl.

994 OKLADNIKOV, ALEKSEY P. 'The Paleolithic of Trans-Baikal. (Trans. from Russian.)', *American Antiquity*, vol. 26, 1960–1, pp. 486–97; Bibl.

995 CHARD, CHESTER S. 'Mesolithic Sites in Siberia', *Asian Perspectives*, vol. 2, no. 1, 1958, pp. 118–27.

996 MICHAEL, HENRY N. 'The Neolithic Age in Eastern Siberia', *Trans APS*, New Series, vol. 48, pt 2, 1958, pp. 1–108; Bibl.

> Rev.: D. B. Shimkin in *American Antiquity*, vol. 24, 1959, pp. 436–437.

997 CHARD, CHESTER S. 'The Oldest Sites of Northeast Siberia', *American Antiquity*, vol. 21, 1955–6, pp. 405–9; Bibl.

998 TOLSTOY, PAUL. 'The Archaeology of the Lena Basin and its New World Relationships. 2 pts.', *American Antiquity*, vol. 23, 1957–8, pp. 397–418 and vol. 24, 1958–9, pp. 63–81; Bibl.

999 JETTMAR, KARL. 'The Altai before the Turks', *Bulletin of the Museum of Far Eastern Antiquities (Stockholm)*, vol. 23, 1951, pp. 135–223; Bibl.

1000 GRIAZNOV, M. P. 'The Pazirik Burial of Altai. (Trans. from Russian and Edited by E. A. Golomshtok.)', *AJA*, vol. 37, 1933, pp. 30–45.

1001 ZAKHAROV, ALEXIS A. 'Antiquities of Katanda (Altai)', *JRAI*, vol. 55, 1925, pp. 37–57.

1002 ZAKHAROV, ALEXIS A. 'Materials on the Archaeology of Siberia: Dr V. V. Radloff's Excavations in the Berēl Steppe', *ESA*, vol. 3, 1928, pp. 132–40.

1003 RUDENKO, SERGEY I. 'The Ust'-Kanskaia Paleolithic Cave Site, Siberia. (Trans. from Russian.)', *American Antiquity*, vol. 27, 1961–2, pp. 203–15.

1004 TALLGREN, A. M. 'The South Siberian Cemetry of Oglatky from the Han Period', *ESA*, vol. 11, 1937, pp. 69–90.

1005 BORTVIN, N. N. 'The Verkhny-Kizil Find', *ESA*, vol. 3, 1928, pp. 122–31.

1006 TALLGREN, A. M. 'Some North-Eurasian Sculptures', *ESA*, vol. 12, 1938, pp. 109–35.

(iv) *The Far East*

1007 OKLADNIKOV, ALEKSEY P. The Soviet Far East in Antiquity: an Archaeological and Historical Study of the Maritime Region of the U.S.S.R. (Trans. from Russian.) (Arctic Institute of North America. Anthropology of the North: Translations from Russian Sources, no. 6.) U. of Toronto P., 1965. Pp. v, 280.

1008 CHARD, CHESTER S. 'Archaeological Work near Magadan', *Anthropological Papers of the University of Alaska*, vol. 8, 1959–60, pp. 77–8; Bibl.

1009 JOCHELSON, WALDEMAR. Archaeological Investigations in Kamchatka. (Carnegie Institution Publications, no. 388.) Washington, 1928. Pp. viii, 88, Bibl.

1010 QUIMBY, GEORGE I. 'The Prehistory of Kamchatka', *American Antiquity*, vol. 12, 1946–7, pp. 173–9; Bibl.

1011 CHARD, CHESTER S. 'Chronology and Culture Succession in the Northern Kuriles', *American Antiquity*, vol. 21, 1955–6, pp. 287–92.

1012 CHARD, CHESTER S. 'Recent Archaeological Work in the Chukchi Peninsula', *Anthropological Papers of the University of Alaska*, vol. 8, 1959–60, pp. 119–30.

1013 OKLADNIKOV, ALEKSEY P. *and* NEKRASOV, I. A. 'New Traces of an Inland Neolithic Culture in the Chukotsk (Chukchi) Peninsula. (Trans. from Russian.)', *American Antiquity*, vol. 25, 1959–60, pp. 247–56; Bibl.

1014 OKLADNIKOV, ALEKSEY P. *and* NEKRASOV, I. A. 'Ancient Settlements in the Main River Valley, Chukchi Peninsula. (Trans. from Russian.)', *American Antiquity*, vol. 27, 1961–2, pp. 546–56; Bibl.

1015 CHARD, CHESTER S. 'An Early Pottery Site in the Chukchi Peninsula', *American Antiquity*, vol. 20, 1954–5, pp. 283–4.

1016 OKLADNIKOV, ALEKSEY P. 'A Note on the Lake El'gytkhyn Finds', *American Antiquity*, vol. 26, 1960–1, pp. 97–8.
   Abstract of Russian report.

1017 GIDDINGS, JAMES L. 'The Archaeology of Bering Strait', *Current Anthropology*, vol. 1, 1960, pp. 121–30, 138; Bibl.

1018 CHARD, CHESTER S., *and others*. 'Comments on Giddings,

J. L., The Archeology of Bering Strait', *Current Anthropology,* vol. 1, 1960, pp. 130–7.

1019   CHARD, CHESTER S. 'Routes to Bering Strait', *American Antiquity,* vol. 26, 1960–1, pp. 283–4.

1020   RUDENKO, S. I. The Ancient Culture of the Bering Sea and the Eskimo Problem. (Trans. from Russian.) (Arctic Institute of North America. Translations from Russian Sources, no. 1.) U. of Toronto P., 1961. Pp. 186. Bibl.

1021   CHARD, CHESTER S. 'Eskimo Archaeology in Siberia', *Southwestern Journal of Anthropology,* vol. 11, 1955, pp. 150–77; Bibl.

1022   GRIFFIN, JAMES B. 'Some Prehistoric Connections between Siberia and America', *Science,* vol. 131, 1960, pp. 801–12; Bibl.

1023   TOLSTOY, PAUL. 'Some Amerasian Pottery Traits in North Asian Prehistory', *American Antiquity,* vol. 19, 1953–4, pp. 25–39; Bibl.

ANTHROPOLOGY, ETHNOLOGY

Bibliography, **1024**. General studies, **1025–1032**; special, **1033**.
Baltic peoples, **1034–1037**; Caucasians, **1038–1046**; Georgians,
1047–1052 (cf. **1757–1758**). On the peoples of Asiatic Russia
generally and especially Central Asia, **1053–1056**; Siberians,
1057–1071. Of these, **1057** is a bibliographic study and **1060**
the most comprehensive work available in English. On the
Buryats, **1064–1065**; Koryaks, **1066**; the Tungus, **1067–1069**;
Samoyeds, **1070** (see also **2050**); Chukchi, **1071**. For works on
the Jews in Russia, see **835–837**.

1024 HALPERN, JOEL, *and others, comp.* Bibliography of
Anthropological and Sociological Publications on Eastern
Europe and the U.S.S.R. With a Supplement of Siberian
Travel Accounts Compiled by R. H. Fisher. (Russian
and East European Studies Center Series, vol. 1, no. 2.)
Los Angeles, 1961. Pp. 142.

1025 WALLACE, ANTHONY F. C., *ed.* Men and Cultures:
Selected Papers of the 5th International Congress of
Anthropological and Ethnological Sciences. Philadelphia,
1956. U. of Pennsylvania P., 1960. Pp. xxxi, 810. Also
Pbk.

1026 FIELD, HENRY, *comp.* Contributions to the Anthropology
of the Soviet Union. (Smithsonian Miscellaneous Collections, vol. 110, no. 13.) Washington, 1948. Pp. vii, 244.

1027 DEBETZ, G. F. 'Summary of Paleo-Anthropological
Investigation in the U.S.S.R.', in **1025**, pp. 34–6.

1028 NIEDERLE, L. 'Historical Records of the Type of the
Ancient Slavs', *Anthropologie* (Prague), vol. 7, 1929,
pp. 62–4.

1029 OBOUKHOFF, NICHOLAS M. 'Racial Origin of the Russian
People', *Southwestern Social Science Quarterly,* vol. 22,
1941, pp. 116–24.

1030 LATHAM, ROBERT G. The Native Races of the Russian
Empire. L., 1854. Pp. viii, 340.

H

1031 TERRAS, VICTOR. 'Leo Diaconus and the Ethnology of Kievan Rus'', *Slavic Rev.*, vol. 24, 1965, pp. 395–406.

1032 SHEVCHENKO, IHOR. 'Sviatoslav in Byzantine and Slavic Miniatures', *Slavic Rev.*, vol. 24, 1965, pp. 709–13.

1033 BOBRI, VLADIMIR. 'Gypsies and Gypsy Choruses of Old Russia', *Journal of the Gypsy Lore Society*, Series 3, vol. 40, 1961, pp. 112–20.

1034 INDREKO, RICHARD. Origin and Area of Settlement of the Fenno-Ugrian Peoples. Heidelberg, 1948. Pp. 24.

1035 MATTHEWS, W. K. 'Medieval Baltic Tribes', *ASEER*, vol. 8, 1949, pp. 126–36.

1036 LOORITS, OSKAR. 'The Development of the Uralian Culture Area', *SEER*, vol. 31, 1952–3, pp. 1–19.
     Particular reference to Estonia.

1037 MAŽIULIS, ANTANAS. 'Lithuanian Ethnographical Studies: a Survey of Ethnographical Museums and Societies', *Lituanus*, vol. 4, 1958, pp. 76–9.

1038 GEIGER, BERNARD, *and others*. Peoples and Languages of the Caucasus . . . (Janua Linguarum, no. 6.) The Hague, 1959. Pp. 77. Bibl.

1039 FIELD, HENRY. Contributions to the Anthropology of the Caucasus. (Papers of the Peabody Museum of American Archaeology and Ethnology, Harvard University, vol. 48, no. 1.) Cambridge, Mass., 1953. Pp. x, 154. Bibl.

1040 JAVAKHISHVILI, ALEXANDER. 'The Caucasian Race', *Georgica*, vol. 1, nos. 2–3, 1936, pp. 92–108; Bibl.

1041 TRAHO, R. 'Literature on Checheno-Ingushes and Karachay-Balkars', *CR*, vol. 5, 1957, pp. 76–96.

1042 ABAZA, R. 'The Abazinians', *CR*, vol. 8, 1959, pp. 34–40.

1043 VERNADSKY, GEORGE V. 'The Riddle of the Gothi Tetraxitae', *Südost-Forschungen*, vol. 11, 1946–52, pp. 281–3.

1044 ADIGHE, R. 'Literature on Dagestan and its People', *CR*, vol. 4, 1957, pp. 101–18.

1045 SAMUEL, JACOB. The Remnant Found; or, The Place of Israel's Hiding Discovered: Being a Summary of Proofs, Showing that the Jews of Daghistan on the Caspian Sea are the Remnant of the Ten Tribes . . . L., 1841. Pp. xxx, 133.

1046   GRIGOLIA, ALEXANDER. 'Milk Relationship in the Caucasus, its Function and Meaning', *BK*, New Series, vol. 13–14, 1962, pp. 148–67.

1047   GUGUSHVILI, A. 'Ethnographical and Historical Division of Georgia', *Georgica*, vol. 1, nos. 2–3, 1936, pp. 53–71.

1048   NAKASHIDSE, GEORGE. 'Georgia and its People', *Ukr Qly*, vol. 18, 1962, pp. 49–60.

1049   ALLEN, W. E. D. 'Ex Ponto 1 and 2: *1*. Heni-Veneti and Os-Alans, *2*. Heni-Veneti and Batavi', *BK*, New Series, vols. 4–5, 1958, pp. 39–54.

1050   ALLEN, W. E. D. 'Ex Ponto 3 and 4: *3*. The Trialetian Goblet for Cormac, *4*. Dogs' Heads and Wolves' Heads', *BK*, New Series, vols. 6–7, 1959, pp. 29–47.

1051   ALLEN, W. E. D. 'Ex Ponto, 5: Heniochi-Aea-Hayasa', *BK*, New Series, vols. 8–9, 1960, pp. 79–92.

1052   BRYER, ANTHONY. 'Some Notes on the Laz and Tzan. 2 pts.', *BK*, New Series, vols. 21–22, 1966, pp. 174–95 and vols. 23–24, 1967, pp. 161–8.

1053   JOCHELSON, WALDEMAR (Iokhelson). Peoples of Asiatic Russia. N.Y., 1928. Pp. 277.

1054   KRADER, LAWRENCE. Peoples of Central Asia. Bloomington, Ind., The Hague, 1963. Pp. xiv, 319.

1055   CZAPLICKA, MARIE A. The Turks of Central Asia in History and at the Present Day... O., 1918. Pp. 242. Bibl.

1056   KRADER, LAWRENCE. Social Organization of the Mongol-Turkic Pastoral Nomads. Indiana U.P., The Hague, 1963. Pp. x, 412. Bibl.
    Rev.: Paula G. Rubel in *Slavic Rev*, vol. 24, 1965, pp. 340–341.

1057   JAKOBSON, ROMAN, *and others, comp.* Paleosiberian Peoples and Languages: a Bibliographical Guide. New Haven, Conn., 1957. Pp. vii, 222.

1058   OKLADNIKOV, ALEKSEY P. Ancient Population of Siberia and its Cultures. (Trans. from Russian.) (Russian Translation Series of the Peabody Museum of Archaeology and Ethnology, Harvard University, vol. 1, no. 1.) Harvard U.P., 1959. Pp. (96). Bibl.

1059   LEVIN, MAKSIM G. Ethnic Origins of the Peoples of Northeastern Asia. (Trans. from Russian.) (Arctic Institute of North America. Anthropology of the North:

Translations from Russian Sources, no. 3.) U. of Toronto P., 1963. Pp. v, 355. Bibl. (Pbk.)

1060 LEVIN, MAKSIM G. *and* POTAPOV, L.P., *ed.* The Peoples of Siberia. (Trans. from Russian.) U. of Chicago P., 1964. Pp. viii, 948.
Translation of *Narody Sibiri*.

1061 CZAPLICKA, MARIE A. Aboriginal Siberia: a Study in Social Anthropology. O., 1914. Pp. xiv, 374. Bibl.

1062 MICHAEL, HENRY N., *ed.* Studies in Siberian Ethnogenesis. (Trans. from Russian.) (Arctic Institute of North America. Anthropology of the North: Translations from Russian Sources, no. 2.) U. of Toronto P., 1962. Pp. vii, 313. (Pbk.)

1063 LOPATIN, IVAN A. 'The Extinct and Near-Extinct Tribes of Northeastern Asia as Compared with the American Indian', *American Antiquity*, vol. 5, 1939–40, pp. 202–8.

1064 KOJEUROFF, GEORGE P. 'Some Contributions to the Anthropology of the Buriats', *Journal of the North-China Branch of the Royal Asiatic Society*, vol. 58, 1927, pp. 142–57; Bibl.

1065 KRADER, LAWRENCE. 'Buryat Religion and Society', *Southwestern Journal of Anthropology*, vol. 10, 1954, pp. (322–51).

1066 JOCHELSON, WALDEMAR (Iokhelson). The Koryak. Leiden, N.Y., 1908. Pp. (842).

1067 JOCHELSON, WALDEMAR (Iokhelson). The Yukaghir and the Yukaghirized Tungus 3 pts. Leiden, N. Y., 1910–26
Not inspected.

1068 SHIROKOGOROV, SERGEY M. Social Organization of the Northern Tungus. Shanghai, 1929. Pp. (427).

1069 SHIROKOGOROV, SERGEY M. 'Northern Tungus Migrations in the Far East: the Goldi and their Ethnical Affinities', *Journal of the North-China Branch of the Royal Asiatic Society*, vol. 57, 1926, pp. 123–83; Bibl.

1070 HAJDÚ, PÉTER. The Samoyed Peoples and Languages. (Trans. from Hungarian.) Indiana U.P., The Hague, 1963. Pp. vii, 114. Bibl.
Rev.: Robert T. Harms in *Slavic Rev*, vol. 23, 1964, pp. 178–179.

1071 LIBBY, DOROTHY. 'Three Hundred Years of Chukchi Ethnic Identity', in **1025,** pp. 298–304.

MYTHOLOGY, FOLKLORE, CUSTOMS

Slavic mythology, **1072–1076.** Slavic folklore, **1077–
1079**; Russian folklore, **1080–1084** (cf. section 16B (iii) on folk
literature). Manners and customs, **1085–1088.** Cheremis studies,
1089–1091; Baltic lands, **1092–1094**; Ukraine, **1095–1096**;
Georgia, **1097**; Crimea, **1098**; Central Asia and Siberia, **1099–
1101.**

1072 MÁCHAL, JAN. 'Slavic Mythology', in Gray, Louis H., *ed.*
Mythology of all Races, vol. 3. Boston Mass., 1918,
pp. 215–330, 351–61; Bibl.: pp. 389–98.

1073 JAKOBSON ROMAN. 'Slavic Mythology', in *Funk and
Wagnall's Standard Dictionary of Folklore, Mythology
and Legend*, vol. 2, N.Y., 1950, pp. 1025–8; Bibl.

1074 ALEXINSKY, G. 'Slavonic Mythology. (Trans. from
French)', in *Larousse Encyclopedia of Mythology*, L.,
N.Y., 1959, pp. 293–310.

1075 CURTIN, JEREMIAH. Myths and Folk-Tales of the
Russians, Western Slavs and Magyars. Boston, Mass.,
1890. Pp. xxv, 555.

1076 DRAGOMANOV, MIKHAIL P. Notes on the Slavic Religio-
Ethical Legends: the Dualistic Creation of the World.
(Trans. from Russian.) Indiana U.P., 1961. Pp. xii, 153.

1077 JAKOBSON, SVATAVA P. 'Slavic Folklore', in *Funk and
Wagnall's Standard Dictionary of Folklore, Mythology
and Legend*, vol. 2, N.Y., 1950, pp. 1019–25; Bibl.

1078 LORD, ALBERT B., *ed.*, Slavic Folklore: a Symposium.
(American Folklore Society. Bibliographical and Special
Series, vol. 6.) Philadelphia, 1956. Pp. viii, 132.
    Rev.: V. Jukova in *SEER*, vol. 29, 1950–51, pp. 602–604; Dimitri
J. F. Matlock in *Rus R*, vol. 17, no. 2, 1958, pp. 154–155.

1079 KIRTLEY, BASIL F. 'Dracula, the Monastic Chronicles
and Slavic Folklore', *Midwest Folklore*, vol. 6, 1956,
pp. (133–9).

1080 OINAS, FELIX J. 'Folklore Activities in Russia', *Journal of American Folklore,* vol. 74, 1961, pp. 362–70.

1081 SOKOLOV, YURI M. Russian Folklore. (Trans. from Russian.) N.Y., L., 1950. Pp. viii, 760. Bibl.
Rev.: V. Jukova in *SEER,* vol. 29, 1950/51, pp. 602–604; Dimitri von Mohrenschildt in *Rus R,* vol. 9, 1950, pp. 336–338.

1082 RALSTON, W. R. S. The Songs of the Russian People as Illustrative of Slavonic Mythology and Russian Social Life. L., 1872. Pp. xvi, 439.
cf. **1373–1374, 1377–1379** and **1506–1508.**

1083 WASSON, *Mrs.* VALENTINA P. *and* WASSON, R. GORDON. Mushrooms, Russia and History. 2 vols. N.Y., 1957. Bibl.

1084 KLAGSTAD, HAROLD L. 'Great Russian Charm Structure', *Indiana Slavic Studies,* vol. 2, 1958, pp. 135–44.

1085 ATKINSON, JOHN A. *and* WALKER, JAMES. A Picturesque Representation of the Manners, Customs and Amusements of the Russians . . . 3 vols. L., 1803–4.

1086 The COSTUME OF THE RUSSIAN EMPIRE. Illustrated by a Series of 73 Engravings . . . L., 1803. 73 Plates.

1087 JOPSON, N. B. 'Early Slavonic Funeral Ceremonies', *SEER,* vol. 6, 1927–8, pp. 59–67.

1088 BULLCY, THOMAS. 'The Names of Certaine Sortes of Drinks Used in Russia . . .', in **1872b,** vol. 2, pp. 448–9.

1089 STUDIES IN CHEREMIS FOLKLORE. Vol. 1. Edited by Thomas A. Sebeok. (Indiana University Publications. Folklore Series, no. 6.) Indiana U.P., 1952. Pp. vii, 213. Bibl.

1090 SEBEOK, THOMAS A. *and* INGEMANN, FRANCES J. Studies in Cheremis: the Supernatural. (Viking Fund Publications in Anthropology, no. 22.) N.Y., 1956. Pp. 357. Bibl.

1091 STUDIES IN CHEREMIS. Vol. 6. Games. By Thomas A. Sebeok and Paul G. Brewster. (Indiana University Publications. Folklore Series, no. 11.) Indiana U.P., 1958. Pp. xi, 123. Bibl.

1092 GIMBUTAS, MARIJA. 'The Ancient Religion of the Balts', *Lituanus,* vol. 8, 1962, pp. 97–109.
Excerpt from **942.**

1093 LOORITS, OSKAR. 'The Stratification of Estonian Folk-Religion', *SEER,* vol. 35, 1956–7, pp. 360–78.

1094 BALYS, JONAS. 'Ancient Wedding Customs [in Lithuania]', *Lituanus*, vol. 6, 1960, pp. 25–6.

1095 STSCHERBAKIWSKYJ, W. 'The Early Ukrainian Social Order as Reflected in Ukrainian Wedding Customs', *SEER*, vol. 31, 1952–3, pp. 325–51.

1096 LUTSIV, VOLODYMYR. 'Kobza-Bandura and "Dumy" and their Significance in the History of the Ukrainian People', *Ukr Rev (L.)*, vol. 13, no. 1, 1966, pp. 53–70.

1097 TSERETELI, M. 'The Asianic (Asia Minor) Elements in National Georgian Paganism . . .', *Georgica*, vol. 1, no. 1, 1935, pp. 28–66.

1098 HOLDERNESS, MARY. Notes Relating to the Manners and Customs of the Crim Tatars . . . L., 1821. Pp. vi, 168.

1099 RANKING, JOHN. Historical Researches on the Wars and Sports of the Mongols and Romans . . . L., 1826. Pp. xv, 516. Bibl.

1100 CURTIN, JEREMIAH. A Journey in Southern Siberia: the Mongols, their Religion and their Myths. L., 1910. Pp. xiv, 319.

1101 MICHAEL, HENRY N., *ed*. Studies in Siberian Shamanism. (Trans. from Russian.) (Arctic Institute of North American Anthropolgy of the North: Translations from Russian Sources, no. 4.) U. of Toronto P., 1963. Pp. iv, 229.

12

CIVILIZATION, CULTURE, PHILOSOPHY

A. GENERAL AND CHRONOLOGICAL

Anthologies of Russian writings in translation, **1102–1103**. Comprehensive general surveys, **1104–1107**; recommended: **1104** and **1107**. Minor general works, arranged primarily by date of publication, **1108–1119**. The culture of Kiev Rus', **1120–0023**. Of these **1123** is the best general introduction. Chiefly on Muscovy, **1124–1127**; 18th century Russian civilization, **1128–1130**. Particularly recommended: **1129**. The religious background to Russian history and the idea of "Holy Russia" is well explored in **1132–1137**. On the doctrine of "Moscow the Third Rome", see **1175–1183**. On science in Russian culture, **1293**.

1102 RIHA, THOMAS, ed. Readings in Russian Civilization. 3 vols. (in 1.) U. of Chicago P., 1964. Pp. xvi, 801. Also Pbk Edition in 3 vols.

1103 BLINOFF, Mrs. MARTHE, comp. Life and Thought in Old Russia. Pennsylvania State U.P., 1961. Pp. xv, 222.
Anthology of writings and documents from the late 15th to the end of the 19th century. Rev.: B. Malnick in *SEER*, vol. 41, 1962–63, pp. 265–266.

1104 MILYUKOV, PAVEL N. (Miliukov). Outlines of Russian Culture. (Trans. from Russian.) 3 vols. U. of Pennsylvania P., 1942. Bibl. Reprinted in one volume 1948.
Partial translation of original Russian work. Rev.: B. H. Sumner in *SEER*, vol. 25, 1946, pp. 253–257. Vol. 1: Religion and the Church, Vol. 2: Literature, Vol. 3: Architecture, Painting and Music.

1105 MASARYK, THOMAS G. The Spirit of Russia: Studies in History, Literature and Philosophy. (Trans. from German.) 2 vols. L., N.Y., 1919. Bibl. 2nd ed. 2 vols. L., N.Y., 1955.
Emphasis on the 19th century. Rev.: D. von Mohrenschildt in *Rus R*, vol. 15, 1956, pp. 211–214; N. Beeson in *ASEER*, vol. 15, 1956, p. 296.

1106 Voyce, Arthur. Moscow and the Roots of Russian Culture. U. of Oklahoma P., 1964. Pp. xiii, 191. Bibl.

1107 Billington, James H. The Icon and the Axe: an Interpretive History of Russian Culture. L., 1966. Pp. xviii, 786, xxxiii. Bibl.

1108 Stephens, Winifred. The Soul of Russia. L., Edinburgh, 1916. Pp. xvii, 307.

1109 Wolkonsky, Prince Sergey (Volkonski). Pictures of Russian History and Russian Literature. (Lowell Lectures.) Boston, Mass., N.Y., L., 1897. Pp. xii, 283.

1110 Foulke, William D. Slav or Saxon: a Study of the Growth and Tendencies of Russian Civilisation. N.Y., 1887. Pp. v, 148. 2nd ed. N.Y., 1899. Pp. vii, 141. 3rd ed. N.Y., 1904. Pp. ix, 210.

1111 Bérard, Victor. The Russian Empire and Czarism. (Trans. from French.) L., 1905. Pp. xxiv, 299.

1112 Muratov, Paul. 'The Age of Russia', *SEER*, vol. 14, 1935–6, pp. 138–45.

1113 Weidlé, Wladimir. Russia: Absent and Present. (Trans. from French.) L., N.Y., 1952. Pp. vi, 153.

1114 Fedotov, George P. 'The Russian', *Rus R*, vol. 13, 1954, pp. 3–17.

1115 Stender-Petersen, Adolf. Russian Studies. (Acta Jutlandica: Aarsskrift for Aarhus Universitet, vol. 28, pt. 2, 1956.) Aarhus, 1956. Pp. 98.

1116 Clarkson, Jesse D. 'Russia: an Essay at Perspective', *Rus R*, vol. 20, 1961, pp. 103–9.

1117 Smith, Robert E. F. 'Russian History and the Soviet Union', *Comparative Studies in Society and History*, vol. 4, 1962, pp. 375–87.

1118 Guins, George C. 'Russia's Place in World History', *Rus R*, vol. 22, 1963, pp. 355–68.

1119 Szeftel, Marc. 'Some Reflections on the Particular Characteristics of the Russian Historical Process', *Rus R*, vol. 23, 1964, pp. 223–37.

1120 Kocevalov, Andriy. 'Ukraine's Participation in the Cultural Activity of the Ancient World', *Ukr Qly*, vol. 5, 1949, pp. 111–21.

1121 Dombrovsky, Aleksandr. 'The Spiritual Trend of Ukraine in Antiquity', *Proceedings of the Shevchenko*

Scientific Society, Historical-Philosophical Section, vol. 1, 1951, pp. 52–5.

1122 CROSS, SAMUEL H. 'Primitive Civilization of the Eastern Slavs', *ASEER*, vol. 5, no. 1, 1946, pp. 51–87.

cf. general Slavic civilization, **108–111**.

1123 GREKOV, BORIS D. The Culture of Kiev Rūs. (Trans. from Russian.) Moscow, 1947. Pp. 153.

1124 BILLINGTON, JAMES H. 'Images of Muscovy', *Slavic Rev*, vol. 21, 1962, pp. 24–34.

1125 ANDREYEV, NIKOLAY. 'Pagan and Christian Elements in Old Russia', *Slavic Rev*, vol. 21, 1962, pp. 16–23.

1126 FLOROVSKY, GEORGES. 'The Problem of Old Russian Culture', *Slavic Rev*, vol. 21, 1962, pp. 1–15 and 35–42.

1127 LIKHACHEV, D. S. 'Further Remarks on the Problem of Old Russian Culture', *Slavic Rev*, vol. 22, 1963, pp. 115–20.

1128 TOMPKINS, STUART R. The Russian Mind from Peter the Great through the Enlightenment. U. of Oklahoma P., 1953. Pp. xi, 291. Bibl.

Rev.: Helene Iswolsky in *Rus R*, vol. 13, 1954, pp. 68–69.

1129 ROGGER, HANS. National Consciousness in Eighteenth-Century Russia. Harvard U.P., 1960. Pp. viii, 319. Bibl.

Rev.: Isabel de Madariaga in *SEER*, vol. 42, 1963–64, pp. 481–482; Alexander Lipski in *ASEER*, vol. 20, 1961, pp. 321–323; Serge A. Zenkovsky in *Rus R*, vol. 20, no. 2, 1961, pp. 156–157.

1130 ROGGER, HANS. 'The Russian National Character: some Eighteenth Century Views', *HSS*, vol. 4, 1957, pp. 17–34.

1131 BRYANCHANINOV, ALEKSANDR N. (Brianchaninov). Ideological Foundations of Russian Slavonism. (Trans. from Russian.) L., 1916. Pp. ii, 30.

1132 IZWOLSKY, HELENE (Iswolsky) (Izvol'ski). The Soul of Russia. N.Y., 1943. Pp. xiii, 200, Bibl.; L., 1944. Pp. xi, 172. Bibl.

1133 CHERNIAVSKY, MICHAEL. 'Holy Russia: a Study in the History of an Idea', *AHR*, vol. 63, 1957–8, pp. 617–37.

1134 SOLOV'EV, ALEKSANDR V. Holy Russia: the History of a Religious-Social Idea. The Hague, 1959. Pp. 61.

1135 CHERNIAVSKY, MICHAEL. Tsar and People: Studies in Russian Myths. Yale U.P., 1961. Pp. xix, 258. Bibl.

Rev.: Marc Raeff in *Slavic Rev*, vol. 21, 1962, pp. 344–346;
Serge A. Zenkovsky in *Rus R*, vol. 22, 1963, pp. 92–93.

1136 FEDOTOV, GEORGE P. 'Religious Background of Russian Culture', *CH*, vol. 12, 1943, pp. 35–51.

1137 BILL, *Mrs.* Valentine T. (Tschebotarioff–Bill). 'Faith and Reason in Russian History', *Rus R*, vol. 13, 1954, pp. 186–92.

1138 RIASANOVSKY, NICHOLAS V. 'Oriental Despotism and Russia', *Slavic Rev*, vol. 22, 1963, pp. 644–9.

1139 SPULER, BERTOLD. 'Russia and Islam', *Slavic Rev*, vol. 22, 1963, pp. 650–5.

1140 VERNADSKY, GEORGE V. 'On some Parallel Trends in Russian and Turkish History', *Transactions of the Connecticut Academy of Arts and Sciences*, vol. 36, 1945, pp. 25–36.

B. RUSSIA BETWEEN EAST AND WEST

General works, **1141–1143**. Russia and the West, **1144–1146** (cf. section 6A-C). Russia and the cultural influence of Byzantium, **1147–1157**. For the early relations of Kiev Rus' with Byzantium, see **692–698**; campaigns against Constantinople, **1570–1577**. On imperialism in Russian history, **1158–1161**. For works on the eastward expansion of Russia, see **320** and **1829–1840**. Eurasianism, see **57–59**. Moscow the "Third Rome", **1175–1183**.

1141 YASHCHENKO, ALEKSANDR. 'The Rôle of Russia in the Mutual Approach of the West and the East', *Universal Races Congress, no. 1, 1911, London: Papers on Inter-Racial Problems*. Edited by G. Spiller, L., Boston, Mass., 1911, pp. 195–207.

1142 KRUPNYTSKY, BORYS (Krupnyckyj). 'The West-East Problem in the Historical Development of Russia', *Ukr Qly*, vol. 4, 1948, pp. 297–307.

1143 CHAMBERLIN WILLIAM H. 'Russia between East and West', *Rus R*, vol. 19, 1960, pp. 309–15.

1144 SUMNER, BENEDICT H. 'Russia and Europe', *OSP*, vol. 2, 1951, pp. 1–16.

1145 CHAMBERLIN, WILLIAM H. 'Russia under Western Eyes', *Rus R*, vol. 16, no. 1, 1957, pp. 3–12.

1146   OLIVA, LAWRENCE J., *comp.* Russia and the West from Peter to Khrushchev. Boston, Mass., L., 1966. Pp. (xxi, 289). Bibl. (Pbk.)

1147   WITTFOGEL, KARL A. 'Russia and the East : a Comparison and Contrast', *Slavic Rev*, vol. 22, 1963, pp. 627–43 and 656–62.

1148   MEYENDORFF, A., *Baron and* BAYNES, NORMAN H. 'The Byzantine Inheritance in Russia', in Baynes, Norman H. *and* Moss, Henry St. L.B., *ed. Byzantium: an Introduction to East Roman Civilization*, O., 1948, chapter 14, pp. 369–91; Bibl.

1149   OBOLENSKY, DMITRI. 'Russia's Byzantine Heritage', *OSP*, vol. 1, 1950, pp. 37–63.

1150   STAMMLER, HEINRICH. 'Russia between Byzantium and Utopia', *Rus R*, vol. 17, no. 2, 1958, pp. 94–103.
    cf. **73**.

1151   RUNCIMAN, STEVEN. 'Byzantium, Russia and Caesaropapism', *Canadian Slavonic Papers*, vol. 2, 1957, pp. 1–10.

1152   DVORNIK, FRANCIS. 'Byzantine Political Ideas in Kievan Russia', *DOP*, nos. 9–10, 1956, pp. 73–121.

1153   DVORNIK, FRANCIS. 'Byzantine Influences in Russia', in Huxley, M., *ed. The Root of Europe*, L., 1952, chapter 10, pp. 95–106.

1154   SHEVCHENKO, IHOR. 'Byzantine Cultural Influences', in **37**, chapter 6, pp. 143–97.

1155   OBOLENSKY, DIMITRI. 'The Heritage of Cyril and Methodius in Russia', *DOP*, no. 19, 1965, pp. 45–65.
    cf. **119–120**.

1156   CROSS, SAMUEL H. 'The Results of the Conversion of the Slavs from Byzantium', *Annuaire de l'Institut de Philologie et d'Histoire Orientales et Slaves (Univ. de Bruxelles)*, vol. 7, 1939–44, pp. 71–82. Also printed N.Y., vol. 7, 1947, pp. 71–82.
    cf. **118**.

1157   DVORNIK, FRANCIS. 'Byzantium and the North', in Huxley, M., *ed. The Root of Europe*, L., 1952, chapter 9, pp. 85–94.

1158   HALECKI, OSKAR. 'Imperialism in Slavic and East European History', *ASEER*, vol. 11, 1952, pp. 1–26.

1159 RIASANOVSKY, NICHOLAS V. 'Old Russia, the Soviet Union and Eastern Europe', *ASEER*, vol. 11, 1952, pp. 171–88.

1160 BACKUS, OSWALD P. 'Was Muscovite Russia Imperialistic?', *ASEER*, vol. 13, 1954, pp. 522–34.

1161 MOSELY, PHILIP E. 'Aspects of Russian Expansion', *ASEER*, vol. 7, 1948, pp. 197–213.
See also **320, 483, 1816, 1821** and **1829–1840.**

C. PHILOSOPHY, POLITICAL IDEOLOGY

In most of the general surveys of Russian philosophy listed below, **1162–1165,** treatment of the earlier period is sketchy. General works on intellectual history and political ideology, **1166–1168**; special topics arranged chronologically, **1169–1174**; studies on "Moscow the Third Rome" arranged by date of publication, **1175–1183.** On Križanić and early Panslavism, see **121–125.** For works on Radishchev, see **504–524.**

1162 EDIE, JAMES M., *and others, ed.* Russian Philosophy. 3 vols. Chicago, 1965.
Anthology in translation. Rev.: Georges Florovsky in *Rus R*, vol. 25, 1966, pp. 409–411; Richard T. de George in *Slavic Rev*, vol. 25, 1966, pp. 361–363.

1163 LOSSKY, NIKOLAY O. History of Russian Philosophy. N.Y., 1951. Pp. 416.
Rev.: R. N. Carew Hunt in *ASEER*, vol. 11, 1952, pp. 226–228.

1164 ZENKOVSKI, VASILI V. A History of Russian Philosophy. (Trans. from Russian.) 2 vols. L., Columbia U.P., 1953.
Rev.: Hans Kohn in *Rus R*, vol. 13, 1954, pp. 296–297.

1165 STAMMLER, HEINRICH. 'The Great Tradition in Russian Philosophy', *Rus R*, vol. 19, 1960, pp. 254–66.

1166 RAEFF, MARC, *comp.* Russian Intellectual History: an Anthology. N.Y., 1966. Pp. x, 404. Bibl.

1167 MCLEAN, HUGH, *and others, ed.* Russian Thought and Politics. (Harvard Slavic Studies, vol. 4.) Harvard U.P., The Hague, 1957. Pp. xi, 513.
Rev.: Ralph T. Fisher in *Rus R*, vol. 17, no. 2, 1958, pp. 142–143.

1168 UTECHIN, SERGE V. Russian Political Thought: a Concise History. N.Y., 1963, L., 1964. Pp. xvi, 320. Bibl. Also Pbk.

Rev.: Stephen F. Cohen in *Rus R*, vol. 23, 1964, pp. 390–392; Barry Hollingsworth in *SEER*, vol. 44, 1966, pp. 220–222.

1169 CHERNIAVSKY, MICHAEL. ' 'Khan' or 'Basileus' : an Aspect of Russian Mediaeval Political Theory', *JHI*, vol. 20, 1959, pp. 459–76.

1170 SHEVCHENKO, IHOR. 'A Neglected Byzantine Source of Muscovite Political Ideology', *HSS*, vol. 2, 1954, pp. (141–79).

1171 RAEFF, MARC. 'An Early Theorist of Absolutism : Joseph of Volokolamsk', *ASEER*, vol. 8, 1949, pp. 77–89.
See note below **1172**.

1172 SZEFTEL, MARC. 'Joseph Volotsky's Political Ideas in a New Historical Perspective', *Jahrbücher für Geschichte Osteuropas*, Neue Folge, vol. 13, 1965, pp. 19–29.
Joseph Volotsky or Sanin was the 1st abbot of Volokolamsk Monastery which he founded in 1479.

1173 ŠERECH, J. 'On Teofan Prokopovič as Writer and Preacher in his Kiev Period', *HSS*, vol. 2, 1954, pp. (211–24.).
Feofan Prokopovich: poet, dramatist, publicist and politician, 1681–1736. cf. **397** and **1251**.

1174 RAEFF, MARC. 'State and Nobility in the Ideology of M. M. Shcherbatov', *ASEER*, vol. 19, 1960, pp. 363–79.
Prince Mikhail M. Shcherbatov: political theorist, 1733–1790.

1175 ZERNOV, NICOLAS. Moscow the Third Rome. L., N.Y., 1937. Pp. 94.

1176 STRÉMOOUKHOFF, DIMITRI (Stremoukhov). 'Moscow the Third Rome: Sources of the Doctrine', *Speculum*, vol. 28, 1953, pp. 84–101.

1177 TOUMANOFF, CYRIL. 'Moscow the Third Rome: Genesis and Significance of a Politico-Religious Idea', *Catholic Historical Review*, vol. 40, 1954–5, pp. 411–47.

1178 WOLFF, ROBERT L. 'The Three Romes: the Migration of an Ideology and the Making of an Autocrat', *Daedalus-Journal of the American Academy of Arts and Sciences*, vol. 88, 1959, pp. 291–311.

1179 ANDREYEV, NIKOLAY. 'Filofey and his Epistle to Ivan Vasil'yevich', *SEER*, vol. 38, 1959–60, pp. 1–31.

1180 HRYSHKO, V. 'The Historical and Legal Basis of the

Theory of the Third Rome', *Ukr Rev* (*L.*), vol. 7, no. 3, 1961, pp. 65–8.

1181 KRUPNYTSKY, BORIS (Krupnyckyj). 'The Idea of the Third Rome in Russian Historical Research', *Ukr Rev* (*L.*), vol. 7, no. 3, 1961, pp. 45–52.

1182 OHLOBLYN, ALEKSANDR P. 'The Theory of Moscow as the Third Rome in the 16th and 17th Centuries', *Ukr Rev* (*L.*), vol. 7, no. 3, 1961, pp. 52–7.

1183 POLONSKA-WASYLENKO, NATALIA D. 'The Evolution of the Theory: "Moscow the Third Rome" during the 18th and 19th Centuries', *Ukr Rev* (*L.*), vol. 7, no. 3, 1961, pp. 57–64.

13

RELIGION

A. GENERAL WORKS, THE RUSSIAN CHURCH

Treatises on the Russian Church, arranged by date of publication, **1185–1202** (cf. **1104**). Of these, **1185** and **1186** are the most informative of the older works; **1192** and **1193** are both useful introductions to the subject, whilst **1202** is very readable if somewhat superficial. On early monasticism, **1203–1206**; missionary activity, **1207**.

1184　JAMES, RICHARD L. L. (R. L. Langford-James). A Dictionary of the Eastern Orthodox Church. L., 1923. Pp. xiv, 144.

1185　PLATON, *Metropolitan of Moscow* (Petr G. Levshin). The Present State of the Greek Church in Russia ... (Trans. from Russian by R. Pinkerton.) Edinburgh, 1814. Pp. xii, 339. N.Y., 1815. Pp. xi, 276.

　　　　Original work published 1765. English translation has an appendix by Robert Pinkerton on the Russian sects.

1186　MURAVEV, ANDREY A. (André Mouravieff). A History of the Church of Russia. (Trans. from Russian.) O., 1842. Pp. xix, 448.

1187　KRASIŃSKI, WALERIAN S., *Count*. Lectures on the Religious History of the Slavonic Nations. L., 1849. Pp. xxviii, 484. 2nd ed., Entitled: Sketch of the Religious History of the Slavonic Nations. Edinburgh, 1851. Pp. xxvi, 332.

1188　WILLIAMS, GEORGE, *ed*. The Orthodox Church of the East in the 18th Century, being the Correspondence between the Eastern Patriarchs and the Non-juring Bishops ... L., 1868.

1189　STANLEY, ARTHUR P. Lectures on the History of the Eastern Church ... L., 1862. Another Edition: L., 1908. Pp. lxxx, 422.

1190　ADENEY, WALTER F. The Greek and Eastern Churches. Edinburgh, N.Y., 1908. Pp. xiv, 634.

　　　　Russian Church: pp. 355–458.

1191 ANGLICAN AND EASTERN CHURCHES ASSOCIATION. The Russian Church: Lectures on its History, Constitution, Doctrine and Ceremonial. L., 1915. Pp. vii, 83.

1192 FRERE, WALTER H. Some Links in the Chain of Russian Church History. L., 1918. Pp. xvi, 200. Bibl.

1193 MINNS, ELLIS H. *and* TROITSKY, S. V. 'Russian Church', in Hastings, James, *ed. Encyclopaedia of Religion and Ethics,* vol. 10, Edinburgh, N.Y., 1918, pp. 867–77; Bibl.

1194 BIGG-WITHER, REGINALD F. A Short History of the Church of Russia, its Teaching and Worship. L., 1920. Pp. 112.

1195 LOWRIE, DONALD A. The Light of Russia: an Introduction to the Russian Church. Prague, 1923, L., 1924. Pp. x, 241. Bibl.

1196 REYBURN, HUGH Y. The Story of the Russian Church. L., N.Y., 1924. Pp. 323. Bibl.

1197 BRYANCHANINOV, NIKOLAY. V. (Brianchaninov). The Russian Church. (Trans. from French.) L., 1931. Pp. xi, 210. Bibl.

1198 DANZAS, YULIYA N. The Russian Church. (Trans. from French.) L., 1936. Pp. viii, 164.

1199 ZERNOV, NICOLAS. The Russians and their Church. L., N.Y., 1945. Pp. v, 193. Bibl. Also Pbk. (S.P.C.K.)

1200 KORPER, RUTH. The Candlelight Kingdom: a Meeting with the Russian Church. N.Y., 1955. Pp. (xi, 83).

1201 IZWOLSKY, HELENE (Iswolsky) (Izvol'ski). Christ in Russia: the History, Tradition and Life of the Russian Church. Milwaukee, 1960, Kingswood, 1962. Pp. 213. Bibl.

Rev.: Veselin Kesich in *Rus R,* vol. 20, no. 2, 1961, pp. 158–160.

1202 ZERNOV, NICOLAS. Eastern Christendom: a Study of the Origin and Development of the Eastern Orthodox Church. L., N.Y., 1961. Pp. 326. Bibl.

Rev.: Georges Florovsky in *Slavic Rev,* vol. 24, 1965, pp. 745–747.

1203 CASEY, ROBERT P. 'Early Russian Monasticism', *OCP,* vol. 19, 1953, pp. 372–423.

1204 HEPPELL, MURIEL. 'The Kievo-Pechersky Monastery from its Origins to the Eleventh Century', *Bulletin of*

the Institute of Historical Research, vol. 25, 1952, pp. 78–80.
Abstract of the author's thesis.

1205 HEPPELL, MURIEL. 'The "Vita Antonii" a Lost Source of the "Paterikon" of the Monastery of Caves', *Byzantinoslavica,* vol. 13, 1952–3, pp. 46–58.

1206 ANDREYEV, NIKOLAY. 'The Pskov-Pechery Monastery in the Sixteenth Century', *SEER,* vol. 32, 1953–4, pp. 318–43.

1207 EDWARDS, *Mrs.* JANE A. S., *née Batty.* Conquests of the Russian Church. L., 1917. Pp. 75. Bibl.
Russian Church missions and missionaries.

B. THE SPIRIT OF ORTHODOXY
CHURCH DOCTRINE AND RITUAL

On Russian spirituality, **1208–1211**, of which the anthology **1209** has been highly praised for its well-chosen texts and scholarly presentation. Covering the period from Kievan Christianity to the 15th century, **1212–1213** may also be recommended. Studies of individual religious thinkers and saints of the Russian Church, arranged chronologically, **1214–1219**; Klyuchevsky on St. Sergius, **1216**. Early hagiography is classed in the section on literature (16B (ii).) General works on Church doctrine and ritual, **1220–1224**. Catechisms, **1225–1227**. See also **1132–1137** on the idea of "Holy Russia".

1208 ZENKOVSKY, VASILY V. 'The Spirit of Russian Orthodoxy', *Rus R,* vol. 22, 1963, pp. 38–55.

1209 FEDOTOV, GEORGE P., *ed.* A Treasury of Russian Spirituality. N.Y., 1948, L., 1950. Pp. xvi, 501. Bibl. Also Pbk. Edition, 1965. (Torchbooks.)
Rev.: George Florovsky in *ASEER,* vol. 8, 1949, pp. 329–330.

1210 NEWMARCH, *Mrs.* ROSA H., *née Jeaffreson.* The Devout Russian: a Book of Thoughts and Counsels Gathered from the Saints and Fathers of the Eastern Church ... L., 1918. Pp. 243.

1211 GRUNWALD, CONSTANTIN DE. Saints of Russia. (Trans. from French by R. Capel.) L., N.Y., 1960. Pp. 180.
Collective biography of 9 saints. Rev.: A. Schmemann in *Slavic Rev,* vol. 21, 1962, pp. 159–160.

1212 FEDOTOV, GEORGE P. The Russian Religious Mind.
Vol. 1. Kievan Christianity. Harvard U.P., 1946. Pp. xvi,
438. Bibl. Also Pbk. (Harper and Row. Torchbooks.)
> Rev.: E. R. Hardy in *ASEER*, vol. 6, pt. 2, 1947, pp. 196–198;
> N. Gorodetzky in *SEER*, vol. 26, 1947–48, pp. 612–614.

1213 FEDOTOV, GEORGE P. The Russian Religious Mind.
[Vol. 2.] The Middle Ages: the Thirteenth to Fifteenth
Centuries. Harvard U.P., 1966. Pp. (423). Bibl.
> Rev.: Serge A. Zenkovsky in *Rus R*, vol. 26, 1967, pp. 296–298.

1214 DAVID, ZDENEK V. 'The Influence of Jacob Boehme on
Russian Religious Thought', *Slavic Rev*, vol. 21, 1962,
pp. 43–64.
> Jacob Boehme, 1575–1624: a German mystic.

1215 DOBBIE-BATEMAN, ARTHUR F. St Seraphim of Sarov
[and Translated Text of]: Concerning the Aim of the
Christian Life. L., 1936. Pp. 60.
> St. Serafim, otherwise Prokhor Isidorovich Moshnin, 1759–1833.

1216 KLYUCHEVSKY, VASILI O. 'St. Sergius: the Importance
of his Life and Work', *Rus R* (*Liverpool*), vol. 2, no. 3,
1913, pp. 45–59.
> Translated text of a speech made in 1892 taken from his: *Sketches
> and Addresses*, Moscow, 1913.

1217 ZERNOV, NICOLAS. St. Sergius—Builder of Russia ... L.,
1938. Pp. xi, 155. Another Edition: L., 1939. Pp. xi,
114.

1218 TRUBETSKOY, EVGENI N., *Prince* (Troubetskoy). Saint
Sophia: Russia's Hope and Calling. (Trans. from
Russian.) L., 1916. Pp. (30).

1219 GORODETSKY, *Mrs.* NADEJDA. St. Tikhon Zadonsky:
Inspirer of Dostoevsky. L., 1951. Pp. xii, 249. Bibl.
> Rev.: Marthe Blinoff in *Rus R*, vol. 11, 1952, pp. 175–176.

1220 DEBIA, JAMES, *comp.* An Account of the Religion,
Rites, Ceremonies and Superstitions of the Moscovites.
Extracted from Several Writers ... L., 1710. Pp. 136.

1221 KING, JOHN GLEN. The Rites and Ceremonies of the
Greek Church in Russia ... L., 1772. Pp. xix, 477.

1222 ROMANOFF, H. C. Sketches of the Rites and Customs
of the Greco-Russian Church. L., 1868. Pp. xiv, 429.

1223 CONSETT, THOMAS, *comp.* The Present State and Regu-
lations of the Church of Russia ... Also in a Second
Volume a Collection of Several Tracts Relating to his

[the Tsar's] Fleet's Expedition to Derbent etc. . . . (Trans. from Russian.) 2 vols. (in 1.) L., 1729. Pp. lxxvi, 455.

1224   BLACKMORE, RICHARD W., *comp*. The Doctrine of the Russian Church . . . Translated from the Slavono-Russian Originals . . . Aberdeen, 1845. Pp. xxviii, 288.

Contains Prokopovich's *Primer or Spelling Book*, Philaret's *Shorter and Longer Catechisms* and Konisski's *Treatise on the Duty of Parish Priests*.

1225   PROKOPOVICH, FEOFAN, *Abp. of Novgorod*. The Russian Catechism. (Trans. from Russian by J. T. Philipps.) L., 1723. Pp. viii, 106. 2nd ed. L., 1725. Pp. xii, 96.

1226   PLATON, *Metropolitan of Moscow* (Petr G. Levshin.) The Great Catechism of the Holy Catholic Apostolic and Orthodox Church. (Trans. from Greek.) L., 1867.

Abridged and translated successively from Russian to Greek to English.

1227   MOGILA, PETR, *Metropolitan of Kiev, ed*. The Orthodox Confession of the Catholic and Apostolic Eastern Church. (Trans. from Russian.) L., 1762. Pp. 206. Another Edition: L., 1898. Pp. 162.

C. ECCLESIASTICAL HISTORY, CHURCH AND STATE

Arrangement of entries in this section is primarily chronological. On the introduction of Christianity into Kiev Rus' and the early history of the Russian Church, **1228–1236.** On the relationship between Church and State, see especially **1240–1242.** On Nikon and the Great Schism, **1243–1249;** Avvakum, **1247– 1249** (cf. **1469**). For works on the Old Believers, see **1255– 1259.** Peter the Great and the Russian Church, **1250–1251.** The Russian Church and the Vatican, **1252–1254** (cf. **1260,** the Catholic Church in Russia). Works on the doctrine of "Moscow the Third Rome", **1175–1183.**

1228   JAKOBSON, ROMAN. 'Minor Native Sources for the Early History of the Slavic Church', *HSS,* vol. 2, 1954, pp. (39– 74).

1229   TIKHOMIROV, MIKHAIL N. 'The Origins of Christianity in Russia. (Trans. from Russian.)', *History,* vol. 44, 1959, pp. 199–211.

1230 ERICSSON, K. 'The Earliest Conversion of the Rus' to Christianity', *SEER*, vol. 44, 1966, pp. 98–121.

1231 HONIGMANN, ERNEST. 'Studies in Slavic Church History, *A* : The Foundation of the Russian Metropolitan Church according to Greek Sources', *Byzantion*, vol. 17, 1944–5, pp. 128–62.

1232 ZERNOV, NICOLAS. 'Vladimir and the Origin of the Russian Church. 2 pts.', *SEER*, vol. 28, 1949–50, pp. 123–38 and 425–38.

1233 VERNADSKY, GEORGE V. 'The Status of the Russian Church during the First Half-Century following Vladimir's Conversion', *SEER*, vol. 20, 1941, pp. 294–314.

1234 STOKES, A. D. 'The Status of the Russian Church, 988–1037', *SEER*, vol. 37, 1958–9, pp. 430–42.

1235 SHEVCHENKO, IHOR. 'The Christianization of Kievan Rus', *Pol R*, vol. 5, no. 4, 1960, pp. 29–35.

1236 OBOLENSKY, DIMITRI. 'Byzantium, Kiev and Moscow : a Study in Ecclesiastical Relations', *DOP*, no. 11, 1957, pp. 21–78.

1237 HALECKI, OSKAR. 'The Ecclesiastical Separation of Kiev from Moscow in 1458', *Wiener Archiv für Geschichte des Slawentums und Osteuropas*, Bd. 2, Teil 1, 1956, pp. 19–32.

1238 SIMPSON, GEORGE W. 'Peter Mohyla : Ecclesiastic and Educator (1647–1947)', *Ukr Qly*, vol. 3, 1946–7, pp. (242 et seq.)

1239 GRAHAM, HUGH, F. 'Peter Mogila—Metropolitan of Kiev', *Rus R*, vol. 14, 1955, pp. 345–56.

1240 TOUMANOFF, CYRIL. 'Caesaropapism in Byzantium and Russia', *Theological Studies*, vol. 7, 1946, pp. 213–43.

1241 KARPOVICH, MICHAEL. 'Church and State in Russian History', *Rus R*, vol. 3, no. 2, 1943–4, pp. 10–20.

1242 MEDLIN, WILLIAM K. Moscow and East Rome : a Political Study of the Relations of Church and State in Muscovite Russia. (Études d'histoire économique, politique et sociale, vol. 1.) Geneva, 1952. Pp. 252. Bibl.
    Rev.: Bertha Malnick in *SEER*, vol. 31, 1952–53, pp. 579–581; Élie Denissoff in *ASEER*, vol. 12, 1953, pp. 267–268.

1243   PALMER, WILLIAM. The Patriarch and the Tsar ...
6 vols. L., 1871–6.
> A collection of primary sources in translation.

1244   ZENKOVSKY, SERGE A. 'The Russian Church Schism:
its Background and Repercussions', *RusR*, vol. 16, no. 4,
1957, pp. 37–58.

1245   SPINKA, MATTHEW, 'Nikon and the Subjugation of the
Russian Church to the State', *CH*, vol. 10, (1941,
pp. 347–66).

1246   LIVES OF EMINENT RUSSIAN PRELATES : *1*. Nikon, 6th
Patriarch of Moscow. By R. Thornton, *2*. Saint Demetrius, Metropolitan of Rostoff, *3*. Michael, Metropolitan
of Novgorod and St. Petersburg. L., 1854. Pp. xvi, 147.
> Pt. 1 is compiled from English materials, pts. 2–3 are translated
> from the Russian.

1247   AVVAKUM, *Archpriest*. The Life of the Archpriest
Avvakum by Himself. (Trans. from Russian by
J. Harrison and H. Mirrlees.) L., 1924. Pp. 156. Also in
1209, pp. 134–81.
> cf. **1469**: Avvakum in Russian literature.

1248   LANZ, HENRY. 'Selected Texts from the Book of Discourses by the Archpriest Avvakum. Commentary and
Translation by H. Lanz', *SEER*, vol. 8, 1929–30, pp.
249–58.

1249   CANT, CATHERINE B. H. 'The Archpriest Avvakum and
his Scottish Contemporaries', *SEER*, vol. 44, 1965–6,
pp. 381–402.

1250   ZERNOV, NICOLAS. 'Peter the Great and the Establish-
ment of the Russian Church', *CQRev*, vol. 125, 1937–8,
pp. 265–93.

1251   GRAHAM, HUGH F. 'Theophan Prokopovich and the
Ecclesiastical Ordinance', *CH*, vol. 25, 1956, pp. 127–35.
> cf. **1173**.

1252   KONCEVIČIUS, JOSEPH B. Russia's Attitude towards
Union with Rome, 9th to 16th Centuries. Washington,
1927. Pp. (xxix, 197).

1253   CHERNIAVSKY, MICHAEL. 'The Reception of the Council of Florence in Moscow', *CH*, vol. 24, 1955, pp. 347–
59.

1254   ALEF, GUSTAVE. 'Muscovy and the Council of Florence',
ASEER, vol. 20, 1961, pp. 389–401.

D. OTHER DENOMINATIONS AND SECTS
NON-RUSSIAN CHURCHES

General works on Russian dissenters, arranged by date, **1255–1259** (see also **1185**). On the Catholic Church in Russia, **1260**; Socialism, **1261**. Doukhobors, **1262–1263**; Quakers, **1264–1265**. Religion in Lithuania, **1266–1267**; the Caucasus, **1268** and Georgia, **1269–1273**; Armenia, **1274**. Alaska, **1275**. On the Jews in Russia, see **835–837**. On Moscow and the Ukrainian Church, see **742**.

1255 HEARD, ALBERT F. The Russian Church and Russian Dissent ... L., N.Y., 1887. Pp. ix, 310. Bibl.

1256 CONYBEARE, FREDERICK C. Russian Dissenters. Harvard U.P., 1921. Pp. 370.

1257 BOLSHAKOFF, SERGEY. Russian Nonconformity: the Story of Unofficial Religion in Russia. Philadelphia, 1950. Pp. 192. Bibl.

1258 CHERNIAVSKY, MICHAEL. 'The Old Believers and the New Religion', *Slavic Rev*, vol. 25, 1966, pp. 1–39.

1259 HACKEL, SERGEI. 'New Perspectives and the Old Believers: Russia and Europe in the Seventeenth Century', *Eastern Churches Review*, vol. 1, 1966, pp. 104–17.

1260 ZATKO, JAMES J. 'The Organisation of the Catholic Church in Russia, 1772–84', *SEER*, vol. 43, 1964–5, pp. 303–13.

1261 LEVYTSKY, OREST. 'Socianism in Poland and South-West Rus' (Trans. from Ukrainian.)', *AUA*, vol. 3, no. 1, 1953, pp. 485–508.
      Anti-Trinitarian Reformation sect active in the 16th–17th centuries.

1262 ELKINGTON, JOSEPH. The Doukhobors: their History in Russia, their Migration to Canada. Philadelphia, 1903. Pp. viii, 336.

1263 MAUDE, AYLMER. A Peculiar People: the Doukhobors. L., 1904. Pp. viii, 336.

1264 DVOICHENKO-MARKOV, EUFROSINA. 'William Penn and Peter the Great', *Proceedings of the American Philosophical Society*, vol. 97, 1953, pp. 12–25.
      Explores Peter's attitude towards the Quakers.

1265   GUR'EV, VAKKH V. Russian Maidens who Suffered as
       Quakers: a Chapter in the Religious History of Russia
       in the Early 18th Century. (Trans. from Russian.) L.,
       1919. Pp. 48.

1266   GIDŽIŪNAS, VIKTORAS. 'The Introduction of Christianity
       into Lithuania', *Lituanus*, vol. 3, no. 4, 1957, pp. 6–13.

1267   DEVEIKĖ, JONĖ. 'The Legal Aspect of the Last Religious
       Conversion in Europe', *SEER*, vol. 32, 1953–4, pp. 117–
       31.

1268   TOUMANOFF, CYRIL. 'Christian Caucasia between Byzan-
       tium and Iran: New Light from Old Sources', *Traditio*,
       vol. 10, 1954, pp. 109–89.

1269   IOSSELIAN, PLATON I. (Ioselian) (Joselian). A Short
       History of the Georgian Church. (Trans. from Russian
       and Edited by Solomon C. Malan.) L., 1866. Pp. xix,
       208.

1270   DOWLING, THEODORE E. Sketches of Georgian Church
       History. L., 1912. Pp. 137.

1271   LANG, DAVID M., *comp*. Lives and Legends of Georgian
       Saints. Selected and Translated from the Original Texts
       L., N.Y., 1956. Pp. 180. Bibl.
           Rev.: G. Bissonnette in *ASEER*, vol. 16, 1957, pp. 218–220.

1272   NINO, *Saint*. The Life of St. Nino. (Trans. from Georgian
       by M. and O. Wardrop.) (Driver, Samuel R., *ed*. Studia
       Biblica et Ecclesiastica, vol. 5, fasc. 1.) O., 1900. Pp. 88.

1273   LANG, DAVID M. 'Peter the Iberian and his Biographers',
       Journal of Ecclesiastical History, vol. 2, 1951, pp. 158–68.

1274   ARPEE, LEON. A History of Armenian Christianity from
       the Beginning to our own Time. N.Y., 1946. Pp. xii,
       386. Bibl.

1275   BASANOFF, V. 'Archives of the Russian Church in Alaska
       in the Library of Congress', *PHR*, vol. 2, 1933, pp. 72–
       84.

14

EDUCATION, SCIENCE AND THE PRESS

General histories of education, arranged by date of publication, **1293–1294;** medical science, **1295–1304** (cf. **842–844, 1425** period, but **1277** gives a fuller account. On the time of Peter the Great, **1282;** Catherine II, **1283.** Other special topics, **1284–1292;** on Lomonosov, **1287–1289.** Science in Russian culture, **1293–1294;** medical science, **1295–1304.** (cf. **842–844, 1425** and **1866).** The Press, **1305–1308.**

1276 SIMKOVICH, VLADIMIR G. 'The History of the School in Russia', *Educational Review,* vol. 33, 1907, pp. 486–522.

1277 KLYUZHEV, I. 'Elementary Public Instruction in Russia. Pt. 1 : From the Foundation of the Empire to the Second Half of the Nineteenth Century', *RusR (Liverpool),* vol. 3, no. 2, 1914, pp. 60–72.

1278 LEARY, DANIEL B. Education and Autocracy in Russia from the Origins to the Bolsheviki. Buffalo, N.Y., 1919. Pp. (127). Bibl.

1279 HANS, NICHOLAS A. History of Russian Educational Policy, 1701–1917. L., 1931. Pp. xiii, 255. Bibl.
cf. **1281.**

1280 JOHNSON, WILLIAM H. E. Russia's Educational Heritage. Pittsburgh, 1950. Pp. xvi, 351. Bibl.
Rev.: N. Hans in *SEER,* vol. 29, 1950–51, pp. 588–589; John Summerville in *ASEER,* vol. 11, 1952, pp. 156–159.

1281 HANS, NICHOLAS A. The Russian Tradition in Education. L., 1963. Pp. vii, 196. Bibl.
Revised version of **1279.** Rev.: Nicholas V. Riasanovsky in *Slavic Rev,* vol. 23, 1964, p. 601.

1282 BISSONNETTE, GEORGES. 'Peter the Great and the Church as an Educational Institution', in Curtiss, John S., *ed. Essays in Russian and Soviet History in Honor of G. T. Robinson,* Leiden, 1963, pp. 3–19.

1283 HANS, NICHOLAS A. 'Dumaresq, Brown and some Early

Educational Projects of Catherine II', *SEER*, vol. 40. 1961–2, pp. 229–35.

1284 SATINA, SOPHIE. Education of Women in Pre-Revolutionary Russia. (Trans. from Russian.) N.Y., 1966. Pp. iii, 153. Bibl. (Pbk.)
cf. **838–839**.

1285 BRYNER, CYRIL. 'Moscow University, 1755–1955', *RusR*, vol. 14, 1955, pp. 201–13.

1286 HANS, NICHOLAS A. 'The Moscow School of Mathematics and Navigation', *SEER*, vol. 29, 1950–1, pp. 532–6.

1287 MENSHUTKIN, BORIS N. Russia's Lomonosov: Chemist, Courtier, Physicist, Poet. (Trans. from Russian by J. E. Thal and E. J. Webster.) Princeton U.P., 1952. Pp. viii, 208. Bibl.
Rev.: Nina Brodiansky in *SEER*, vol. 31, 1952–53, pp. 596–597.

1288 KUDRYAVTSEV, B. B. The Life and Work of Mikhail Vasilyevich Lomonosov. Moscow, 1954. Pp. 117.

1289 HUNTINGTON, W. CHAPIN. 'Michael Lomonosov and Benjamin Franklin: Two Self-Made Men of the Eighteenth Century', *RusR*, vol. 18, 1959, pp. 294–306.

1290 HANS, NICHOLAS A. 'Polish Schools in Russia, 1772–1831', *SEER*, vol. 38, 1959–60, pp. 394–414.

1291 HALECKI, OSKAR. 'The Universities of the Polish-Lithuanian Commonwealth from the 14th to the 17th Century . . .', *PolR*, vol. 5, no. 3, 1960, pp. 21–9.

1292 HANS, NICHOLAS A. 'Russian Students at Leyden in the 18th Century', *SEER*, vol. 35, 1956–7, pp. 551–62.

1293 VUCINICH, ALEXANDER (Vukinich). Science in Russian Culture: a History to 1860. Stanford U.P., 1963; L., 1965. Pp. xv, 463. Bibl.
Rev.: John Turkevich in *Rus R*, vol. 23, 1964, pp. 399–400; David Joravsky in *Slavic Rev*, vol. 25, 1966, pp. 367–369; W. F. Ryan in *History of Science*, vol. 5, 1966, pp. 52–61.

1294 RYAN, WILLIAM F. 'Some Russian Contributions to the History of the Microscope', *Proceedings of the Royal Microscopical Society*, vol. 2, 1967, pp. 362–5.

1295 DÖRBECK, FRANZ. 'Origins of Medicine in Russia', *Medical Life*, vol. 30, 1923, pp. (223–34).

1296 EMBDEN, VON, *Dr. of Hamburg*. 'An Historical Sketch of Medicine in the Russian Empire from the Earliest to the Present Time', *Edinburgh Medical and Surgical Journal*, vol. 13, 1817, pp. 455–65.

1297 LEFEVRE, GEORGE. 'Sketch of the Origin and Present State of Medicine and of Medical Institutions in Russia. Pt. 1', *British and Foreign Medical Review*, vol. 1, 1836, pp. 597–606.

1298 '[History of Medicine in Russia: Review Article]', *British and Foreign Medico-Chirurgical Review*, 1862, vol. 30, pp. 285–305.

1299 'MEDICINE PAST AND PRESENT IN RUSSIA', *The Lancet*, 1897, vol. 2, pp. 343–74.

1300 GARRISON, F. H. 'Russian Medicine under the Old Regime', *Bulletin of the New York Academy of Medicine*, Series 2, vol. 7, 1931, pp. 693–734.

1301 GANTT, WILLIAM A. H. Russian Medicine. N.Y., 1937.

1302 KEEVIL, JOHN J. Hamey the Stranger. L., 1952. Pp. xvi, 192. Bibl.

Baldwin Hamey, physician at the Russian court, 1594–1597.

1303 CLEMOW, FRANK G. 'English Physicians at the Court of Moscow in the 16th and 17th Centuries', *Proceedings of the Anglo-Russian Literary Society*, no. 21, Apr.–Jun., 1898, pp. 35–48.

1304 CLEMOW, FRANK G. 'Medical Men and Matters in Russia in the 18th Century', *Proceedings of the Anglo-Russian Literary Society*, no. 28, May–Jul., 1900, pp. 5–23.

1305 PROSTOV, EUGENE V. 'Origins of Russian Printing', *Library Quarterly*, vol. 1, 1931, pp. 255–77. Bibl.

1306 SWINDLER, WILLIAM F. 'Recent Research Material on Russian Journalism: a Survey of Important Studies of the Russian Press from its 17th Century Beginnings to the Present', *Journalism Quarterly*, vol. 32, 1955, pp. 70–5.

1307 WYNAR, LUBOMYR R. History of Early Ukrainian Printing, 1491–1600. (University of Denver. Graduate School of Librarianship. Studies in Librarianship, vol. 1, no. 2, 1962.) Denver, 1962.

1308 TARNAWSKY, MARTA. 'The Founding Fathers of Ukrainian Printing: Shvaipolt Fiol and Ivan Fedorov', *Ukr Qly*, vol. 21, 1965, pp. 206–18.

15

ART AND ARCHITECTURE

A. GENERAL

Bibliography, **1309**. General surveys, arranged by date, **1310–1318**; of these, **1316–1317** may be particularly recommended, whilst **1318** is a useful modern primer. Special aspects of Russian art, **1319–1322**. On Scythian art and the animal style in South Russia, **1323–1329**. See also **1104**.

1309   ETTLINGER, AMREI *and* GLADSTONE, JOAN M., *comp.* Russian Literature, Theatre and Art: a Bibliography of Works in English, Published 1900–1945. L., 1946. Pp. 96.

1310   MASKELL, ALFRED. Russian Art and Art Objects in Russia. (South Kensington Museum Art Handbooks.) L., 1884. Pp. xii, 278.

1311   NEWMARCH, *Mrs.* ROSA H., *née Jeaffreson*. The Russian Arts. L., N.Y., 1916. Pp. xvi, 293.

1312   RICE, DAVID TALBOT, *ed.* (Talbot-Rice). Russian Art. L., Edinburgh, 1935. Pp. viii, 136.

1313   BUNT, CYRIL G. E. Russian Art from Scyths to Soviets. L., N.Y., 1946. Pp. 272. Bibl.

1314   RICE, *Mrs.* TAMARA T. (Talbot-Rice). Russian Art. (Pelican Books.) West Drayton, 1949. Pp. 276. Bibl.

1315   ALPATOV, MIKHAIL V., *ed.* Russian Impact on Art. (Trans. from Russian.) N.Y., 1950. Pp. xx, 352. Bibl.
   Rev.: Leon Stilman in *ASEER*, vol. 10, 1951, pp. 155–157: Nadejda Gorodetsky in *SEER*, vol. 29, 1950–51, pp. 328–330.

1316   HAMILTON, GEORGE H. The Art and Architecture of Russia. (Pelican History of Art.) Harmondsworth, Baltimore, 1954. Pp. xxi, 320.
   Rev.: T. J. McCormick in *Rus R*, vol. 15, 1956, pp. 285–286.

1317   RICE, *Mrs.* TAMARA T. (Talbot-Rice). A Concise History of Russian Art. L., N.Y., 1963. Pp. 288. Bibl. Also Pbk.
   Expanded version of **1314**. Rev.: Albert J. Schmidt in *Slavic Rev*, vol. 23, 1964, pp. 601–602.

1318 HARE, RICHARD. The Art and Artists of Russia. L., 1965. Pp. 294. Bibl.

1319 WEIDLÉ, WLADIMIR. 'Some Common Traits in Early Russian and Western Art', *OSP,* vol. 4, 1953, pp. 17–37.

1320 HOLME, CHARLES, *ed.* Peasant Art in Russia. (The Studio. Special Autumn Number, 1912.) L., 1912. Pp. x, 52.

1321 NEWMARCH, *Mrs.* ROSA H., *née Jeaffreson.* 'Life and Legend in Russian Art', *Proceedings of the Anglo-Russian Literary Society,* no. 34, May–Jul., 1902, pp. 5–27.

1322 MURATOV, PAUL. 'The Traditionalism of Ancient Russian Art', *SEER,* vol. 8, 1929–30, pp. 259–268.

1323 BOROVKA, GREGORY. Scythian Art. (Trans. from German by V. G. Childe.) L., N.Y., 1928. Pp. 111 + 74 Plates.

1324 MINNS, ELLIS H. 'The Art of the Northern Nomads', *Proceedings of the British Academy,* vol. 28, 1942, pp. 47–99 + 28 Plates.

1325 VERNADSKY, GEORGE V. 'The Eurasian Nomads and their Art in the History of Civilization', *Saeculum,* vol. 1, 1950, pp. 74–86.

1326 ROSTOVTZEFF, MIKHAIL I. (Rostovtsev). The Animal Style in South Russia and China. Princeton U.P., 1929. Pp. xvi, 112.

1327 CARTER, *Mrs.* DAGNY. The Symbol of the Beast: the Animal-Style Art of Eurasia. N.Y., 1957. Pp. ix, 204. Bibl.
     Rev.: Malcolm Burgess in *SEER,* vol. 36, 1957–58, pp. 558–562.

1328 HANČAR, FRANZ. 'The Eurasian Animal Style and the Altai Complex', *AA,* vol. 15, 1952, pp. 171–94.

1329 RUDENKO, S. I. 'The Mythological Eagle, the Gryphon, the Winged Lion and the Wolf in the Art of the Northern Nomads', *AA,* vol. 21, 1958, pp. 101–22.

B. PAINTING AND SCULPTURE

General studies on Russian painting, **1330–1334.** On icons, **1335–1353.** Of these, **1336** is the classic work on the subject. Sculpture, **1354–1356** (cf. **1006**).

1330 CHAMOT, MARY. Russian Painting and Sculpture. (Perg-

amon and Oxford Russian Series.) O., 1963. Pp. xiii, 55. Bibl.; N.Y., 1964. Pp. 56. Bibl. (Pbk.)
Rev.: Arthur Voyce in *Slavic Rev*, vol. 24, 1965, pp. 353–354.

1331 LAZAREV, VIKTOR N. Old Russian Murals and Mosaics, from the 11th to the 16th Century. (Trans. from Russian.) L., 1966. Pp. 290.

1332 FARBMAN, MICHAEL S., *ed*. Masterpieces of Russian Painting: Russian Icons and Frescoes from the 11th to the 18th Centuries. L., 1930. Pp. 125. Bibl.

1333 CHEN, JACK. Russian Painting of the 18th and 19th Centuries: a Commentary and a Catalogue [of an Exhibition Held in London.] L., 1948. Pp. 30.

1334 BENOIS, ALEXANDRE. The Russian School of Painting. (Trans. from Russian.) N.Y., 1916, L., 1919. Pp. 199.
Emphasis on 19th and 20th centuries.

1335 RICE, DAVID T. (Talbot-Rice). The Beginnings of Russian Icon Painting. (Ilchester Lecture for 1937.) O.U.P., 1938. Pp. 24.

1336 KONDAKOV, NIKODIM P. The Russian Icon. (Trans. from Russian by E. H. Minns.) O., 1927. Pp. xxvi, 226.
Rev.: D. S. Mirsky in *SEER,* vol. 6, 1927–28, pp. 471–474.

1337 MINNS, ELLIS H. 'The Exhibition of Icons at the Victoria and Albert Museum', *SEER,* vol. 8, 1929–30, pp. 627–35.

1338 CONWAY, *Sir* MARTIN. 'The History of Russian Icon Painting', in **1332**, pp. 11–33.

1339 ANISIMOV, A. I. 'Russian Icon Painting: its Bloom, Over-Refinement and Decay', in **1332**, pp. 61–93.

1340 OLSUFIEV, Y. A. 'The Development of Russian Icon Painting from the 12th to the 19th Century', *Art Bulletin,* vol. 12, 1930, pp. 347–73.

1341 RICE, DAVID T. (Talbot-Rice). Russian Icons. (King Penguin Books.) Harmondsworth, L., N.Y., 1947. Pp. 40 + 16 Plates.

1342 SCHWEINFURTH, PHILIPP. Russian Icons. L., N.Y., 1953. Pp. 61.

1343 HACKEL, ALEXEI A. The Icon. (Trans. from German.) Freiburg-im-Breisgau, 1954. Pp. 20 + 16 Plates.
Plates reproduced from **1336**.

1344 OUSPENSKY, LEONIDE (Uspenski) *and* LOSSKY, VLADI-

MIR. The Meaning of Ikons. (Trans. from French.) Boston, Mass., 1956. Pp. (222).

1345 UNITED NATIONS EDUCATIONAL, SCIENTIFIC AND CULTURAL ORGANIZATION. U.S.S.R. Early Russian Icons. Texts by Victor Lasareff and Otto Demus. Greenwich, Conn., N.Y., 1958. Pp. (28). Bibl.

1346 RICE, *Mrs.* TAMARA T. (Talbot-Rice). Icons. L., 1959. Pp. 195. Reprinted 1960.

    English, German and French texts. Rev.: Nikolay Andreyev in *SEER,* vol. 38, 1959–60, pp. 238–240.

1347 ONASCH, KONRAD. Icons. (Trans. from German.) L., 1963. Pp. 427. Bibl.

1348 SCHEFFER, N. 'Symbolism of the Russian Icon', *Gazette des Beaux Arts,* vol. 25, 1944, pp. (77–94).

1349 FRY, ROGER. 'Russian Icon Painting from the West European Point of View', in **1332**, pp. 35–59.

1350 OSIAKOVSKI, S. 'Six Hundred Years of Rublev', *Anglo-Soviet Journal,* vol. 21, no. 4, 1960, pp. 13–16.

1351 ANDREYEV, NIKOLAY. 'Nikon and Avvakum on Icon-Painting', *Revue des Études Slaves,* vol. 38, 1961, pp. 37–44.

1352 ANISIMOV, ALEKSANDR I. Our Lady of Vladimir. (Abridged Trans. from Russian.) Prague, 1928. Pp. 36 + 7 Plates. Bibl.

1353 LEVINSON, N. 'The Restoration of Old Russian Paintings. (Trans. from Russian.)', *SEER,* vol. 3, 1924–5, pp. 350–5.

1354 FALCONET, ÉTIENNE M. *and* DIDEROT, DENIS. Pieces ... on Sculpture in General, and Particularly on the Celebrated Statue of Peter the Great Now Finished by [E. M. Falconet] at St. Petersburg. (Trans. from French by W. Tooke.) L., 1777. Pp. 72.

1355 BISCHOFF, ILSE. 'Étienne Maurice Falconet: Sculptor of the Statue of Peter the Great', *Rus R,* vol. 24, 1965, pp. 369–86.

1356 POMERANTSEV, N. Russkaya derevyannaya skul'ptura. Russian Wooden Sculpture. Moscow, 1967. Pp. 132.

    Parallel Russian and English texts.

C. ARCHITECTURE

General treatises, **1357–1361**. On Ukrainian and particularly Kievan architecture, **1362–1366**; Leningrad, **1367**; the Kremlin, **1368**. The best introductions to this subject are **1357** and **1359**.

1357   BUXTON, DAVID R. Russian Mediaeval Architecture ... C.U.P., N.Y., 1934. Pp. xi, 112. Bibl.
   Rev.: Ellis H. Minns in *SEER*, vol. 13, 1934–35, pp. 217–218.

1358   VOYCE, ARTHUR. 'National Elements in Russian Architecture', *Journal of the Society of Architectural Historians*, vol. 16, no. 2, 1957, pp. (6–16).

1359   CROSS, SAMUEL H. Mediaeval Russian Churches. Cambridge, Mass., 1949. Pp. xiv, 95.
   Rev.: Nicholas V. Riasanovsky in *Rus R*, vol. 9, 1950, pp. 236–239.

1360   CONANT, KENNETH JOHN. 'Novgorod, Constantinople, and Kiev in Old Russian Church Architecture', *SEER*, vol. 22, no. 2, 1944, pp. 75–92.

1361   REKLAITIS, POVILAS, 'The Problem of the Eastern Borders of Gothic Architecture', *Lituanus*, vol. 10, no. 2, 1964, pp. 33–49.

1362   SICHYNSKY, VOLODYMYR. 'Early Christian Architecture in Ukraine', *Proceedings of the Shevchenko Scientific Society, Historical-Philosophical Section*, vol. 1, 1951, pp. 63–6.

1363   CROSS, SAMUEL, H. 'The Earliest Mediaeval Churches of Kiev', *Speculum*, vol. 11, 1936, pp. 477–99.

1364   POWSTENKO, OLEXA. The Cathedral of St. Sophia in Kiev. (*AUA*, vols. 3–4, 1954. Special Issue.) N.Y., 1954. Pp. 471.
   Texts in English and Ukrainian. Rev.: Arthur Voyce in *ASEER*, vol. 15, 1956, pp. 298–300; G. H. Hamilton in *Rus R*, vol. 15, 1956, pp. 140-141.

1365   CROSS, SAMUEL H. 'The Mosaic Eucharist of St. Michael's, Kiev', *ASEER*, vol. 6, no. 1, 1947, pp. 56–61.

1366   MILLER, D. A. 'The Pečerskij Assumption and its Influence on Medieval Russian Orthodoxy', *Jahrbücher für Geschichte Osteuropas*, Neue Folge, vol. 14, 1966, pp. 321–6.

1367   PETERSEN, ZOÉ B. 'The Architectural Heritage of Leningrad', *ASEER*, vol. 4, no. 3–4, 1945, pp. 18–34.

1368 VORONIN, NIKOLAY N., *ed.* Palaces and Churches of the Kremlin. L., Prague, Moscow, 1966. Pp. 151.

1369 LUKOMSKI, GEORGI K. (Loukomski). Charles Cameron, 1740–1812 : his Life and Work in Russia. (Trans. from Russian.) L., 1943, N.Y., 1944. Pp. 102. Bibl.

  Scottish architect commissioned for work in Russia by Catherine II. New York edition has variant title.

D. MUSIC, THEATRE AND BALLET

General works on Russian music, **1370–1372,** are mostly sketchy on the early period. Folk music, **1373–1374.** Pre-18th century Polish influences in Russian music, **1375.** Eighteenth century opera and folk-song, **1376–1378.** Georgian folk music, **1379.**

On the theatre, **1380–1387.** Of the general studies in this group, **1380–1382,** the best treatment of the early period is to be found in **1381,** whilst **1383** is entirely on the early period. See also **686** on English plays in St. Petersburg. Bibliography, **1309.** Russian ballet, **1388–1390.**

1370 POUGIN, ARTHUR. A Short History of Russian Music. (Trans. from French.) L., 1915. Pp. x, 332.

1371 ALLEN, WARREN D. 'Music in Russia and the West', *Rus R,* vol. 8, no. 1, 1949, pp. 102–10.

1372 LEONARD, RICHARD A. A History of Russian Music. L., N.Y., 1956. Pp. 395. Bibl.

1373 SWAN, ALFRED J. 'The Nature of the Russian Folk-Song', *Musical Quarterly,* vol. 29, 1943, pp. (498–516).

1374 SWAN, ALFRED J. 'The Mainsprings of Russian Music : Folk Song and Religious Chant', *Rus R,* vol. 24, 1965, pp. 177–81.

1375 GOŁOS, JERZY S. 'Polish Influences in Russian Music before the Eighteenth Century', *Pol R,* vol. no. 2, 1960, pp. 8–17.

1376 WHAPLES, MIRIAM K. 'Eighteenth Century Russian Opera in the Light of Soviet Scholarship', *Indiana Slavic Studies,* vol. 2, 1958, pp. 113–34.

1377 SEAMAN, GERALD. 'Folk-Song in Russian Opera of the 18th Century', *SEER,* vol. 41, 1962–3, pp. 144–57.

1378 SEAMAN, GERALD. 'Russian Folksongs in the Eighteenth Century', *Music and Letters,* vol. 40, 1959, pp. 253–60.

K

1379   JORDANIA, R. 'Georgian Folk Music and its Importance in European Folklore', *CR*, vol. 1, 1955, pp. 128–37.

1380   FUELOP–MILLER, RENÉ *and* GREGOR, JOSEPH. The Russian Theatre: its Character and History. (Trans. from German.) L., 1930. Pp. 136.

1381   VARNEKE, BORIS V. History of the Russian Theatre: Seventeenth through Nineteenth Century. (Trans. from Russian.) N.Y., 1951. Pp. xiii, 459.
    Rev.: Andrew M. Haufman in *Rus R*, vol. 10, 1951, pp. 319–321.

1382   SLONIM, MARC. Russian Theater from the Empire to the Soviets. N.Y., 1961, L., 1963. Pp. 354.
    Rev.: George Gibian in *Rus R*, vol. 21, 1962, pp. 387–388.

1383   MALNICK, BERTHA. 'The Origin and Early History of the Theatre in Russia', *SEER*, vol. 19, 1939–40, pp. 203–27.

1384   VELIMIROVIĆ, MILOŠ M. 'Liturgical Drama in Byzantium and Russia', *DOP*, no. 16, 1962, pp. 349-85.

1385   PARGMENT, LILA. 'Serf Theatres and Serf Actors', *AATSEEL Jnl*, vol. 14, no. 3, 1956, pp. 71–8.

1386   MALNICK, BERTHA. 'Russian Serf Theatres', *SEER*, vol. 30, 1951–2, pp. 393–411.

1387   BURGESS, MALCOLM. 'Russian Public Theatre Audiences of the 18th and Early 19th Centuries', *SEER*, vol. 37, 1958–9, pp. 160–83.

1388   BEAUMONT, CYRIL W. A History of Ballet in Russia, 1613–1881. L., 1930. Pp. xix, 140.

1389   LIFAR, SERGE. A History of Russian Ballet from its Origins to the Present Day. (Trans. from Russian.) L., N.Y., 1954. Pp. 328.

1390   CROSS, SAMUEL H. 'The Russian Ballet before Dyagilev', *SEER*, vol. 22, no. 4, 1944, pp. 19–49.

E. ART OF THE BORDERLANDS

Lithuania, **1391–1395**. Ukraine, **1396–1397**. Georgia, **1398**. Armenia, **1399**. Central Asia and Siberia, **1400–1405** (cf. **1006**).

1391   REKLAITIS, POVILAS. 'The Development of Monumental Art in Ancient Lithuania', *Lituanus*, vol. 3, no. 2, 1957, pp. 9–21.

1392   GIMBUTAS, MARIJA. Ancient Symbolism in Lithuanian

Folk Art. (Memoirs of the American Folklore Society, vol. 49.) Philadelphia, 1958, Pp. 148. Bibl.
Rev.: René Fuelop-Miller in *Rus R*, vol. 18, 1959, pp. 73–75.

1393 GIMBUTAS, MARIJA. 'The Origins of Folk Art', *Lituanus*, vol. 7, 1961, pp. 13–17.

1394 BALTRUŠAITIS, JURGIS. 'Arts and Crafts in the Lithuanian Homestead', *Lituanus*, vol. 7, 1961, pp. 18–20.

1395 REKLAITIS, POVILAS. 'Iconography of the Lithuanian Peasant in Lithuania Minor', *Lituanus*, vol. 10, no. 1, 1964, pp. 61–71.

1396 UKRAINIAN ARTS: a Collection of Authoritative Articles on the Ukraine's Folk and Fine Arts. Compiled by Olya Dmytriw. Edited by Anne Mitz. (Ukrainian Youth's League of North America.) N.Y., 1952. Pp. 212. 2nd ed. N.Y., 1955. Pp. 217.

1397 HORDYNSKY, SVIATOSLAV. 'Ukrainian Art in Past and Present', *Ukr Rev (L.)*, vol. 4, no. 1, 1957, pp. 51–4.

1398 KAKABADZE, S. 'The Date of the Building of the Cathedral: the Living Pillar', *Georgica*, vol. 1, nos. 2–3, 1936, pp. 78–91.

1399 DER NERSESSIAN, SIRARPIE. Armenia and the Byzantine Empire: a Brief Study of Armenian Art and Civilization. Harvard U.P., 1947. Pp. xxi, 148 + 32 Plates. Bibl.

1400 RICE, *Mrs.* TAMARA T. (Talbot-Rice). Ancient Arts of Central Asia. L., 1965. Pp. 288. Bibl. Also Pbk.

1401 HRBAS, MILOŠ *and* KNOBLOCH, EDGAR. The Art of Central Asia. (Trans. from Czech.) L., 1965. Pp. 140. Bibl.

1402 BUSSAGLI, MARIO. Painting of Central Asia. (Trans. from Italian by L. Small.) Geneva, 1963. Pp. 138. Bibl.

1403 TALLGREN, A. M. 'Inner Asiatic and Siberian Rock Pictures', *ESA*, vol. 8, 1933, pp. 175–210.

1404 FRUMKIN, GRÉGOIRE. 'On some Ancient Wall-Paintings in Soviet Central Asia', *Bibliotheca Orientalis*, vol. 19, 1962, pp. 122–5.

1405 DALTON, ORMONDE M. The Treasure of the Oxus, with other Examples of Early Oriental Metal-Work. L., 1905. 2nd ed. L., 1926. Pp. lxxvi + 75 Plates, xl. 3rd ed. L., 1964.

16

LANGUAGE AND LITERATURE

A. LANGUAGE

The works listed in this section represent a very restricted selection of the available literature on the subject. Only those works considered to have some relevance for the historian have been included. Readers wishing to explore the subject more thoroughly are referred to the bibliographies cited below, **1406–1407**. The best general introduction for the non-specialist is **1417**.

1406 STANKIEWICZ, EDWARD *and* WORTH, DEAN S., *comp.* A Selected Bibliography of Slavic Linguistics. Vol. 1. The Hague, 1966.
  To be completed in 2 volumes. Rev.: G. Shevelov in *SEEJ*, vol. 11, 1967, pp. 339–345.

1407 UNBEGAUN, B. O. *and* SIMMONS, JOHN S. G., *comp.* A Bibliographical Guide to the Russian Language. O., 1953. Pp. xiv, 174.

1408 MATTHEWS, W. K. 'The Language Pattern of the U.S.S.R.', *SEER*, vol. 25, 1946–7, pp. 427–54.

1409 HALLE, MORRIS, *and others, comp.* For Roman Jakobson: Essays on the Occasion of his Sixtieth Birthday ... The Hague, 1956. Pp. xii, 681. Bibl.

1410 TALVJ, *pseud.* [*Mme.* Thérèse A. Louise v. Jakob]. Historical View of the Slavic Language in its Various Dialect ... Andover, 1834. Another Edition, Entitled: Historical Review of the Languages and Litterature [sic] of the Slavic Nations ... N.Y., 1850. Pp. xvi, 412.

1411 SHEVELOV, GEORGE Y. A Prehistory of Slavic: the Historical Phonology of Common Slavic. Heidelberg, 1964; N.Y., 1965. Pp. xx, 662. Bibl.

1412 MATTHEWS, W. K. 'Sources of Old Church Slavonic', *SEER*, vol. 28, 1949–50, pp. 466–85.

1413 LUNT, HORACE G. 'The Beginnings of Written Slavic', *Slavic Rev*, vol. 23, 1964, pp. 212–9.

1414 AUTY, ROBERT. 'Community and Divergence in the History of the Slavonic Languages', *SEER*, vol. 42, 1963–4, pp. 257–73.

1415 TRUBETSKOY, NIKOLAY S., *Prince*. (Trubetzkoy). The Common Slavic Element in Russian Culture. (Trans. from Russian.) Edited by Leon Stilman. Columbia U.P., 1949. 2nd ed. Columbia U.P., 1950. Pp. vii, 39.

1416 MATTHEWS, W. K. 'The Russian Language before 1700', *SEER*, vol. 31, 1952–3, pp. 364–87.

1417 MATTHEWS, W. K. The Structure and Development of Russian. C.U.P., 1953. Pp. ix, 225.
    Rev.: N. B. Jopson in *SEER*, vol. 32, 1953–54, pp. 242–245.

1418 SOKOLSKY, A. A. A History of the Russian Language. Tampa, Fla., 1966. Pp. (222).

1419 UNBEGAUN, B. O. 'The Language of Muscovite Russia in Oxford Vocabularies', *OSP*, vol. 10, 1962, pp. 46–59.

1420 MATTHEWS, W. K. 'Observations on the Study of 17th-Century Russian', *SEER*, vol. 34, 1955–6, pp. 487–90.

1421 GARDINER, S. C. 'Translation Technique in 17th-Century Russia', *SEER*, vol. 42, 1963–4, pp. 110–35.

1422 MATTHEWS, W. K. 'The Pronunciation of Mediaeval Russian', *SEER*, vol. 30, 1951–2, pp. 87–111.

1423 VASMER, MAX 'The Meaning of Russian River Names', *OSP*, vol. 6, 1955, pp. 44–55.

1424 TICHOVSKIS, H. 'An 18th-Century Controversy on the Relation between Baltic and Slavonic Languages', *SEER*, vol. 42, 1963–4, pp. 429–34.

1425 LEEMING, H. 'Polish and Polish-Latin Medical Terms in Pre-Petrine Russian', *SEER*, vol. 42, 1963–4, pp. 89–109.
    cf. **1295–1304**.

B. LITERATURE

(i) *General Works*

Despite the more general concern with the great Russian writers of the 19th Century, some excellent studies are available in English on early Russian literature. Anthologies and dictionaries, **1426–1429**; see also **1209**. Works exclusively on the earlier period, **1430–1435** (cf. **1212–1213**). General histories of Russian literature, **1436–1445**; recommended, **1441–1443**. See also **1104**.

For translations and commentaries on the early chronicles, see **128–131**.

1426   WIENER, LEO, *comp*. Anthology of Russian Literature from the Earliest Period to the Present Time. (Trans. from Russian.) 2 vols. N.Y., L., 1902–3.
Volume 1 contains texts from the 10th century to the close of the 18th.

1427   GUERNEY, BERNARD G., *comp*. A Treasury of Russian Literature . . . (Trans. from Russian.) N.Y., 1943. Pp. xx, 1048. L., 1948. Pp. xx. 1037. Also Pbk. Edition, Entitled: An Anthology of Russian Literature.

1428   SNOW, VALENTINE, *comp*. Russian Writers: a Bio-Bibliographical Dictionary from the Age of Catherine II to . . . 1917. N.Y., 1946. Pp. 222.

1429   HARKINS, WILLIAM E., *comp*. Dictionary of Russian Literature. N.Y., 1956. Pp. vi, 439.

1430   GUDZI, NIKOLAY K. History of Early Russian Literature. (Trans. from Russian.) N.Y., 1949. Pp. xix, 545.
Rev.: A. Stender–Petersen in *ASEER*, vol. 9, 1950, pp. 312–315; J. A. Posin in *Rus R*, vol. 8, 1949, pp. 351–353.

1431   CHIZHEVSKY, DMITRI (Čiževskij). History of Russian Literature from the Eleventh Century to the End of the Baroque. The Hague, 1960. Pp. 451.

1432   MIRSKY, DMITRI S., *Prince*. 'Old Russian Literature: its Place in the History of Civilisation', *SEER*, vol. 3, 1924–5, pp. 74–91.

1433   TRUBETSKOY, NIKOLAY S., *Prince* (Trubetzkoy). 'Introduction to the History of Old Russian Literature', *HSS*, vol. 2, 1954, pp. (91–103).

1434   GUDZI, NIKOLAY K. 'The Artistic Heritage of Old Russian Literature', *OSP*, vol. 7, 1957, pp. 17–26.

1435   CHIZHEVSKY, DMITRI (Čiževskij). 'On the Question of Genres in Old Russian Literature', *HSS*, vol. 2, 1954, pp. (105–15).

1436   OTTO, FRIEDRICH. The History of Russian Literature . . . (Trans. from German.) O., 1839. Pp. xxiv, 408.

1437   WALISZEWSKI, KAZIMIERZ. A History of Russian Literature: Comprising . . . [**1441**] and Contemporary Russian

1438   HAPGOOD, ISABEL F. A Survey of Russian Literature. N.Y., 1902. Pp. 279.

1439   BRUECKNER, ALEXANDER. A Literary History of Russia.
        (Trans. from German.) L., 1908. Pp. xix, 558.

1440   SHAKHNOVSKI, I. K. A Short History of Russian Liter-
        ature. (Trans. from Russian.) L., 1921. Pp. 180.

1441   MIRSKY, DMITRI S., *Prince*. A History of Russian Liter-
        ature from the Earliest Times to the Death of
        Dostoievsky. L., N.Y., 1927. Pp. xiv, 388. Bibl.

1442   MIRSKY, DMITRI S., *Prince*. A History of Russian Liter-
        ature : Comprising . . . [**1441**] and Contemporary Russian
        Literature. Edited and Abridged by F. J. Whitfield. L.,
        N.Y., 1949. Pp. xi, 518, xxiv. Bibl.
          Rev.: Kenneth E. Harper in *ASEER*, vol. 9, 1950, pp. 229–231.

1443   MIRSKY, DMITRI S., *Prince*. History of Russian Liter-
        ature from its Beginnings to 1900. N.Y., 1958. Pp. 383.
          Comprises text of **1441** with the addition of the 1st two chapters of
          his: *Contemporary Russian Literature.*

1444   SLONIM, MARC L. The Fpic of Russian Literature from
        its Origins through Tolstoy. N.Y., O.U.P., 1950. Pp. vii,
        367. (Pbk.).
          Rev.: D. Brown in *ASEER*, vol. 9, 1950, pp. 227–229.

1445   SLONIM, MARC. An Outline of Russian Literature.
        O.U.P., N.Y., 1958. Pp. 253. Bibl.

(ii) By Period

Included in this section are both original texts in translation
and commentaries. Arrangement is primarily chronological.
Bibliography, **1446** (see also **1309**). Writings from the Kiev
period, **1447–1466**; the *Tale of Igor* (translations and commentaries), **1453–1465**. Seventeenth century literature, **1467–
1470**; 18th century, **1471–1484**. Early chronicles: **128–131**.

1446   HEPPELL, MURIEL. 'Slavonic Translations of Early
        Byzantine Ascetical Literature : a Bibliographical Note',
        Journal of Ecclesiastical History, vol. 5, 1954, pp. 86–
        100.

1447   CALDERON, GEORGE. 'The Tale of Sorrow', *Rus R*
        (*Liverpool*), vol. 3, no. 1, 1914, pp. 26–37.
          Commentary on *Povest' o gore-zlochastii*, cf. **1500**.

1448   STANKIEWICZ, EDWARD. 'The Life of Methodius in the
        Light of Related Sources', *Indiana Slavic Studies*, vol. 2,
        1958, pp. 145–61.

1449　CROSS, SAMUEL H. 'The Earliest Allusion in Slavic Literature to the "Revelations" of Pseudo-Methodius', *Speculum*, vol. 4, 1929, pp. 329–39.

1450　CHIZHEVSKY, DMITRI (Čiževskij). 'Epiphanius the Wise: Medieval Russian Hagiographer', *St. Vladimir's Seminar Quarterly*, vol. 3, 1956, pp. 15–26.

1451　DANE, MICHAEL M. 'Epiphanius' Image of St. Stefan', *Canadian Slavonic Papers*, vol. 5, 1961, pp. 72–86.

1452　'Two National Saints: the Life and Martyrdom of Michael, Prince of Chernigov and of his Boyar Theodore [and] The Life of Father Irenarch, the Hermit. (Trans. from Russian by Mrs. A. Zvegintsev.)', *Rus R* (*Liverpool*), vol. 2, no. 3, 1913, pp. 21–44.

1453　YARMOLINSKY, AVRAHM. 'The "Slovo" in English', *Memoirs of the American Folklore Society*, vol. 42, 1949, [i.e. **1497** below], pp. 203–23; Bibl.

1454　SLOVO O POLKU IGOREVE. The Tale of the Armament of Igor, A.D. 1185: a Russian Historical Epic. Edited and Translated by Leonard A. Magnus. O.U.P., 1915. Pp. lxiii, 122. Bibl.
　　　　Parallel Russian and English texts.

1455　SLOVO O POLKU IGOREVE. The Tale of Igor. Adapted . . . by H. de Vere Beauclerk. L., 1918. Pp. 23.

1456　SLOVO O POLKU IGOREVE. The Song of Igor's Campaign: an Epic of the Twelfth Century. Translated by Vladimir Nabokov. N.Y., 1960, L., 1961. Pp. 135. (Pbk.).

1457　SOLOV'EV, ALEKSANDR V. 'New Traces of the Igor Tale in Old Russian Literature', *HSS*, vol. 1, 1953, pp. 73–81.

1458　MANNING, CLARENCE A. 'Classical Influence on the Slovo', *Memoirs of the American Folklore Society*, vol. 42, 1949, [i.e. **1497** below], pp. 87–97.

1459　BESHAROV, JUSTINIA. Imagery of the Igor' Tale in the Light of Byzantino-Slavic Poetic Theory. Leiden, 1956. Pp. vii, 115. Bibl.
　　　　Rev.: N. Andreyev in *SEER*, vol. 35, 1956–57, pp. 636–637; W. E. Harkins in *ASEER*, vol. 16, 1957, pp. 225–226.

1460　JAKOBSON, ROMAN. 'The Puzzles of the Igor Tale on the 150th Anniversary of its First Edition', *Speculum*, vol. 27, 1952, pp. 43–66.

1461　BIDA, CONSTANTINE. 'Linguistic Aspects of the Controversy over the Authenticity of Igor's Campaign', *Canadian Slavonic Papers,* vol. 1, 1956, pp. 76–88.

1462 SHARLEMAN, M. 'The "Song of Igor" from the Aspect of Natural Science', *Ukr Rev (L),* vol. 10, no. 3, 1963, pp. 38–61; Bibl.

1463 MENGES, KARL H. 'The Oriental Elements in the Vocabulary of the Oldest Russian Epos, the Igor's Tale', *Word,* vol. 7, 1951; Supplement, pp. vi, 98.

1464 SCHLAUCH, MARGARET. 'Scandinavian Influence on the Slovo?', *Memoirs of the American Folklore Society,* vol. 42, 1949, [i.e. **1497** below], pp. 99–124.

1465 TARTAK, ELIAS L. 'Prince Igor in America', *Rus R,* vol. 8, 1949, pp. 230–3.

1466 'The Homily of Adam in Hades to Lazarus. (Trans. from Russian.)', *SEER,* vol. 10, 1931–2, pp. 244–52.

1467 KARLINSKY, SIMON. 'Domostroi as Literature', *Slavic Rev.,* vol. 24, 1965, pp. 497–502.

1468 HARKINS, WILLIAM E. 'The Pathetic Hero in Russian Seventeenth Century Literature', *ASEER,* vol. 14, 1955, pp. 512–7.

1469 ZENKOVSKY, SERGE A. 'The Old Believer Avvakum: his Role in Russian Literature', *Indiana Slavic Studies,* vol. 1, 1956, pp. 1–51.
    cf. **1247–1249** and **1351**.

1470 'Tsar Alexis and his Rules of Falconry [i.e. the Preface to his: New Falconry Regulation of 1656]', *SEER,* vol. 3, 1924–5, pp. 63–4.

1471 STRUVE, GLEB. 'Russian 18th-Century Literature through Party-Colored Spectacles', *SEEJ,* vol. 15, 1957, pp. 22–33.

1472 WELSH, DAVID J. Russian Comedy, 1765–1823. The Hague, 1966. Pp. 133. Bibl.

1473 COLEMAN, ARTHUR P. Humor in the Russian Comedy from Catherine to Gogol. (Columbia University Slavonic Studies, vol. 2.) Columbia U.P., 1925. Pp. 94. Bibl.

1474 WELSH, DAVID J. 'Satirical Themes in 18th-Century Russian Comedies', *SEER,* vol. 42, 1963–4, pp. 403–14.

1475 WELSH, DAVID J. ' "Philosophers" and "Alchemists" in some 18th Century Russian Comedies', *SEEJ,* New Series, vol. 8, 1964, pp. 149–58.

1476   DRAGE, C. L. 'The Anacreonta and 18th-Century Russian Poetry', *SEER*, vol. 41, 1962–3, pp. 110–34.

1477   EVANS, R. J. M. 'Antioch Kantemir and his First Biographer and Translator', *SEER*, vol. 37, 1958–9, pp. 184–95.

1478   EVANS, R. J. M. 'Antiokh Kantemir and his German Translators', *SEER*, vol. 36, 1957–8, pp. 150–8.

1479   MALYSHEV, V. 'The "Confession" of Ivan Filippov, 1744', *OSP*, vol. 11, 1964, pp. 17–27.

1480   LANG, DAVID M. 'Boileau and Sumarokov: the Manifesto of Russian Classicism', *Modern Language Review*, vol. 43, 1948, pp 500–6.

1481   KARAMZIN, NIKOLAY M. Russian Tales of Karamzin. (Trans. from Russian by J. B. Elrington.) L., 1803. Pp. (262).

1482   KARAMZIN, NIKOLAY M. Tales from the Russian of Nicolai Karamsin. (Trans. from Russian by A. A. Feldborg.) L., 1804. Pp. xii, 262.

1483   KARAMZIN, NIKOLAY M. Letters of a Russian Traveller, 1789–1790 . . . Translated and Abridged by F. Jonas. Columbia U.P., O.U.P., 1957. Pp. ix, 351.
       Rev.: N. V. Riasanovsky in *ASEER*, vol. 17, 1958, pp. 545–546.

1484   STENBOCK-FERMOR, ELISABETH. 'Story of Van'ka Kain', *Journal of American Folklore*, vol. 69, 1956, pp. 254–65.
       Popular character in 18th-century folk literature.

(iii) Folk Literature

Bibliography, **1485**. General surveys of the subject, **1486–1487**. Epic literature, byliny, ballads, **1488–1503** (cf. the *Slovo o Polku Igoreve*, classed in the preceding section, **1453–1465**). Historical song, **1504–1505**. Folk song, **1506–1508**. (See also: **1082**, **1373–1374** and **1377–1379**). Folk tales and fairy tales, **1509–1521**. Russian proverbs, **1522–1527**. On Slavic and Russian folklore, see **1077–1084**. Folk literature of Russia's borderlands is classed in section 16B (iv).

1485   HARKINS, WILLIAM E., *comp*. Bibliography of Slavic Folk Literature. N.Y., 1953. Pp. 28.

1486   GASTER, MOSES. Greeko-Slavonic Literature and its

Relation to the Folklore of Europe during the Middle Ages. (Ilchester Lecture for 1886.) L., 1887. Pp. x, 229, iv.

1487 CHADWICK, HECTOR M. *and* CHADWICK, *Mrs.* NORAH, *née Kershaw*. The Growth of Literature. 3 vols. C.U.P., 1932–40.
Russian Oral Literature, vol. 2, pt. 1, pp. 1–298; The Oral Literature of the Tatars, vol. 3, pt. 1, pp. 1–226.

1488 JAKOBSON, ROMAN. Selected Writings. Vol. 4. Slavic Epic Studies. The Hague, 1966. Pp. xii, 751.
Articles in French, German, English and Russian.

1489 HAPGOOD, ISABEL F., *comp.* The Epic Songs of Russia. (Trans. from Russian). N.Y., L., 1886, Pp. xiii, 358. 2nd ed. L., 1915. Pp. xxxix, 282.

1490 CHADWICK, *Mrs.* NORAH, *née Kershaw, comp.* Russian Heroic Poetry. (Trans. from Russian.) C.U.P., 1932. Pp. xv, 294.

1491 ZENKOVSKY, SERGE A., *comp.* Medieval Russia's Epics, Chronicles and Tales. (Trans. from Russian.) N.Y., 1963. Pp. xii, 436. Also Pbk.
Rev.: Horace W. Dewey in *Slavic Rev*, vol. 22, 1963, pp. 755–756; Nicholas E. Alessen in *Rus R*, vol. 23, 1964, pp. 74–75; A. D. Stokes in *SEER*, vol. 43, 1964–65, pp. 435–438.

1492 BYLINY BOOK: Hero Tales of Russia. Told from the Russian by Marion C. Harrison. Cambridge, 1915. Pp. xv, 70.

1493 'Folk Tales of Ancient Russia—Byliny of Lord Novgorod the Great. Translated by Kate Blakey', *SEER*, vol. 3, 1924–5, pp. 52–62.
Contents: 1. *Vasili Buslaevich the Brave of Novgorod*, 2. *Sadko: the Rich Merchant Guest*.

1494 MAGNUS, LEONARD A. The Heroic Ballads of Russia. L., 1921. Pp. xxi, 210.

1495 BLAKEY, KATE. 'Early Russian Folk Epics', *SEER*, vol. 1, 1922–3, pp. 525–32.

1496 ENTWISTLE, WILLIAM J. 'Russian Ballads', in his: *European Balladry*, O., 1939, pp. 354–80.

1497 JAKOBSON, ROMAN *and* SIMMONS, ERNEST J., *ed.* Russian Epic Studies. (Memoirs of the American Folklore Society, vol. 42, 1949.) Philadelphia, 1949. Pp. 224.
Rev.: W. K. Matthews in *SEER*, vol. 29, 1950–51, pp. 310–312; A. Stender-Petersen in *ASEER*, vol. 9, 1950, pp. 225–227.

1498   CHIZHEVSKY, DMITRI (Čiževskij). 'On Alliteration in Ancient Russian Epic Literature', *Memoirs of the American Folklore Society,* vol. 42, 1949 [i.e. **1497** above], pp. 125–30.

1499   JAKOBSON, ROMAN. 'Balladic Byliny Recorded in the South Ladoga Basin', *Journal of American Folklore,* vol. 69, 1956, pp. 236–8.

1500   HARKINS, WILLIAM E. 'Russian Folk Ballads and The Tale of Misery and Ill Fortune', *ASEER,* vol. 13, 1954, pp. 402–13.
    cf. **1447**.

1501   JAKOBSON, ROMAN O. *and* SZEFTEL, MARC. 'The Vseslav Epos', *Memoirs of the American Folklore Society,* vol. 42, 1949 [i.e. **1497** above], pp. 13–86.

1502   CHIZHEVSKY, DMITRI (Čiževskij). 'Yaroslav the Wise in East-Slavic Epic Poetry', *Journal of American Folklore,* vol. 69, 1956, pp. 236–8.

1503   ENTWISTLE, WILLIAM J. 'Bride-Snatching and the "Deeds of Digenis" ', *OSP,* vol. 4, 1953, pp. 1–16.

1504   STIEF, CARL. Studies in the Russian Historical Song. Copenhagen, 1953. Pp. iii, 265.
    Rev.: G. Nandris in *SEER,* vol. 32, 1953–54, pp. 539–542.

1505   STIEF, CARL. 'A Muscovite Lampoon [on Prince Vasili Vasil'evich Golitsyn]', *Scandoslavica,* vol. 1, 1954, pp. 78–86.

1506   LINEVA, EVGENIYA E., *comp.* (Lineff) (Linieff) (Liniova). The Peasant Songs of Great Russia. 2 vols. St. Petersburg, 1905, Moscow, 1911.
    English and Russian texts.

1507   SCHINDLER, KURT, *comp.* Sixty Russian Folk Songs. 3 vols. N.Y., Boston, Mass., 1918–9.
    Not inspected.

1508   VERNADSKY, NINA. 'The Russian Folk Song', *Rus R,* vol. 3, no. 2, 1943–4, pp. 94–9.

1509   RALSTON, W. R. S., *comp.* Russian Folk-Tales. (Trans. from Russian.) L., 1873. Pp. xvi, 382.

1510   HODGETTS, EDITH M. S., *comp.* Tales and Legends from the Land of the Tzar: a Collection of Russian Stories. (Trans. from Russian.) L., 1890. Pp. x, 324.

1511   BAIN, ROBERT N., *comp.* Russian Fairy Tales. Selected and Translated from the *Skazki* of [Petr N.] Polevoi. L., 1892. Pp. ix, 264. 2nd ed. L., 1893. Pp. viii, 264. 3rd ed. L., 1915. Pp. 283.

1512 BLUMENTHAL, VERRA X. DE, *comp.* Folk Tales from the Russian. L., Chicago, 1903. Pp. (153).

1513 HOUGHTON, LOUISE S., *comp.* The Russian Grandmother's Wonder Tales. L., N.Y., 1906. Pp. xx, 348.
Adapted and translated from: Strauss, F. S., *ed. Sagen und Märchen der Südslaven.*

1514 DOLE, NATHAN H., *comp.* The Russian Fairy Book. (Trans. from Russian.) N.Y., 1907. Pp. (126).

1515 MAGNUS, LEONARD A., *comp.* Russian Folk Tales. (Trans. from Russian.) L., 1915. Pp. xv, 350.

1516 ZEITLIN, IDA, *comp.* Skazki: Tales and Legends of Old Russia. L., N.Y., 1926. Pp. 335.

1517 HARRISON, JANE E. *and* MIRRLEES, HOPE, *comp.* The Book of the Bear: Being 21 Tales Newly Translated from the Russian. L., 1926. Pp. xiii, 108.
Folk tales and 19th-century short stories.

1518 AFANAS'EV, ALEKSANDR N. Russian Fairy Tales. (Trans. from Russian.) N.Y., 1945, L., 1946. Pp. 661.

1519 VERNADSKY, GEORGE V. *and* DZANTY, DZAMBULAT. 'The Ossetian Tale of Iry Dada and Mstislav', *Journal of American Folklore,* vol. 69, 1956, pp. 216–35.
Includes original text with English translation.

1520 VERNADSKY, GEORGE V. 'Problems of Ossetic and Russian Epos', *ASEER,* vol. 18, 1959, pp. 281–94.
Arguments in defence of the genuineness of **1519** above.

1521 HENNING, W. B. 'A Spurious Folktale', *BSOAS,* vol. 21, 1958, pp. 315–8.
An attack on the authenticity of **1519**.

1522 SEGAL, LOUIS, *comp.* Russian Proverbs and their English Equivalents. L., N.Y., 1917. Pp. 63.

1523 BAUER–CZARNOMSKI, FRANCIS, *comp.* Proverbs in Russian and English. L., 1920. Pp. 103.

1524 CHAMPION, SELWYN G., *ed.* Racial Proverbs: a Selection of the World's Proverbs . . . L., 1938. 2nd ed. L., 1950. Pp. cxxix, 767. Reprinted 1963.
Contains 790 Russian and 202 Ukrainian proverbs.

1525 GUERSHOON, ANDREW I. Certain Aspects of Russian Proverbs. L., 1941. Pp. 204.
Lists 1,361 Russian proverbs in English translation.

1526 LANGNAS, ISAAC A., *comp.* 1200 Russian Proverbs . . . (Trans. from Russian.) N.Y., 1960. Pp. (91).

1527 RUSSIAN PROVERBS. Newly Translated . . . for the Peter Pauper Press. N.Y., 1960. Pp. 61.

(iv) *Literature of the Borderlands*

Estonia, **1528**. Latvia, **1529**. Lithuania, **1530–1545**; Donelaitis, **1540–1545**. Ukraine, **1546–1550**. The Caucasus, **1551**; Georgia, **1552–1567**; Armenia, **1568**. Siberian folk tales, **1569**.

1528 KALLAS, OSKAR P. 'Estonian Folk Literature', *SEER,* vol. 9, 1930–1, pp. 107–15.

1529 ANDRUPS, JANIS *and* KALVE, VITAUTS. Latvian Literature: Essays. (Trans. from Latvian.) Stockholm, 1954. Pp. xvi, 206. Bibl.

1530 KATZENELENBOGEN, URIAH, *ed.* The Daina: an Anthology of Lithuanian and Latvian Folk-Songs. Chicago, 1935. Pp. xii, 165.

1531 SRUOGA, BALYS. 'Lithuanian Folk Songs (Dainos) [and] Lithuanian Song (Daina) Literature. (Trans. from Lithuanian.)', *Folk-Lore,* vol. 43, 1932, pp. 301–24 and 324–37.

1532 BALYS, JONAS. Lithuanian Narrative Folksongs: a Description of Types and a Bibliography. Washington, 1954. Pp. (144).

1533 PATERSON, ADRIAN. Old Lithuanian Songs. Kaunas, Pribačis, 1939. Pp. (xxiv, 95).

1534 BALYS, JONAS. 'The Lithuanian Daina', *Lituanus,* vol. 7, 1961, pp. 21–3.

1535 PAYNE, ROBERT. 'On the Dainos', *Lituanus,* vol. 9, 1963, pp. 134–8.

1536 MACEINA, ANTANAS. 'Folksong and the National Character', *Lituanus,* vol. 7, 1961, pp. 27–9.

1537 ZOBARSKAS, STEPAS, *comp.* Lithuanian Folk Tales. N.Y., 1958. Pp. 200. 2nd ed. N.Y., 1959. Pp. 240.

1538 'Devyniabrolė. (Trans. from Lithuanian.)', *Lituanus,* vol. 7, 1961, pp. 103–4.

1539 KAUPAS, JULIUS. 'An Interpretation of Devyniabrolė', *Lituanus,* vol. 7, 1961, pp. 105–8.

1540 Maciūnas, Vincas *and* Ostrauskas, Kostas, *comp.* 'Bibliography [of] Kristijonas Donelaitis', *Lituanus,* vol. 10, no. 1, 1964, pp. 87–96.

1541 Donelaitis, Kristijonas. 'The Braggart Oak. (Trans. from Lithuanian.)', *Lituanus,* vol. 10, no. 1, 1964, pp. 52–3.

1542 Donelaitis, Kristijonas. 'Excerpts from The Seasons. (Trans. from Lithuanian.)', *Lituanus,* vol. 10, no. 1, 1964, pp. 35–51.

1543 Vaškelis, Aleksas. 'The Life and Age of Kristijonas Donelaitis', *Lituanus,* vol. 10, no. 1, 1964, pp. 8–33.

1544 Vaškelis, Aleksas. 'Pietist Spirit in Donelaitis' Poetry', *Lituanus,* vol. 10, nos. 3–4, 1964, pp. 80–92.

1545 Šešplaukis, Alf. 'A Question of Influences: Donelaitis and German Literature', *Lituanus,* vol. 10, no. 1, 1964, pp. 54–60.

1546 Manning, Clarence A. Ukrainian Literature: Studies of the Leading Authors. Jersey City, 1944. Pp. 126. Bibl.

1547 Dz'obko, Iosafat, *comp.* (J. Dziobko). My Songs: a Selection of Ukrainian Folksongs in English Translation. Winnipeg, 1958. Pp. 103.

1548 Lineva, Evgeniya E., *comp.* (*Lineff*) (*Linieff*) (*Liniova*). Folk Songs of the Ukraine. (Trans. from Ukrainian.) Godfrey, Ill., 1958. Pp. vii, 65.

1549 Nandris, G. 'The Relations between Moldavia and Ukraine according to Ukrainian Folklore', *Ukr Rev* (L.), vol. 5, no. 1, 1958, pp. 26–48.

1550 Bain, Robert N., *comp.* Cossack Fairy Tales and Folk Tales. (Trans. from Ukrainian.) L., 1894. Pp. xii, 290. Another Edition: L., 1902.

1551 Dirr, Adolf, *comp.* Caucasian Folk Tales. Translated by L. Menzies. L., 1925. Pp. xiii, 306.

1552 Toumanoff, Cyril. 'Mediaeval Georgian Historical Literature, 7th—15th Centuries', *Traditio,* vol. 1, 1943, pp. 139–82.

1553 Blake, Robert P. 'Georgian Secular Literature, Epic, Romantic and Lyric, 1100–1800', *Harvard Studies and Notes in Philology and Literature,* vol. 15, 1933, pp. 25–48.

1554 Lang, David M. 'Saint Euthymius the Georgian and

the Barlaam and Ioasaph Romance', *BSOAS,* vol. 17, 1955, pp. 306–25.

1555   LANG, DAVID M. 'The Life of the Blessed Iodasaph: a New Oriental Christian Version of the Barlaam and Ioasaph Romance', *BSOAS,* vol. 20, 1957, pp. 389–407.

1556   LANG, DAVID M. 'Georgia's Great Bard, Shota Rustaveli, 1166–1966', *Anglo-Soviet Journal,* vol. 27, no. 2, 1966, pp. 19–23.

1557   RUSTAVELI, SHOTA (Shot'ha Rust'hveli). The Man in the Panther's Skin: a Romantic Epic. (Trans. from Georgian by Marjory S. Wardrop.) L., 1911. Pp. xviii, 273. Reprinted Tbilisi, 1966. Pp. (376).

1558   RUSTAVELI, SHOTA. (Shot'ha Rust'hveli). The Knight in the Tiger's Skin. (Trans. from Georgian by Marjory S. Wardrop.) Supplemented and Revised by E. Orbelyani and S. Jordanishvili. N.Y., Moscow, 1938. Pp. xlviii, 300.

1559   MARGVELASHVILI, TITUS. 'The Georgian Epic: the Man in the Panther's Skin', *Georgica,* vol. 1, nos. 2–3, 1936, pp. 24–43.

1560   STEVENSON, R. H. 'A Note on Rust'aveli's Panther-Symbol', *BK,* New Series, vols. 2–3, 1957, pp. 79–80.

1561   AMIRAN-DAREJANIANI: a Cycle of Medieval Georgian Tales Traditionally Ascribed to Mose Khoneli. Translated by R. H. Stevenson. N.Y., O.U.P., 1958. Pp. xxxiii, 240.

> Rev.: F. Kazemzadeh in *ASEER,* vol. 18, 1959, pp. 612–613; David M. Lang in *SEER,* vol. 38, 1959–60, pp. 240–243.

1562   LANG, DAVID M. *and* MEREDITH-OWENS, G. M. 'Amiran-Darejaniani: a Georgian Romance and its English Rendering', *BSOAS,* vol. 22, 1959, pp. 454–90.

1563   STEVENSON, R. H. 'The Background to Amiran-Darejaniani', *BK,* New Series, vol. 1, 1957, pp. 17–19.

1564   STEVENSON, R. H. 'Omaïniani: a Georgian Romance of the Early Seventeenth Century', *BK,* New Series, vol. 17–18, 1964, pp. 178–83.

1565   STEVENSON, R. H. 'Didmouraviani: a Narrative Poem of the Seventeenth Century', *BK,* New Series, vol. 13–14, 1962, pp. 168–70.

1566   The BOOK OF WISDOM AND LIES: [Traditional Stories]

of the 18th Century [from Georgia.] By Sulkhan
Orbeliani. (Trans. from Georgian by *Sir* Oliver Wardrop.) L., 1894. Pp. xvi, 256.

1567 WARDROP, MARJORY S., *comp*. Georgian Folk Tales.
(Trans. from Georgian.) L., 1894. Pp. xii, 175.

1568 DAREDEVILS OF SASSOUN : the Armenian National
Epic. Edited and Translated by Leon Surmelian. Denver,
1964. Pp. 280.

1569 COXWELL, C. F., *comp*. Siberian and other Folk Tales :
Primitive Literature of the Empire of the Tsars. L.,
1925. Pp. 1056.

L

17

MILITARY HISTORY, WARS, CAMPAIGNS

Arrangement in this section is primarily chronological. Early campaigns against Constantinople, **1570–1577** (relations with Byzantium, **692–698**). Other campaigns of the Kievan period, **1578–1579**. Fourteenth—sixteenth century wars and campaigns, **1580–1582**; 17th century, **1583–1585**. Wars of Peter the Great, **1586–1591**. Eighteenth century, **1592–1603**. On Suvorov, **1595–1602**. On the Astrakhan Regiment, **1603**.

1570 VERNADSKY, GEORGE V. 'The Problem of the Early Russian Campaigns in the Black Sea Area', *ASEER*, vol. 8, 1949, pp. 1–9.

1571 BOAK, ARTHUR E. R. 'Earliest Russian Moves against Constantinople', *Queen's Quarterly*, vol. 55, 1948, pp. 308–17.

1572 VASILIEV, ALEKSANDR A. The Russian Attack on Constantinople in 860. (Publications of the Medieval Academy of America, no. 46.) Cambridge, Mass., 1946. Pp. xii, 245.

1573 DOLLEY, R. H. 'Oleg's Mythical Campaign against Constantinople', *Bulletin de la Classe des Lettres de l'Académie Royale de Belge*, Series 5, vol. 35, 1949, pp. 106–30.

1574 JENKINS, R. J. H. 'The Supposed Russian Attack on Constantinople in 907 : Evidence of the Pseudo-Symeon', *Speculum*, vol. 24, 1949, pp. 403–6.

1575 DOLLEY, R. H. 'Pseudo-Symeon (Pp. 705–7) and the Oleg Controversy', *SEER*, vol. 30, 1951–2, pp. 551–5.

1576 VASILIEV, ALEKSANDR A. 'The Second Russian Attack on Constantinople', *DOP*, no. 6, 1951, pp. 161–225.

1577 VERNADSKY, GEORGE V. 'The Byzantine-Russian War of 1043', *Südost-Forschungen*, vol. 12, 1953, pp. 47–67.

1578 STOKES, A. D. 'The Background and Chronology of the

Balkan Campaigns of Svyatoslav Igorevich', *SEER*, vol. 40, 1961–2, pp. 44–57.

1579 STOKES, A. D. 'The Balkan Campaigns of Svyatoslav Igorevich', *SEER*, vol. 40, 1961–2, pp. 466–96.

1580 FENNELL, JOHN L. I. 'The Campaign of King Magnus Eriksson against Novgorod in 1348 : an Examination of Sources', *Jahrbuch für Geschichte Osteuropas*, Neue Folge, vol. 14, 1966, pp. 1–9.

1581 The RUSSIAN INVASION OF POLAND IN 1563 : Being a Translation of a Contemporary Account in Latin. L., 1874. Also in *Aungervyle Society Reprints*, 2nd Series, 1884, pp. 285–90.

1582 BILLERBEGE, FRAUNCIS. Most Rare and Strange Discourses, of Amurathe the Turkish Emperor . . . with the Warres betweene Him and the Persians, and also of the Tartars and the Muscovites . . . L., c. 1585. Pp. 16.

1583 A SHORT SURVEY OR HISTORY OF THE KINGDOME OF SVEDEN . . . Something also more Particularly Concerning . . . Gustavus Adolphus the III and of his Wars with the Russian, Denmarke and Poland . . . L., 1632. Pp. 103.

1584 TYS-KROKHMALIUK, YURIY. 'The Victory at Konotop', *Ukr Rev (L.)*, vol. 6, no. 3, 1959, pp. 34–45.

Russian troops defeated by a force under the command of Hetman I. Vykhovsky, July 8th, 1659.

1585 PÉTIS DE LA CROIX, FRANÇOIS. The Wars of the Turks with Poland, Muscovy and Hungary. (Trans. from French.) L., 1705.

Rare work cited in **4**.

1586 NIKOLAIEFF, ALEXANDER M. 'Peter the Great as a Military Leader', *Army Quarterly and Defence Journal*, vol. 80, 1960, pp. 76–86.

1587 JACKSON, W. G. F. Seven Roads to Moscow. L., 1957, N.Y., 1958. Pp. x, 334.

Discusses the three principal invasions of Russia by Charles XII, Napoleon and Hitler. Rev.: Marc Raeff in *Rus R*, vol. 18, 1959, pp. 348–349.

1588 TOKARZEWSKI-KARACZEWICZ, *Prince* Jan. 'The Battle of Poltava', *Ukr Rev (L.)*, vol. 6, no. 2, 1959, pp. 13–20 and no. 3, pp. 49–67.

1589   ANDRUSIAK, NICHOLAS. 'From Muscovy to Russia : the Battle of Poltava, 1709', *Ukr Qly*, vol. 18, 1962, pp. 167–74.

1590   KURAT, ARDES NIMET. 'Letters of Poniatowski on the Pruth Campaign, 1711', *SEER*, vol. 26, 1947–8, pp. 239–58.

1591   LEMERCIER-QUELQUEJAY, CHANTAL. 'An Unpublished Document on the Campaign of Peter the Great in the Caucasus', *RCAJ*, vol. 54, 1967, pp. 174–8.

1592   ROLT, RICHARD. Memoirs of the Life of John, Earl of Craufurd : Describing the Campaigns against the Turks, Wherein His Lordship Served in Both the Imperial and Russian Armies . . . L., 1753. Reprinted 1769. Pp. xi, 336.

       The Earl fought in the Russo-Turkish wars of 1736–1739, joining the Russian side in 1738.

1593   TIELKE, JOHANN G. An Account of Some of the Most Remarkable Events of the War between the Prussians, Austrians and Russians from 1756 to 1763 . . . (Trans. from German.) 2 vols. L., 1787–8.

1594   TIELKE, JOHANN G. The Field Engineer; or, Instructions upon Every Branch of Field Fortification, Demonstrated by Examples which Occurred in the 7 Years War between the Prussians, the Austrians and the Russians. (Trans. from German by Edwin Hewgill.) 2 vols. L., 1789.

1595   ANTHING, JOHANN F. History of the Campaigns of Count Alexander Suworow-Rymnikski. (Trans. from German.) 2 vols. L., 1799.

1596   LA VERNE, LÉGER M. P. T. DE (De La Verne) (Tranchant de la Verne). The Life of Field Marshal Souvarof . . . (Trans. from French.) N.Y., 1814. Pp. (305).

1597   MACREADY, EDWARD N. A Sketch of Suwarow and his Last Campaign . . .L., 1851. Pp. xvi, 300.

1598   SPALDING, HENRY. Suvóroff. L., 1890. Pp. 243.

1599   BLEASE, W. L. Suvorof. L., 1920. Pp. xxiii, 366.

1600   OSIPOV, K. Alexander Suvorov : a Biography. (Trans. from Russian.) L., 1944. Pp. 207.

1601   ESSAME, H. 'The Suvorov Legend', *Military Review*, vol. 41, no. 1, 1961, pp. (14–23).

1602   LONGWORTH, PHILIP. The Art of Victory: the Life and Achievements of Generalissimo Suvorov, 1729–1800. L., 1965. Pp. 350.
Rev.: P. S. Squire in *SEER*, vol. 45, 1967, pp. 250-251.

1603   POLLEN, JOHN. 'The Story of a Russian Regiment', *Proceedings of the Anglo-Russian Literary Society*, no. 18, May–Jul., 1897, pp. 33–46.
A history of the 12th Grenadier or Astrakhan Regiment.

18

MARITIME AND NAVAL HISTORY

General works, **1604–1609.** Contemporary accounts of Peter the Great's emergent navy, **1610–1612.** British connections with the Russian Navy in the 18th century, **1613–1614** and **1616–1617** (cf. note to **1605**). See also **2063–2064** on Sir Samuel Bentham.

1604 CLARKE, *Sir* GEORGE S. Russia's Sea-Power, Past and Present. L., 1898. Pp. xix, 202.

1605 JANE, FREDERICK T. (John F. T. Jane). The Imperial Russian Navy: its Past, Present and Future. L., 1899. Pp. 755. 2nd ed. L., 1904. Pp. 735.
An appendix lists British and American officers who served in the Russian Navy, cf. **1614.**

1606 MITCHELL, MAIRIN. The Maritime History of Russia, 848–1948. L., 1949, N.Y., 1950. Pp. xvi, 543. Bibl.
Rev.: A. E. Sokol in *Rus R,* vol. 9, 1950, pp. 334–336.

1607 WOODWARD, DAVID. The Russians at Sea: a History of the Russian Navy. L., 1965, N.Y., 1966. Pp. 254.
Rev.: Thomas W. Wolfe in *Rus R,* vol. 25, 1966, pp. 414–416.

1608 ANDERSON, ROGER C. Naval Wars in the Baltic during the Sailing-Ship Epoch, 1522–1850. L., 1910. Pp. vi, 423. Bibl.

1609 ANDERSON, ROGER C. Naval Wars in the Levant, from the Battle of Lepanto to the Introduction of Steam, 1559–1853. Liverpool U.P., Princeton U.P., 1952. Pp. ix, 619. Bibl.
Rev.: A. E. Sokol in *ASEER,* vol. 12, 1953, pp. 140–141.

1610 HISTORY OF THE RUSSIAN FLEET DURING THE REIGN OF PETER THE GREAT. By a Contemporary Englishman (1724). Edited by Vice-Admiral [Sir] Cyprian A. G. Bridge. (Publications of the Navy Records Society, vol. 15.) L., 1899. Pp. xxvi, 161.

1611 DEANE, JOHN. A Letter from Moscow to the Marquess of

Carmarthen, Relating to the Czar of Muscovy's For-
wardness in his Great Navy ... L., 1699. Pp. 2.

1612   CONSETT, THOMAS, *comp.* 'A Collection of Several Tracts
Relating to ... [the Tsar's] Fleet's Expedition to
Derbent etc. ... (Trans. from Russian.)', in **1223**, vol. 2.

1613   ANDERSON, MATTHEW S. 'Great Britain and the Growth
of the Russian Navy in the Eighteenth Century',
Mariner's Mirror, vol. 42, 1956, pp. 132–46.

1614   ANDERSON, ROGER C. 'British and American Officers in
the Russian Navy', *Mariners' Mirror,* vol. 33, 1947,
pp. 17–27.
    Supplements the list of officers given in **1605**.

1615   An AUTHENTIC NARRATIVE of the Russian Expedition
against the Turks by Sea and Land ... By an Officer on
Board the Russian Fleet. L., 1772. Pp. viii, 168, viii.

1616   ANDERSON, MATTHEW S. 'Great Britain and the Russian
Fleet, 1769–70', *SEER,* vol. 31, 1952–3, pp. 148–63.

1617   SOKOL, A. E. 'Nelson and the Russian Navy', *Military
Affairs,* vol. 13, 1949, pp. (129–37).

1618   THÖRNQVIST, CLARA. 'Old Barge-Builders' Terms from the
Volga Area', *SEER,* vol. 32, 1953–4, pp. 140–50.

19

LOCAL AND REGIONAL HISTORY

A. BALTIC LANDS: LIVONIA, LATVIA, ESTONIA

Bibliography, **1619–1620**. General works, **1621–1624** (cf. **942–944**). Livonia, **1625–1626**. Latvia, **1627–1629**; of these **1627** is a bibliographic study, **1629** a scholarly introduction. Estonia, **1630–1633**; bibliography, **1630**.

1619   BALYS, JONAS, *comp.* 'The More Important Works on the Baltic States: a Survey of the Last Ten Years', *Lituanus,* vol. 8, 1962, pp. 110–9.
    Reprint with additions of his article: 'The Baltic States, a Ten-Year Survey', *Library of Congress Quarterly Journal,* vol. 20, no. 1, 1962, pp. 80-92.

1620   JONAITIS, B., *comp.* 'Baltic States: Selected Western Sources, 1962–1963', *Lituanus,* vol. 10, no. 2, 1964, pp. 71–7.

1621   SPEKKE, ARNOLDS. The Ancient Amber Routes and the Geographical Discovery of the Eastern Baltic. (Trans. from Lettish.) Stockholm, 1957. Pp. xiii, 120. Bibl.
    Rev.: M. Gimbutas in *ASEER,* vol. 17, 1958, pp. 571–572. cf. **902** and **942–944.**

1622   MANNING, CLARENCE A. The Forgotten Republics: [the Baltic States.] N.Y., 1952. Pp. xii, 264. Bibl.
    Rev.: H. E. Ronimois in *ASEER,* vol. 12, 1953, pp. 572–573.

1623   SPEKKE, ARNOLDS. Balts and Slavs, their Early Relations. Washington, 1966. Pp. 129, vi. Bibl.

1624   SCHREIBER, HERMANN. Teuton and Slav: the Struggle for Central Europe. (Trans. from German.) L., 1965. Pp. 392. Bibl.

1625   BLOMBERG, CARL J., *Freiherr von.* An Account of Livonia. With a Relation of the Rise, Progress and Decay of the Marian Teutonick Order ... L., 1701. Pp. vi, 336.

1626   KIRCHNER, WALTHER. The Rise of the Baltic Question. U. of Delaware P., 1954. Pp. xi, 283. Bibl.
    An account of Livonia. Rev.: A. Bruce Boswell in *SEER,* vol. 33,

1954–55, pp. 532–534; J. Mayda in *ASEER,* vol. 14, 1955, pp. 288–289.

1627 OZOLS, SELMA A., *comp.* Latvia: a Selected Bibliography. Washington, 1963. Pp. (144).

1628 BILMANIS, ALFRED. A History of Latvia. Princeton U.P., 1951. Pp. x, 441. Bibl.
> Rev.: Malbone W. Graham in *ASEER,* vol. 11, 1952, pp. 237–239; Gustavs Celmins in *Rus R,* vol. 12, 1953, pp. 196–198.

1629 SPEKKE, ARNOLDS. History of Latvia: an Outline. Stockholm, 1951. Pp. xx, 436. Bibl.
> Rev.: C. L. Lundin in *Rus R,* vol. 12, 1953, pp. 56–58; A. Bruce Boswell in *SEER,* vol. 31, 1952–53, pp. 261–263.

1630 U.S.A. LIBRARY OF CONGRESS. *Slavic and Central European Division.* Estonia: a Selected Bibliography. Compiled by Salme Kuri. Washington, 1958. Pp. iv, 74.

1631 UUSTALU, EVALD. The History of Estonian People. L., 1952. Pp. 268. Bibl.
> Rev.: A. Bruce Boswell in *SEER,* vol. 32, 1953–54, pp. 247–248.

1632 ASPECTS OF ESTONIAN CULTURE. Edited by Evald Uustalu [and others.] L., 1961. Pp. 332.
> Rev.: K. Ericsson in *SEER,* vol. 41, 1962–63, pp. 553–555.

1633 NODEL, EMANUEL. Estonia: Nation on the Anvil. N.Y., 1964. Pp. (207).

B. WESTERN BORDERLANDS, LITHUANIA, BELORUSSIA

1634 is scholarly. Lithuania, **1635–1653.** Lithuanian bibliography, **1635;** historiography, **1636–1638;** general surveys, **1639–1642,** the best of which is **1641.** Special topics, arranged chronologically, **1643–1651.** On the Polish-Lithuanian state, see **1645–1648.** For the travels of Ghillebert de Lannoy in Lithuania, see **1929.** Belorussia, **1654–1660;** bibliography, **1654;** historiography, **1655–1657.**

1634 HALECKI, OSKAR. Borderlands of Western Civilization: a History of East Central Europe. N.Y., 1952. Pp, xvi, 503. Bibl.
> Rev.: A. Bruce Boswell in *SEER,* vol. 31, 1952–53, pp. 259–261; Bruce C. Hopper in *ASEER,* vol. 12, 1953, pp. 147–149.

1635 BALYS, JONAS, *comp.* Lithuania and Lithuanians: a Selected Bibliography. N.Y., 1961. Pp. (x, 190).

1636   TRUMPA, VINCAS. 'The Work of Lithuanian Historians', *Lituanus,* vol. 6, 1960, pp. 75–9.

1637   JAKŠTAS, JUOZAS. 'Russian Historiography on the Origin of the Lithuanian State: Some Critical Remarks on V. T. Pashuto's Study', *Lituanus,* vol. 11, no. 4, 1965, pp. 25–46.

1638   TRUMPA, VINCAS. 'Simonas Daukantas: Historian and Pioneer of Lithuanian National Rebirth', *Lituanus,* vol. 11, no. 1, 1965, pp. 5–17.

1639   GABRYŚ, J. A Sketch of the Lithuanian Nation. Paris, 1911. Pp. 24.

1640   JUSAITIS, KUNIGAS A. The History of the Lithuanian Nation ... Philadelphia, 1918. Pp. ix, 156.

1641   CHASE, THOMAS G. The Story of Lithuania. N.Y., 1946. Pp. xiii, 392. Bibl.
     Rev.: Oskar Halecki in *ASEER*, vol. 6, no. 1, 1947, pp. 202–204.

1642   JURGELA, CONSTANTINE R. History of the Lithuanian Nation ... N.Y., 1948. Pp. 544. Bibl.

1643   PUZINAS, JONAS. 'In Search of the Origins of the Lithuanian People', *Lituanus,* vol. 3, no. 1, 1957, pp. 7–11.

1644   CHASE, THOMAS G. Significance of Ruthenian and Muscovite Elements in Lithuanian History. N.Y., 1944. Pp. 31.

1645   BACKUS, OSWALD P. 'The Problem of Unity in the Polish-Lithuanian State', *Slavic Rev,* vol. 22, 1963, pp. 411–31 and 450–5.

1646   BOSWELL, ALEXANDER BRUCE. 'Poland and Lithuania in the Fourteenth and Fifteenth Centuries', *C Med H,* vol. 8, C.U.P., 1936, chapter 18, pp. 556–86; Bibl.: pp. 948–60.

1647   JAKŠTAS JOSEPH. 'How Firm was the Polish-Lithuanian Federation?', *Slavic Rev,* vol. 22, 1963, pp. 442–9.

1648   DEVEIKE, JONE. 'The Lithuanian Diarchies', *SEER,* vol. 28, 1949–50, pp. 392–405.

1649   BACKUS, OSWALD P. Motives of West Russian Nobles in Deserting Lithuania for Moscow, 1377–1514. U. of Kansas P., 1957. Pp. 174. Bibl.

1650   JAKŠTAS, JOSEPH. 'The Battle of Tannenberg, 1410', *Baltic Review,* no. 20, 1960, pp. 18–37.

1651 SRUOGA, VANDA. 'The Battle of Gruenwald—Tannen-berg', *Lituanus*, vol. 6, 1960, pp. 121–3.

1652 SENIOUTOVITCH-BEREZNY, VIATCHESLAV. 'The Creation of the Volhynian Nobility and its Privileges', *Proceedings of the Shevchenko Scientific Society, Historical-Philo-sophical Section*, vol. 2, 1957, pp. 44–6.

1653 SENN, ALFRED. 'Lithuanian Surnames', *ASEER*, vol. 4, nos. 1–2, 1945, pp. 127–37.

1654 VAKAR, NICHOLAS P., *comp*. A Bibliographical Guide to Belorussia. Harvard U.P., 1956. Pp. xii, 63.

1655 VARONIČ, L. 'The History of Belorussia in the Works of Soviet Historiography', *Belorussian Review*, vol. 2, 1956, pp. 73–97.

1656 STANKIEVIČ, JAN. 'The Soviet Falsification of Belorussian History', *Belorussian Review*, vol. 4, 1957, pp. 56–82.

1657 BACKUS, OSWALD P. 'The History of Belorussia in Recent Soviet Historiography', *Jahrbücher für Geschichte Osteuropas*, Neue Folge, vol. 11, 1963, pp. 79–96.

1658 VAKAR, NICHOLAS P. Belorussia: the Making of a Nation . . . Harvard U.P., 1956. Pp. xiv, 297.
   Chiefly modern. Rev.: Oskar Halecki in *ASEER*, vol. 16, 1957, pp. 95–96; H. Seton-Watson in *SEER*, vol. 35, 1956–57, pp. 309–312.

1659 OSTROWSKI, R. Fragments from the History of Byelo-russia to 1700. L., 1961. Pp. 103.

1660 VAKAR, NICHOLAS P. 'The Name "White Russia"', *ASEER*, vol. 8, 1949, pp. 201–13.

<h2 style="text-align:center">C. UKRAINE</h2>

(i) *General Works*

For the early history of the Ukraine before the middle of the 13th century see section 5C. Bibliography of the Ukraine, **1661–1662**. Historiography, **1663–1670**. Encyclopaedias and other general works, **1671–1676**. General histories of the Ukraine, arranged by date, **1677–1688**. The best of these include **1681–1683** and **1685**. Contemporary descriptions and travellers' accounts, **1997, 2052** and **2078**.

1661 PELENSKYJ, EUGEN J., *comp*. Ucrainica: Ausgewählte Bibliographie über die Ukraine in West-Europäischen

Sprachen. (Mitteilungen der Ševčenko-Gesellschaft der Wissenschaften, Bd. 158.) Munich, 1948. Pp. (111).

1662   WERES, ROMAN, *comp.* The Ukraine : Selected References in the English Language. Kalamazoo, 1961. Pp. (233).

1663   OHLOBLYN, ALEKSANDR. 'Ukrainian Historiography, 1917–1956', *AUA,* vols. 5–6, 1957, pp. 307–435.

1664   PELENSKI, JAROSLAW. 'Soviet Ukrainian Historiography after World War II', *Jahrbücher für Geschichte Osteuropas,* Neue Folge, vol. 12, 1964, pp. 375–418.

1665   KRUPNYTSKY, BORYS. 'Trends in Modern Ukrainian Historiography', *Ukr Qly,* vol. 6, 1950, pp. 337–45.

1666   DOROSHENKO, DMYTRY. 'A Survey of Ukrainian Historiography', *AUA,* vols. 5–6, 1957, pp. 13–304.

1667   HORAK, STEPHAN M. 'Ukrainian Historiography, 1953–1963', *Slavic Rev,* vol. 24, 1965, pp. 258–72.

1668   CHUBATY, NICHOLAS D. (Czubatyj). 'The Conceptions of Ukrainian Nationality in their Historical Development', *Proceedings of the Shevchenko Scientific Society, Historical-Philosophical Section,* vol. 2, 1957, pp. 10–16.
     cf. **60–63.**

1669   SIMPSON, GEORGE W. 'Hrushevsky, Historian of Ukraine', *Ukr Qly,* vol. 1, 1944–5, pp. 132–9.

1670   OHLOBLYN, ALEKSANDR. 'Research Studies on "Istoriya Rusov" ', *Proceedings of the Shevchenko Scientific Society, Historical-Philosophical Section,* vol. 2, 1957, pp. 32–6.

1671   UKRAINE : a Concise Encyclopaedia. Edited by Volodymyr Kubijovyč. Prepared by the Shevchenko Scientific Society. Vol. 1. U. of Toronto P., 1963. Pp. xxxviii, 1185.
     In progress. To be completed in 3 volumes. Rev.: Lowell R. Tillett in *Slavic Rev,* vol. 24, 1965, pp. 164–167.

1672   MIRCHUK, IVAN, *ed.* Ukraine and its People : a Handbook with Maps, Statistical Tables and Diagrams. Munich, 1949. Pp. vii, 280. Bibl.

1673   SIMPSON, GEORGE W. Ukraine : a Series of Maps and Explanations Indicating the Historic and Contemporary Geographical Position of the Ukrainian People. N.Y., 1941, O.U.P., 1942. Pp. (48 + Maps).

1674   KRAWCIW, BOHDAN. 'Ukraine in Western Cartography

and Science in the 17th and 18th Centuries', *Ukr Qly*, vol. 18, 1962, pp. 24–39.

1675 KOVALIV, PANTELEMON. 'Name of Ukraine in Foreign Languages', *Ukr Qly*, vol. 6, 1950, pp. 346–51.

1676 SICHYNSKY, VOLODYMYR. Ukraine in Foreign Comments and Descriptions from the Sixth to Twentieth Century. N.Y., 1953. Pp. 236.

1677 SANDS, BEDWIN, *pseud.* The Ukraine ... Ukrainian History and Present-Day Political Problems. L., 1914. Pp. 72, viii. Bibl.

1678 HRUSHEVSKY, MIKHAILO S. The Historical Evolution of the Ukrainian Problem. (Trans. from Ukrainian.) L., 1915. Pp. 58.

1679 RUDNITSKY, STEFAN. The Ukraine and the Ukrainians. (Trans. from German.) Jersey City, 1915. Pp. 36, iv. Bibl.

1680 RUDNITSKY, STEFAN. Ukraine: the Land and its People. (Trans. from German.) N.Y., 1918. Pp. 369.

1681 DOROSHENKO, DMYTRY. History of the Ukraine. (Trans. from Ukrainian and Abridged.) Edmonton, 1939. Pp. 686. Bibl. Reprinted 1941.

> Rev.: O. J. Frederiksen in *SEER*, vol. 20, 1941, pp. 355–357.

1682 ALLEN, W. E. D. The Ukraine: a History. C.U.P., 1940. Pp. xvi, 404. Reprinted N.Y., 1963.

> Rev.: O. J. Frederiksen in *SEER*, vol. 20, 1941, pp. 355–357.

1683 HRUSHEVSKY, MIKHAILO S. A History of Ukraine. Edited by O. J. Frederiksen. Yale U.P., 1941. Pp. xviii, 629. Bibl.

1684 CHAMBERLIN, WILLIAM H. The Ukraine: a Submerged Nation. N.Y., 1944. Pp. 91.

1685 MANNING, CLARENCE A. The Story of the Ukraine. N.Y., 1947. Pp. 326. Bibl.

> Rev.: O. J. Fredriksen in *ASEER*, vol. 6, no. 2, 1947, pp. 182–184.

1686 KRUPNYTSKY, BORYS. 'Ten Centuries of Ukraine', *Ukr Rev (L.)*, vol. 2, no. 1, 1955, pp. 67–77.

1687 NAHAYEWSKY, ISIDORE (Nahaevs'kii). History of Ukraine. Philadelphia, 1962. Pp. 295.

1688 PRITSAK, OMELJAN *and* RESHETAR, JOHN S. 'The Ukraine

and the Dialectics of Nation-Building', *Slavic Rev,* vol. 22, 1963, pp. 224–55.

1689　O———CH, L. 'Direct Popular Rule in the Central Government of Ukraine of the 17th Century', *Ukr Qly,* vol. 6, 1950, pp. 151–7.

(ii) *Chronological*

Entries, chiefly biographical studies, are arranged chronologically. Khmelnitski, **1690–1694**; in Soviet historiography, **1690**; Mazepa, **1697–1709**, Pylyp Orlyk, **1712–1716**.

1690　KRUPNYTSKY, BORYS. 'Bohdan Khmelnitsky and Soviet Historiography', *Ukr Rev (Munich),* vol. 1, 1955, pp. 65–75.

1691　VERNADSKY, GEORGE V. Bohdan, Hetman of Ukraine. Yale U.P., 1941, O.U.P., 1942. Pp. vii, 150. Bibl.
　　Rev.: Philip E. Mosely in *SEER,* vol. 21, no. 1, 1943, pp. 269–270.

1692　CHUBATY, NICHOLAS D. (Czubatyj). 'Bohdan Khmelnytsky, Ruler of Ukraine', *Ukr Qly,* vol. 13, no. 3, 1957, pp. 197–204.

1693　MOSKALENKO, ANDRIY. Khmel'nyts'kyi and the Treaty of Pereyaslav in Soviet Historiography. (Trans. from Ukrainian and Edited by John A. Armstrong.) N.Y., 1955. Pp. (40).

1694　WEERD, HANS DE. 'Report of the Netherlands Ambassador to the Polish Court on Bohdan Khmelnytsky in 1654', *Ukr Qly,* vol. 13, no. 1, 1957, pp. 56–8.

1695　LYPYNSKY, VYACHESLAV. 'The Ukraine at the Turning Point (Trans. from Ukrainian.)', *AUA,* vol. 3, no. 2, 1953, pp. 605–19.

1696　BORSCHAK, ELIE. 'A Little-Known French Biography of Yuras' Khmelnytsky', *AUA,* vol. 3, no. 1, 1953, pp. 509–17.

1697　MACKIW, THEODORE. 'Mazepa in the Light of Contemporary English and American Sources', *Ukr Qly,* vol. 15, no. 4, 1959, pp. 346–62.
　　cf. **1730.**

1698　MACKIW, THEODORE. 'Mazeppa in the Light of the Contemporary English Press', *Ukr Rev (L.),* vol. 7, no. 1, 1960, pp. 30–6.
　　cf. **1730.**

1699 MACKIW, THEODORE. Mazepa (1632–1709) in Contemporary German Sources. (Shevchenko Scientific Society. Papers, vol. 9). N.Y., 1959. Pp. (43).

1700 KRUPNYTSKY, BORYS. 'Mazepa and Soviet Historiography', *Ukr Rev (Munich)*, vol. 3, 1956, pp. 49–53.

1701 MANNING, CLARENCE A. Hetman of Ukraine: Ivan Mazeppa. N.Y., 1957. Pp. (234).

1702 VOGÜÉ, *Viscount* E. MELCHIOR DE. The True Story of Mazeppa. The Son of Peter the Great. A Change of Reign [i.e. the Death of Catherine II and the Accession of Paul I.] (Trans. from French.) L., 1884. Pp. 294.
   Mazeppa: pp. 1–71; Alexis Petrovich: pp. 75–237; death of Catherine: pp. 241–294.

1703 ANDRUSIAK, MYKOLA. 'Ivan Mazepa: Hetman of Ukraine', *Ukr Qly*, vol. 3, 1946–7, pp. (31 et seq.).

1704 MANNING, CLARENCE A. 'The World of Mazepa', *Ukr Qly*, vol. 15, no. 3, 1959, pp. 260–70.

1705 KENTRSCHYNSKYJ, BOHDAN. 'The Political Struggle of Mazepa and Charles XII for Ukrainian Independence', *Ukr Qly*, vol. 15, no. 3, 1959, pp. 241–59.

1706 SICHYNSKY, VOLODYMYR. 'Ivan Mazepa—Patron of Culture and Arts of Ukraine', *Ukr Qly*, vol. 15, no. 3, 1959, pp. 271–80.

1707 MANNING, CLARENCE A. 'Mazepa in English Literature', *Ukr Qly*, vol. 15, no 2, 1959, pp. 133–44.

1708 HOLUBNYCHY, LYDIA. 'Mazepa in Byron's Poem and in History', *Ukr Qly*, vol. 15, no. 4, 1959, pp. 336–45.

1709 MACKIW, THEODORE. 'Mazepa or Mazeppa?' *Ukr Rev* (*L.*), vol. 10, no. 4, 1963, pp. 42–5.

1710 OHLOBLYN, ALEKSANDR. 'The Year 1709', *Ukr Rev* (*L.*), vol. 6, no. 4, 1959, pp. 19–30.

1711 KRUPNYTSKY, BORYS. 'Hetman Danylo Apostol, 1654–1734', *Ukr Rev* (*L.*), vol. 10, no. 1, 1963, pp. 53–7.

1712 KRUPNYTSKY, BORYS. 'General Characteristics of Pylyp Orlyk', *AUA*, vol. 6, 1958, pp. 1247–59.

1713 'A Famous Ukrainian Hetman and Emigrant . . . Pylyp Orlyk', *Ukr Rev* (*L.*), vol. 9, no. 4, 1962, pp. 81–4.

1714 VASYLENKO, MYKOLA. 'The Constitution of Pylyp Orlyk', *AUA*, vol. 6, 1958, pp. 1260–95.

1715 ORLYK, PYLYP. 'Pylyp Orlyk's Devolution of the

Ukraine's Rights. Presentation and Introduction by Elie Borschak', *AUA*, vol. 6, 1958, pp. 1296–1312.

1716   OHLOBLYN, ALEKSANDR. 'Hetman Orlyk's Manifesto', *Ukr Rev (L.)*, vol. 4, no. 3, 1957, pp. 42–7.

1717   POLONSKA-VASYLENKO, NATALIA D. The Settlement of the Southern Ukraine, 1750–1755. *AUA*, vols. 4–5, Summer-Fall, 1955.) N.Y., 1955. Pp. (350).

1718   OHLOBLYN, ALEKSANDR. 'Ukrainian Autonomists of the 1780's and 1790's and Count P. A. Rumyantsev-Zadunaysky', *AUA*, vol. 6, 1958, pp. 1313–26.

(iii) *The Cossacks, Foreign Relations of Ukraine*

Works on the Cossacks, arranged by date of publication, **1719–1729.** Foreign relations of the Ukraine, **1730–1739.** England and the Ukraine, **1730–1733** (cf. **1697–1698**). Relations with Sweden, **1734–1735**; with France, **1736–1737**; with the Vatican, **1738**; America, **1739.** For Russo-Ukrainian relations, see: **722–744.**

1719   CHEVALIER, PIERRE. A Discourse of the Original Countrey, Manners, Government and Religion of the Cossacks, with Another of the Precopian Tartars . . . (Trans. from French.) L., 1672. Pp. x, 195.

1720   KITTLE, SAMUEL. A Concise History of the Cossacks . . . Edinburgh, 1814. Pp. viii, 107.

1721   HEBER, *Mrs.* AMELIA. The Life of Reginald Heber . . . With Selections from his Correspondence . . . Together with a Journal of his Tour in Norway, Sweden, Russia . . . and a History of the Cossaks. 2 vols. L., 1830.

1722   KRASIŃSKI, HENRYK, *Count*. The Cossacks of the Ukraine . . . L., 1848. Pp. xv, 312.

1723   CZAPLICKA, MARY A. C. The Evolution of the Cossack Communities. Guildford, 1918. Pp. 17.
     Article originally published in the *Journal of the Central Asian Society.*

1724   CRESSON, WILLIAM P. The Cossacks: their History and Country. N.Y., 1919. Pp. x, 239.

1725   HINDUS, MAURICE. The Cossacks: the Story of a Warrior People. N.Y., 1945. Pp. xiv, 321. Another Edition with Abbreviated Title: L., 1946. Pp. 319.

1726 BILYI, I. 'The Cossacks and their Struggle for Freedom', *Eastern Quarterly*, vol. 4, no. 2, 1951, pp. 32–7.
Emphasizes 19th–20th centuries.

1727 HAVELOCK, H. 'The Cossacks in the Early Seventeenth Century', *EHR*, vol. 13, 1898, pp. 242–60.

1728 FIELD, CECIL. The Great Cossack: the Rebellion of Sten'ka Razin against Alexis Michaelovitch, Tsar of all the Russias. L., 1947. Pp. 125. Bibl.
For contemporary accounts of the rebellion, see **383–386**.

1729 EFREMOV, I. 'The Don Cossacks', *Rus R* (*Liverpool*), vol. 3, no. 2, 1914, pp. 116–21.

1730 MACKIW, THEODORE. 'Ukraine as Seen by the "London Gazette", 1665–1965', *Ukr Rev* (*L.*), vol. 13, no. 1, 1966, pp. 71–7.
cf. **1697–1698**.

1731 WYNAR, LUBOMYR (Vynar). The Question of Anglo-Ukrainian Relations during the Rule of the Great Ukrainian Hetman Bohdan Khmelnytsky', *Ukr Rev* (*L.*), vol. 10, no. 1, 1963, pp. 28–52.

1732 WYNAR, LUBOMYR (Vynar). 'The Question of Anglo-Ukrainian Relations in the Middle of the Seventeenth Century', *AUA*, vol. 6, 1958, pp. 1411–8.

1733 BORSHAK, ELIE. 'Early Relations between England and Ukraine', *SEER*, vol. 10, 1931–2, pp. 138–60.
17th–18th centuries.

1734 HALECKI, OSKAR. 'Ukraine, Poland and Sweden at the Time of Ivan Mazepa', *Ukr Qly*, vol. 15, no. 2, 1959, pp. 128–32.

1735 KRUPNYTSKY, BORYS. 'The Swedish-Ukrainian Treaties of Alliance, 1708–1709', *Ukr Qly*, vol. 12, no. 1, 1956, pp. 47–57.

1736 CHUBATY, NICHOLAS D. (Czubatyj). 'Mazeppa's Champion in the "Secret du Roi" of Louis XV, King of France', *Ukr Qly*, vol. 5, 1949, pp. 37–51.

1737 KIRCHNER, WALTHER. 'Ukrainian Tobacco for France', *Jahrbücher für Geschichte Osteuropas*, Neue Folge, vol. 10, 1962, pp. 497–512.

1738 WYNAR, LUBOMYR (Vynar). 'Ukrainian Kozaks and the Vatican in 1594', *Ukr Qly*, vol. 21, 1965, pp. 65–78.
cf. **1252**.

M

1739   OHLOBLYN, ALEKSANDR. 'American Revolution and Ukrainian Liberation Ideas during the Late 18th Century', *Ukr Qly*, vol. 11, no. 3, 1955, pp. 203–12.

D. SOUTHERN BORDERS. THE CAUCASUS, GEORGIA, ARMENIA AND THE CRIMEA

The most prominent names in the field of Caucasian and Georgian studies are those of the early pioneers: the Wardrops and their able successors, W. E. D. Allen, D. M. Lang, V. F. Minorsky and C. Toumanoff. This relatively small band of scholars is responsible for more than half of the works listed in this section.

General works on Caucasian history, **1740–1744**; specially recomended: **1742** and **1744**. Studies of particular periods, arranged primarily in chronological order, **1745–1752**. Bibliography of Circassia, **1753**. Georgia, **1754–1775**. The best general work covering the whole period is **1755**; **1756** emphasises 19th century history. **1757** is an excellent study of the early history of Georgia, whilst **1769** is good on the later period. Armenia, **1776–1780**. Crimea, **1781–1787**. Of the three general works on the Crimea, **1781–1783,** all are occasional publications; **1784** is scholarly. Contemporary descriptions of the Caucasus and the Crimea are listed in the introduction to section 20 B.

1740   TOUMANOFF, CYRIL. 'Caucasia and Byzantine Studies', *Traditio,* vol. 12, 1956, pp. 409–25.

1741   GAMBASHIDZE, DAVID V. (Ghambashidze). The Caucasus: its People, History, Economics and Present Position. L., 1918. Pp. 20.

1742   MINORSKY, VLADIMIR F. Studies in Caucasian History ... L., 1953. Pp. 178+Appendices.

1743   TOUMANOFF, CYRIL. Studies in Christian Caucasian History. Georgetown U.P., 1963. Pp. 600. Bibl.

1744   TOUMANOFF, CYRIL. 'Armenia and Georgia', *C Med H,* 2nd ed., vol. 4, pt. 1, C.U.P., 1966, chapter 14, pp. 593–637; Bibl.: pp. 983–1009.

1745   GRIGOLIA, ALEXANDER. 'The Caucasus and the Ancient Pre-Greco-Roman Culture World', *BK,* New Series, vols. 8–9, 1960, pp. 97–104.

1746 MINORSKY, VLADIMIR F. A History of Sharvān and Darband in the 10th–11th Centuries. Cambridge, 1958. Pp. 187.

1747 MINORSKY, VLADIMIR F. 'Caucasica in the History of Mayyāfāriqīn', *BSOAS*, vol. 13, 1949–50, pp. 27–35.

1748 MINORSKY, VLADIMIR F. 'Caucasica II: *1*. The Georgian Maliks of Ahar, *2*. The Princess Orbeli in Persia', *BSOAS*, vol. 13, 1949–50, pp. 868–77.

1749 DASXURANCI, MOVSĒS. The History of the Caucasian Albanians. (Trans. from Armenian by C. J. F. Dowsett.) (London Oriental Series, vol. 8). O.U.P., 1961. Pp. xx, 252.

> A history of the Azerbaijan area from the 4th to the 11th century. Probably written at the end of the 11th or early in the 12th century. Emphasis is on church history. Rev.: Karl H. Menges in *Rus R*, vol. 21, 1962, p. 200.

1750 ALLEN, W. E. D. 'A Note on the Princely Families of Kabarda', *BK*, New Series, vols. 13–4, 1962, pp. 140–7.

1751 TOUMANOFF, CYRIL. 'Chronology of the Kings of Abasgia and other Problems', *Le Muséon*, vol. 69, 1956, pp. 73–90.

1752 BADDELEY, JOHN F. The Russian Conquest of the Caucasus. L., N.Y., 1908. Pp. xxxviii, 518.

> First 4 chapters deal with the 18th century.

1753 TRAHO, R., *comp.* 'Literature on Circassia and the Circassians', *CR*, vol. 1, 1955, pp. 145–62.

1754 WARDROP, *Sir* OLIVER. The Kingdom of Georgia ... L., 1888. Pp. xii, 202. Bibl.

1755 ALLEN, W. E. D. A History of the Georgian People from the Beginning down to the Russian Conquest in the Nineteenth Century. L., 1932. Pp. xxiv, 429. Bibl.

> Rev.: Z. Avalov in *SEER*, vol. 12, 1933–34, pp. 220–226.

1756 LANG, DAVID M. A Modern History of Georgia. L., N.Y., 1962. Pp. xiv, 298.

> Emphasis on 19th century. American edition has slightly variant title. Rev.: Richard Pipes in *Rus R*, vol. 22, 1963, pp. 89–90.

1757 LANG, DAVID M. The Georgians. (Ancient Peoples and Places, vol. 51.) L., 1966. Pp. 244. Bibl.

> Rev.: W. E. D. Allen in *BK*, New Series, vols. 23–24, 1967, pp. 187–191.

1758 LEHMANN-HAUPT, C. F. 'On the Origin of the

Georgians', *Georgica*, vol. 1, nos. 4–5, 1937, pp. 43–79.

1759   MANTSKAVA, I. 'The Golden Age of Georgia. (Trans. from Georgian). 2 pts.', *Asiatic Review*, vol. 37, 1941, pp. 366–76 and 798–809; Bibl.

1760   TOUMANOFF, CYRIL. 'Iberia on the Eve of Bagratid Rule : an Enquiry into the Political History of Eastern Georgia between the 6th and the 9th Century', *Le Muséon*, vol. 65, 1952, pp. 17–49 and 199–258.

1761   GUGUSHVILI, A. 'The Chronological-Genealogical Table of the Kings of Georgia', *Georgica*, vol. 1, nos. 2–3, 1936, pp. 109–53.

1762   T'AQAISHVILI, E. 'Georgian Chronology and the Beginning of Bagratid Rule in Georgia', *Georgica*, vol. 1, no. 1, 1935, pp. 9–27.

1763   TOUMANOFF, CYRIL. 'The Early Bagratids : Remarks in Connexion with Recent Publications', *Le Muséon*, vol. 62, 1949, pp. 21–54.

1764   TOUMANOFF, CYRIL. 'On the Relationship between the Founder of the Empire of Trebizond and the Georgian Queen Thamar', *Speculum*, vol. 15, 1940, pp. 299–312.

1765   LANG, DAVID M. 'Georgia in the Reign of Giorgi the Brilliant, 1316–1346', *BSOAS*, vol. 17, 1955, pp. 74–91.

1766   TOUMANOFF, CYRIL. 'The Fifteenth-Century Bagratids and the Institution of Collegial Sovereignty in Georgia', *Traditio*, vol. 7, 1949–51, pp. 169–221.

1767   TOUMANOFF, CYRIL. 'The Oldest Manuscript of the Georgian Annals : the Queen Anne Codex, 1479–1495', *Traditio*, vol. 5, 1947, pp. 340–4.

1768   LANG, DAVID M. 'Georgia and the Fall of the Safavī Dynasty', *BSOAS*, vol. 14, 1952, pp. 523–39.

1769   LANG, DAVID M. The Last Years of the Georgian Monarchy, 1658–1832. Columbia U.P., 1957. Pp. xvi, 333. Bibl.

     Rev.: F. Kazemzadeh in *ASEER*, vol. 17, 1958, pp. 544–555; W. E. D. Allen in *SEER*, vol. 37, 1958–59, pp. 272–275 and in *BK*, N.S., vols. 4–5, 1958, pp. 107–110.

1770   ALLEN, W. E. D. 'Trivia Historiae Ibericae. Pt. 1. Gerfalcons for the King', *BK*, New Series, vols. 11–12, 1961, pp. 104–10.

1771   ALLEN, W. E. D. 'Trivia Historiae Ibericae. Pts. 2–4

(*2* : Aristop Sonski, *3* : Sonskaya Zemlya, *4* : The Daryal Gorge.)', *BK,* New Series, vols. 17–18, 1964, pp. 164–77.

1772 LANG, DAVID M. 'Georgian Manuscripts in Oxford', *BK,* New Series, vols. 2-3, 1957, pp. 74–8.

1773 LANG, DAVID M. 'The New Oxford Edition of Proclus Diadochus', *BK,* New Series, vols. 13–14, 1962, pp. 171–2.

Ioane Petritsi's translation of Proclus Diadochus' (410–485) *Elements of Theology.*

1774 BRYER, ANTHONY. 'Ludovico Da Bologna and the Georgian and Anatolian Embassy of 1460–1461', *BK,* New Series, vols. 19–20, 1965, pp. 178–98.

1775 LANG, DAVID M. 'Georgian Relations with France during the Reign of Wakhtang VI, 1711–1724', *JRAS,* 1950, pp. 114–26.

1776 CʻʿAMčʻEAN, MIKʻAYÉL (Michael Chamich). History of Armenia from B.C. 2247 to the Year of Christ 1780 . . . (Trans. from Armenian.) 2 vols. Calcutta, 1827.

1777 MACLER, FRÉDÉRIC. 'Armenia', *C Med H,* vol. 4, C.U.P., 1923, chapter 6, pp. 153–82; Bibl.: 814–8.

1778 KURKJIAN, VAHAN M. A History of Armenia. N.Y., 1958. Pp. (526).

1779 MIKIRTITCHIAN, L. 'Was There an Armenian Renaissance?', *CR,* vol. 5, 1957, pp. 26–33.

1780 HABLIZL, CARL L. The National History of East Tartary . . . (Trans. from French.) L., 1789. Pp. viii, 199.

Translation of the French translation of original Russian.

1781 MILNER, THOMAS. The Crimea : its Ancient and Modern History . . . L., 1855. Pp. xiii, 368.

1782 BARKER, WILLIAM B. A Short Historical Account of the Crimea . . . Hertford, L., 1855. Pp. xvi, 236.

1783 GRANT, ANTHONY. An Historical Sketch of the Crimea. L., 1855. Pp. viii, 111.

1784 VASILIEV, ALEXANDER A. The Goths in the Crimea. (Monographs of the Mediaeval Academy of America, no. 11.) Cambridge, Mass., 1936. Pp. x, 292.

1785 KORTEPETER, C. M. 'Gāzī Girāy II, Khan of the Crimea, and Ottoman Policy in Eastern Europe and the Caucasus, 1588–94', *SEER,* vol. 44, 1966, pp. 139–66.

1786 ETON, WILLIAM. Survey of the Turkish Empire. In which

are Considered ... the State of the Provinces, Including the Ancient Government of the Crim Tatars ... [and] a Developement of the Political System of the Late Empress of Russia. L., 1798. Pp. xxviii, 516. 2nd ed. L., 1799. 3rd ed. L., 1801.

1787 STOKES, A. D. 'Tmutarakan', *SEER*, vol. 38, 1959–60, pp. 499–514.
Province of Kiev Rus' on Black Sea.

E. CENTRAL ASIA, THE MONGOLS

For the history of Russia under Mongol rule, see section 5D. General works on the history of Central Asia, arranged by date of publication, **1788–1792**. Of this group, **1790** and **1792** are both scholarly and informative; **1789** is a pioneer work still useful for the early period. Background studies, **1793–1794**. Studies on Mongol history, **1795–1814**. Of the general works, **1795–1803**, arranged by date, **1796** is the most comprehensive study available in English; **1802** the best general introduction. See also **322** on this subject. On Genghis Khan, **1804–1807**. On Timur, **1808–1814**. References to early descriptive accounts of the Mongols and Central Asia are listed in the introduction to section 20B.

1788 BRETSCHNEIDER, EMIL. Mediaeval Researches from Eastern Asiatic Sources: Fragments towards the Knowledge of the Geography and History of Central and Western Asia from the 13th to the 17th Century. 2 vols. L., 1888. 2nd ed. 2 vols. L., 1910.

1789 SKRINE, FRANCIS H. B. *and* ROSS, EDWARD D. The Heart of Asia: a History of Russian Turkestan and the Central Asian Khanates from the Earliest Times. L., 1899. Pp. 444.

1790 BARTOL'D, VASILI V. (Barthold). Turkestan down to the Mongol Invasion. (Trans. from Russian and Revised by the Author.) (E. J. W. Gibb Memorial Publications, New Series, vol. 5.) L., 1928. Pp. xix, 513. Bibl. Reprinted L., 1958.

1791 NARSHAKHĪ. The History of Bukhara. Translated from a Persian Abridgement of the Arabic Original by R. N. Frye. Cambridge, Mass., 1954. Pp. xx, 178.

1792 BARTOL'D, VASILI V. (Barthold). Four Studies on the History of Central Asia. (Trans. from Russian.) Vols. 1–3. Leiden, 1956–62.

1793 PEISKER, T. 'The Asiatic Background [to Early Mediaeval History]', *C Med H,* vol. 1, C.U.P., 1911, chapter 12, pp. 323–59; Bibl.: pp. 660–4.

1794 GRØNBECH, KAARE. 'The Steppe Region in World History', *Acta Orientalia (Havniae),* vol. 23, 1958–9, pp. 43–56.

1795 BAHÂDUR, ABÛ AL-GHÂZÎ (Abúl Ghazi Bahadour). A General History of the Turks, Moguls and Tatars... (Trans. from French.) 2 vols. L., 1729–30.

1796 HOWORTH, *Sir* HENRY H. History of the Mongols from the Ninth to the Nineteenth Century. 4 vols. (in 5.) L., 1876–1927.

1797 MUHAMMAD, HAIDAR, *Dughlát* (Mirza Muhammad Haidar). The Tarikh-i-Rashidi: a History of the Moghuls of Central Asia. Translated by E. D. Ross. L., 1895. Pp. xxiv, 535.

1798 PARKER, EDWARD H. A Thousand Years of the Tartars. L., 1895. Pp. iv, 371. 2nd ed. L., N.Y., 1924. Pp. xii, 288.
   Chiefly translations of Chinese sources.

1799 KENNEDY, PRINGLE. A History of the Great Moghuls... With an Introduction Concerning the Mongols and Moghuls of Central Asia. Calcutta, 1905, Pp. iv, 319.

1800 CURTIN, JEREMIAH. The Mongols: a History. L., Boston, Mass., 1908. Pp. xxvi, 426.

1801 LOEWE, HERBERT M. J. 'The Mongols', *C Med H,* vol. 4, C.U.P., 1923, chapter 20, pp. 627–52; Bibl.: pp. 880–2.

1802 PRAWDIN, MICHAEL. The Mongol Empire: its Rise and Legacy. (Trans. from German.) L., N.Y., 1940. Pp. 581. Bibl.
   Rev.: George Vernadsky in *SEER,* vol. 21, 1943, pp. 244–245.

1803 ISHBOLDIN, BORIS (Ischboldin). Essays on Tatar History. New Delhi, 1963. Pp. (182).
   Rev.: Bertold Spuler in *Slavic Rev,* vol. 23, 1964, pp. 587–588.

1804 PÉTIS DE LA CROIX, FRANÇOIS, *comp.* The History of Genghizcan the Great ... Collected from Several

Oriental Authors and European Travellers . . . (Trans. from French). L., 1722. Pp. (ix, 448).

1805   LAMB, HAROLD. Genghis Khan: the Emperor of all Men. L., 1928. Pp. 287. Bibl. Also Pbk. (Bantam Books Ltd.).

1806   VLADIMIRTSOV, B. YA. The Life of Chingis-Khan. (Trans. from Russian by D. S. Mirsky.) L., 1930. Pp. xii, 172.

1807   FOX, RALPH W. Genghis-Khan. L., N.Y., 1936. Pp. xiii, 285. Bibl.

1808   ALHACEN. The Historie of the Great Emperour Tamerlan . . . (Trans. from the French of Jean du Bec.) L., 1597. Pp. 265. Abridged Version also in **1873,** vol. 11, pp. 401–68.

1809   The LIFE OF TAMERLANE THE GREAT, with his Wars against the Great Duke of Moso [sic]. L., 1653. Pp. 61.
        Attributed to Samuel Clarke and Richard Knolles.

1810   SHARAF AL-DĪN'ALĪ (Yazdī) (Cherefeddin Ali). The History of Timur-Bec . . . Tamerlain the Great Emperor of the Moguls and Tartars . . . (Trans. from French.) 2 vols. L., 1723.
        Translation from French translation of Persian original.

1811   LAMB, HAROLD. Tamerlane the Earth Shaker. N.Y., 1928. Pp. ix, 340. Bibl.; L., 1929. Pp. 318. Bibl.

1812   HOOKHAM, H. Tamburlaine the Conqueror. L., 1962. Pp. xv, 344.

1813   WHITE, JOSEPH. A Specimen of the Civil and Military Institutes of Timour or Tamerlane . . . O., 1780. Pp. 39.

1814   TOGAN, ZEKI V. 'Timur's Campaign of 1395 in the Ukraine and North Caucasus', *AUA,* vol. 6, 1958, pp. 1358–71.

1815   KINGSMILL, T. W. 'The Intercourse of China with Central and Western Asia in the 2nd Century B.C.', *Journal of the North-China Branch of the Royal Asiatic Society,* New Series, vol. 14, 1879, pp. 1–29.

1816   CHESHIRE, HAROLD T. 'The Expansion of Imperial Russia to the Indian Border', *SEER,* vol. 13, 1934–5, pp. 85–97.

F. SIBERIA AND THE FAR EAST, RUSSIA'S EASTWARD EXPANSION

Bibliography, **1817–1818** (cf. **1024**). General works on

Siberia, **1819–1823**; recommended, **1821**. Of the more specialized studies, **1824–1828**, Lantzeff's study of Siberia in the 17th century merits special attention. On Russian eastward expansion, **1829–1840**; the most important studies on this topic are **1834, 1836, 1838** and **1840**. See also **320, 1161** and **1821**. On the question of imperialism in Russian history, see **1158–1160**. Kamchatka and Russian discoveries in the Far East and the Pacific, **1841-1853**. On Alaska, **1854–1858** (cf. **1275**). For works on archaeological discoveries in Siberia, see sections 9B (iii–iv). On ethnology and anthropology, **1057–1071**. Social and economic studies, **907–908**. References to contemporary accounts of travel in Siberia are listed in the introduction to section 20B.

1817   KERNER, ROBERT J., *comp*. Northeastern Asia : a Selected Bibliography . . . 2 vols. U. of California P., 1939.

1818   KERNER, ROBERT J., *comp*. 'Russian Expansion to America : its Bibliographical Foundations', *Papers of the Bibliographical Society of America,* vol. 25, 1931, pp. 111–29.

1819   MUELLER, GERHARD F. *and* PALLAS, PETER S. Conquest of Siberia and the History of the Transactions, Wars, Commerce etc., etc., Carried on between Russia and China from the Earliest Period. (Trans. from Russian.) L., 1842. Pp. v, 153.

1820   BAIKALOV, ANATOLE V. 'The Conquest and Colonisation of Siberia', *SEER,* vol. 10, 1931–2, pp. 557–71.

1821   FISHER, RAYMOND H. The Russian Fur Trade, 1550–1700. (University of California Publications in History, vol. 31.) U. of California P., 1943. Pp. xi, 275. Bibl.

     Rev.: A. G. Mazour in *SEER,* vol. 22, no. 4, 1944, pp. 132–133.

1822   SEMENOV, YURI N. (Semyonov). The Conquest of Siberia : an Epic of Human Passions. (Trans. from German.) L., 1944. Pp. xi, 356.

1823   SEMENOV, YURI N. (Semyonov). Siberia : its Conquest and Development. (Trans. from German.) L., Baltimore, 1963. Pp. 414. Bibl.

     Rev.: Ronald F. Drew in *Slavic Rev,* vol. 23, 1964, pp. 581–582.

1824 ARMSTRONG, TERENCE E. Russian Settlement in the North. (Scott Polar Research Institute. Special Publications, no. 4.) C.U.P., 1965. Pp. xii, 224. Bibl.
Rev.: Raymond H. Fisher in *Rus R*, vol. 25, 1966, pp. 418–419.

1825 BAIKALOV, ANATOLE V. 'Notes on the Origin of the Name "Siberia" ', *SEER*, vol. 29, 1950–1, pp. 287–9.

1826 LANTZEFF, GEORGE V. 'The Siberian Khanate: a Chip of the Jenghiz Khan Empire', *Slavia*, vol. 16, 1942–3, pp. (39–47).

1827 LANTZEFF, GEORGE V. Siberia in the Seventeenth Century: a Study of the Colonial Administration. (University of California Publications in History, vol. 30.) U. of California P., 1943. Pp. viii, 235. Bibl.
Rev.: A. G. Mazour in *SEER*, vol. 22, no. 4, 1944, pp. 132–133.

1828 FISHER, RAYMOND H. 'Mangazeia: a Boom Town of Seventeenth Century Siberia', *Rus R*, vol. 4, no. 1, 1944–5, pp. 89–99.

1829 RAVENSTEIN, ERNEST G. The Russians on the Amur: its Discovery, Conquest and Colonisation . . . L., 1861. Pp. xx, 467.

1830 KRAUSSE, ALEXIS S. Russia in Asia: a Record and a Study, 1558–1899. L., N.Y., 1899. Pp. xii, 411. 2nd ed. L., N.Y., 1900. Pp. xxxi, 411. Bibl.

1831 RAMBAUD, ALFRED. 'The Expansion of Russia: Problems of the East and Problems of the Far East', *International Monthly*, vol. 2, Oct., 1900, pp. 211–51 and 341–61.

1832 BEAZLEY, C. RAYMOND. 'The Russian Expansion towards Asia and the Arctic in the Middle Ages to 1500', *AHR*, vol. 13, 1907–8, pp. 731–41.

1833 LOBANOV-ROSTOVSKY, A. 'Russian Imperialism in Asia: its Origin, Evolution and Character', *SEER*, vol. 8, 1929–30, pp. 28–47.

1834 VERNADSKY, GEORGE V. 'The Expansion of Russia', *Transactions of the Connecticut Academy of Arts and Sciences*, vol. 31, July, 1933, pp. 391–425.

1835 HENDERSON, DANIEL M. From the Volga to the Yukon: the Story of the Russian March to Alaska and California . . . N.Y., 1944. Pp. (x, 256).

1836 KERNER, ROBERT J. 'The Russian Eastward Movement:

some Observations on its Historical Significance', *PHR*, vol. 17, 1948, pp. 135–48.

1837 FOUST, C. M. 'Russian Expansion to the East through the Eighteenth Century', *JEH*, vol. 21, 1961, pp. 469–82.

1838 LENSEN, GEORGE A., *ed*. Russia's Eastward Expansion. Englewood Cliffs., 1964. Pp. viii, 184. (Pbk.)

1839 LENSEN, GEORGE A. 'Russia and the United States in Asia', *Rus R*, vol. 24, 1965, pp. 99–110.

1840 TREADGOLD, D. W. 'Russian Expansion in the Light of [Frederick J.] Turner's Study of the American Frontier', *Agricultural History*, vol. 26, 1952, pp. 147–52.

1841 KRASHENINNIKOV, STEPAN P. The History of Kamtschatka and the Kurilski Islands, with the Countries Adjacent ... (Abridged and Translated from Russian by Sir James Grieve.) Glocester, 1764. Pp. 280. Facsimile Reprint, Chicago, 1962. Pp. vi+vii, 288.

Rev.: Raymond H. Fisher in *Slavic Rev*, vol. 22, 1963, pp. 560-561.

1842 MUELLER, GERHARD F. Voyages from Asia to America ... To which is Prefixed a Summary of the Voyages Made by the Russians on the Frozen Sea, in Search of a North East Passage ... (Trans. from German by Thomas Jefferys.) L., 1761. Pp. viii+xliii, 76. 2nd ed., L., 1764. Pp. viii, 120.

1843 COXE, WILLIAM. Account of the Russian Discoveries between Asia and America. To Which are Added, the Conquest of Siberia, and the History of the Transactions and Commerce between Russia and China. L., 1780. Pp. xxii, 344, xvi. 2nd ed. L., 1780. Pp. xxiii, 344. 3rd ed. L., 1787. Pp. xxviii, 454. 4th ed. L., 1804. Pp. xxiv, 500.

1844 BARROW, *Sir* JOHN. A Chronological History of Voyages into the Arctic Regions ... L., 1818. Pp. 379+48.

1845 BURNEY, JAMES. A Chronological History of North-Eastern Voyages of Discovery and of the Early Eastern Navigations of the Russians. L., 1819. Pp. viii, 310.

1846 ANDREEV, ALEKSANDR I., *ed*. Russian Discoveries in the Pacific and in North America in the Eighteenth and Nineteenth Centuries ... (Trans. from Russian.) Ann Arbor, 1952. Pp. (214).

Rev.: A. E. Sokol in *ASEER*, vol. 13, 1954, pp. 440-441.

1847   SOKOL, A. E. 'Russian Expansion and Exploration in the Pacific', *ASEER*, vol. 11, 1952, pp. 85–105.

1848   GOLDER, FRANK A. Russian Expansion on the Pacific, 1641–1850 ... Cleveland, 1914. Pp. (368). Bibl. Reprinted Gloucester, Mass., 1960.

1849   LAURIDSEN, PETER. Vitus Bering: the Discoverer of Bering Strait. (Trans. from Danish.) Chicago, 1889. Pp. (xvi, 223).

1850   GOODHUE, CORNELIA. Journey into the Fog: the Story of Vitus Bering and the Bering Sea. N.Y., 1944. Pp. (179).

1851   DAVIDSON, GEORGE. The Tracks and Landfalls of Bering and Chirikof on the North-West Coast of America ... 1741. San Francisco, 1901. Pp. 44.

1852   GOLDER, FRANK A. Bering's Voyages: an Account of the Efforts of the Russians to Determine the Relations of Asia and America. 2 vols. N.Y., 1922–5.

1853   MASTERSON, JAMES R. *and* BROWER, HELEN. 'Bering's Successors, 1745–1780: Contributions of Peter Simon Pallas to the History of Russian Exploration toward Alaska', *Pacific North West Quarterly*, vol. 38, 1947, pp. 35–83 and 109–55. Also in Book Form: U. of Washington P., 1948. Pp. vii, 96.

1854   MANNING, CLARENCE A. Russian Influences on Early America. N.Y., 1953. Pp. (216).

       Rev.: Richard B. Morris in *ASEER*, vol. 14, 1955, pp. 561–562.

1855   BANCROFT, HUBERT H. History of Alaska, 1730–1885. (The Works of H. H. Bancroft, vol. 33.) San Francisco, 1886. Pp. xxxviii, 775. Bibl.

1856   CHEVIGNY, HECTOR. Russian America: the Great Alaskan Venture, 1741–1867. L., N.Y., 1965. Pp. x, 274.

       Rev.: Albert Parry in *Rus R*, vol. 24, 1965, pp. 421-423.

1857   FARRELLY, THEODORE S. 'A Lost Colony of Novgorod in Alaska', *SEER*, vol. 22, no. 3, 1944, pp. 33–8.

       Examines the evidence for a settlement of Russian refugees in Alaska, founded ca. 1571.

1858   CHEVIGNY, HECTOR. Lord of Alaska: Baranov and the Russian Adventure. N.Y., 1942. Pp. 320. L., 1946. Pp. 255. Bibl.

G. INDIVIDUAL TOWNS AND CITIES

For a general account of individual towns and cities in the Middle Ages, see **291.** Kiev, **1859.** Moscow, **1860–1866.** St. Petersburg, **1867–1868.** On Novgorod see **131, 342, 825, 936–939** and **1580.** Architectural studies of individual cities are classed in section 15 C.

1859 SHULGIN, BASIL. 'Kiev: Mother of Russian Towns', *SEER*, vol. 19, 1939–40, pp. 62–82.

1860 SULKOWSKI, I. A. M. An Historical Account and Description of the City of Moscow . . . L., 1813. Pp. 47.

1861 LYALL, ROBERT. The Character of the Russians and a Detailed History of Moscow . . . L., 1823. Pp. 28, cliv, 639.

1862 GERRARE, WIRT, *pseud.* [William O. Greener]. The Story of Moscow. (Mediaeval Towns Series.) L., 1900. Pp. xii, 315. 2nd ed. 1903. 3rd ed. 1910.

1863 BIRKETT, G. A. 'Slavonic Cities, 4: Moscow, 1147–1947', *SEER*, vol. 25, 1946–7, pp. 336–55.

1864 VOYCE, ARTHUR. The Moscow Kremlin: its History, Architecture and Art Treasures. U. of California P., 1954, L., 1955. Pp. xiii, 147. Bibl.
Rev.: Kenneth J. Conant in *Rus R*, vol. 15, 1956, pp. 73–74; E. R. Hapgood in *ASEER*, vol. 14, 1955, pp. 575–576.

1865 VOYCE, ARTHUR. Moscow and the Roots of Russian Culture. U. of Oklahoma P., 1964. Pp. xiii, 191. Bibl.

1866 MERTENS, CHARLES DE. An Account of the Plague which Raged at Moscow in 1771. (Trans. from French.) L., 1799. Pp. x, 122.
Originally written in Latin. See also **842–843** and **1295–1304.**

1867 MARSDEN, CHRISTOPHER. Palmyra of the North: the First Days of St. Petersburg. L., 1942. Pp. 280. Reprinted 1943.

1868 GOSLING, NIGEL. Leningrad: History, Art, Architecture. L., N.Y., 1965. Pp. 252. Bibl.

20

TRAVEL AND DESCRIPTION, CONTEMPORARY ACCOUNTS

A. BIBLIOGRAPHIES, COLLECTIONS, HISTORIES OF TRAVEL

Bibliographies, **1869–1871** (cf. **4, 1024** and **1817**). General collections of voyages and travels, arranged by date of publication (of first edition), **1872–1881**. Of these, **1872** and **1873** contain an abundance of relevant material, much of it unobtainable elsewhere. Minor collections of two or more works specifically on Russian travel, **1882–1887**. Histories of travel in Russia, sometimes including original texts, **1888–1902**.

1869 ADELUNG, FRIEDRICH VON. Kritisch-Literärische Übersicht der Reisenden in Russland bis 1700 ... 2 vols. St. Petersburg, 1846. Facsimile Reprint : Amsterdam, 1960.
Contains an appendix giving a chronological list of travellers to Russia to the end of the 17th century.

1870 PINKERTON, JOHN, comp. 'Catalogue of Books of Voyages and Travels', in **1879**, vol. 17, pp. 1–255.

1881 HAKLUYT SOCIETY. Works. Series 1, vols. 1–100; of Travel. Vol. 1. The Old World. U. of Washington P., 1935. Pp. 404. Reprinted 1948.

1872 HAKLUYT, RICHARD. The Principall Navigations, Voiages and Discoveries of the English Nation ... L., 1589. Facsimile Reprint in 2 vols. C.U.P., 1965. 2nd ed. 3 vols. L., 1598–1600. Other Editions : a. 5 vols. L., 1809–12. b. 12 vols. Glasgow, 1903–5. c. 8 vols. L., 1907 (i.e.— Everymans Series. Many Reprints.)
Title varies slightly with 2nd edition. References to individual texts quoted elsewhere in this bibliography have been made throughout to the 12-volume Glasgow edition.

1873 PURCHAS, SAMUEL. Purchas his Pilgrimes. 4 vols. L., 1625. Another Edition, Entitled : Hakluytus Posthumus; or, Purchas his Pilgrimes ... 20 vols. Glasgow, 1905–7.
The 1st edition was supplied with an engraved title-page, bearing the alternative title: *Hakluytus Posthumus etc.* The above work

should not be confused with another work by Purchas, entitled: *Purchas his Pilgrimage; or, Relations of the World* ... The 4th edition of the latter, however, published in 1626, ranks as a 5th volume of *Purchas his Pilgrimes*.

References to individual items in Purchas have been made to the more generally available Glasgow edition.

1874 CHURCHILL, AWNSHAM *and* CHURCHILL, JOHN. A Collection of Voyages and Travels. 4 vols. L., 1704. 2nd ed. 6 vols. L., 1732. 3rd ed. 6 vols. L., 1744–6. Another Edition: 8 vols. L., 1752.

Volumes 7–8 of the 1752 edition are a re-issue of **1876**. References quoted elsewhere in the bibliography to individual items in Churchill are made to the 1st edition.

1875 HARRIS, JOHN. Navigantium atque Itinerantium Bibliotheca; or, A Compleat Collection of Voyages and Travels ... 2 vols. L., 1705. 2nd ed., Edited by John Campbell and Entitled: A Collection of Voyages Originally Published by John Harris. 2 vols. L., 1715. 3rd ed. 2 vols. L., 1744–8. 4th ed. 2 vols. L., 1764.

3rd and 4th editions also edited by John Campbell.

1876 A COLLECTION OF VOYAGES AND TRAVELS ... Compiled from the ... Library of the Late Earl of Oxford ... Printed for Thomas Osborne. 2 vols. L., 1745.

Reprinted L., 1752 as vols. 7–8 of **1874**.

1877 MOORE, JOHN H. A New and Complete Collection of Voyages and Travels ... 2 vols. L., 1780.

1878 PELHAM, CAVENDISH. The World; or, The Present State of the Universe ... 2 vols. L., 1808–10.

1879 PINKERTON, JOHN. A General Collection of the Best and Most Interesting Voyages and Travels in all Parts of the World. 17 vols. L., 1808–14.

1880 KERR, ROBERT. A General History and Collection of Voyages and Travels. 18 vols. Edinburgh, 1811–24. Bibl. (in vol. 18.)

1881 HAKLUYT SOCIETY. Works. Series 1, vols. 1–100; Series 2, vol. 1——

In progress.

1882 PUTNAM, PETER, *ed*. Seven Britons in Imperial Russia, 1698–1812. O.U.P., Princeton U.P., 1952. Pp. xxxiv, 424. Bibl.

Rev.: Albert Parry in *ASEER*, vol. 12, 1953, pp. 258–259; Kenneth I. Dailey in *Rus R*, vol. 12, 1953, pp. 198–199.

1883 BOND, *Sir* EDWARD A., *ed*. Russia at the Close of the

16th Century: Comprising the Treatise 'Of the Russe Common Wealth' by Giles Fletcher and the Travels of Sir Jerome Horsey. (**1881**, Series 1, vol. 20.). L., 1856. Pp. cxxxiv, 392.

1884 MOORE, JOHN H., *comp.* 'Travels in Russia, Siberia etc. by Mr. Hanway and Others', in **1877**, vol. 1, pp. 558–75.

1885 HAMEL, JOSEPH VON. England and Russia: Comprising the Voyages of John Tradescant the Elder, Sir Hugh Willoughby, Richard Chancellor, Nelson and Others to the White Sea etc. (Trans. from German.) L., 1854. Pp. xi, 422. Another Edition, Entitled: Early English Voyages to Northern Russia. L., 1857.

1886 MORGAN, E. D. *and* COOTE, C. H., *ed.* Early Voyages and Travels to Russia and Persia by Anthony Jenkinson and other Englishmen ... 2 vols. (**1881**, Series 1, vols. 72–3.) L., 1886. Pp. clxii, 496.

1887 HAKLUYT, RICHARD. The Discovery of Muscovy. L., 1889. Pp. 192. Another Edition: L., 1904. Pp. 192.
Abstracts of passages relating to Russia taken from **1872**.

1888 BEAZLEY, *Sir* RAYMOND. 'Early Glimpses of Moscovite Russia', *Contemporary Review*, vol. 168, 1945, pp. 288–93.

1889 FOSTER, *Sir* WILLIAM. England's Quest of Eastern Trade. L., 1933, N.Y., 1934. Pp. xiv, 355.

1890 VAUGHN, ERNEST V. 'English Trading Expeditions into Asia under the Authority of the Muscovy Company, 1557–1581', in **638**, pp. 127–214.

1891 STEUART, ARCHIBALD F. Scottish Influences in Russian History from the End of the 16th Century to the Beginning of the 19th Century ... Glasgow, 1913. Pp. xviii, 142.

1892 KIRCHNER, WALTHER. 'Emigration to Russia', *AHR*, vol. 55, 1949–50, pp. 552–66.
18th–19th centuries.

1893 MURRAY, HUGH. Historical Account of Discoveries and Travels in Asia from the Earliest Ages ... 3 vols. Edinburgh, 1820. Bibl.

1894 KOMROFF, MANUEL, *ed.* Contemporaries of Marco Polo ... N.Y., 1928, L., 1929. Pp. 255.

Contains reports of the journeys of William of Rubruck (pp. 73–217), John of Plano-Carpini (pp. 25-71) and Friar Odoric (pp. 219–255). See also **1914** and **1910**.

1895 DAWSON, CHRISTOPHER, ed. (Henry C. Dawson). The Mongol Mission: Narratives and Letters of the Franciscan Missionaries in Mongolia and China in the 13th and 14th Centuries. L., N.Y., 1955. Pp. xli, 246. Bibl. William of Rubruck: pp. 89–220; John of Plano-Carpini: pp. 1–72. cf. **1910–1914.**

1896 SYKES, Sir PERCY. The Quest for Cathay. L., 1936. Pp. xii, 280.

1897 'Accounts of Independent Tartary', in **1879,** vol. 9, pp. 320–85.

1898 PURCHAS, SAMUEL. 'Of the Armenians, Medes, Persians, Parthians, Scythians, Tartarians, Chinois and of their Religions', in his: *Purchas his Pilgrimage; or, Relations of the World* . . . 4th ed., L., 1626, Booke 4, pp. 343–476. See note to **1873.**

1899 MOORE, JOHN H., comp. 'Travels through Tibet, Western Tartary, Karazm and Bukharias by Thevenot, Kircher, Duhalde, Gruebar, Dorevile etc', in **1877,** vol. 2, pp. 609–37.

1900 MOORE, JOHN H., comp. 'Travels from Astracan through Asiatic Russia to China by Father Averil, the Muscovite Ambassadors etc', in **1877,** vol. 1, pp. 575–86.

1901 BRICE, W. C. 'Caravan Traffic across Asia', *Antiquity,* vol. 28, 1954, pp. 78–84.

1902 LANE, HENRY. 'A Letter . . . to . . . M. William Sanderson, Conteining a Briefe Discourse of that which Passed in the North-East Discovery for the Space of Three and Thirtie Yeres', in **1872b,** vol. 3, pp. 330–6. Also in **1873,** vol. 12, pp. 49–54.

1903 EDWARDS, ARTHUR. 'Distances of Certaine Places in Russia', in **1872 b,** vol. 3, pp. 68–72. [**A.D. 1567.**]

B. INDIVIDUAL ACCOUNTS BY DATE OF VOYAGE OR SOJOURN

Entries are arranged chronologically. The dates given in parentheses after each item are based for the most part on the list of travellers to Russia contained in **1869.** The list only extends to the year 1700, thus many of the 18th century dates are only

N

given here approximately, based as they are on information contained in the texts of the entries concerned.

Contemporary accounts of specific historical events are classed with the general history of the period (section 5). Among the more important of the sources listed in this section are the following: 1932–1933, 1938–39, 1964, 1972–1975, 1999, 2018–2020, 2031, 2044, 2061 and 2078.

Ukraine: 1997, 2052, 2078. Crimea: 1907, 1965, 2026, 2055, 2070–2071, 2077, 2080. Caucasus: 1907, 2005, 2009–2010, 2012, 2015, 2022, 2026, 2081. Central Asia and the Tatars: 1908–1928, 1935, 2012, 2014–2015, 2031. Siberia: 1987, 1994, 1996, 2008, 2014, 2030–2032, 2034, 2046–2048, 2050, 2056, 2060, 2063–2065, 2072, 2074. See also 1024 which contains a bibliography of Siberian travel accounts.

1904   OCHTHER. 'The Voyage of Ochther Made to the Northeast Parts Beyond Norway, Reported by Himselfe unto Alfred the Famous King of England about the Yere 890', in 1872 b, vol. 1, pp. 11–14. [ca. 890.]

1905   EKBLOM, R. 'King Alfred and Bearings in the Borderland between the West Slavs and the Balts', *Scandoslavica*, vol. 4, 1958, pp. 117–26. [ca. 890.]

1906   BEAZLEY, C. RAYMOND. 'The Oldest Monument of Russian Travel', *Trans RHS*, New Series, vol. 14, 1900, pp. 175–85. [A.D. 1106–7.]
     The journey of Archimandrite Daniel of Kiev to the Holy Land ca. 1106–1107.

1907   PETACHIAS, *Rabbi of Ratisbon*. Travels ... in the Latter End of the 12th Century [in] Poland, Russia, Little Tartary, the Crimea, Armenia [etc.] (Trans. from Hebrew.) L., 1856. 2nd ed. L., 1861. Pp. viii, 106.
     Parallel Hebrew and English texts.

1908   WENDOVER, R. *and* PARIS, MATTHEW. 'Relations Touching the Tartars', in 1873, vol. 11, pp. 173–82. [A.D. 1240—41.]

1909   Yvo, *of Narbonne*. 'Part of an Epistle Written ... unto the Archbishop of Burdeaux, Containing the Confession of an Englishman, as Touching the ... Tartars, Which had Lived among Them ... Recorded by Matthew Paris in the Yeare ... 1243', in 1873, vol. 11, pp. 183–7. Also in **1872 b**, vol. 1, pp. 50–54 and **1880**, vol. 1, pp. 114–7. [**A.D. 1243.**]

1910 JOHN, *of Plano-Carpini*. 'The Journey of Friar John of Pian de Carpine to the Court of Kuyuk Khan, 1245–1247 . . .', in **1914** [i.e. **1881**, Series 2, vol. 4], pp. 1–32. Also in **1880**, vol. 1, pp. 125–61; **1894**, pp. 25-71; **1895**, pp. 1–72. [**A.D. 1245–7.**]

1911 BENEDICT, *the Pole*. 'A Narrative of Friar John of Pian de Carpine's Mission, Derived from an Oral Statement of his Companion, Friar Benedict the Pole', in **1914** [i.e. **1881**, Series 2, vol. 4], pp. 33–9. [**A.D. 1245–7.**]

1912 BEAZLEY, C. RAYMOND, *ed*. The Texts and Versions of John de Plano Carpini and William de Rubruquis, as Printed for the First Time by Hakluyt in 1598 . . . (Hakluyt Society Works, Extra Series, vol. 13.) L., 1903. Pp. xx, 345. [**A.D. 1245–7; 1253–5.**]

1913 VINCENTIUS, *Bellovacensis*. 'Relations of Vincentius Beluacensis, the Most of Which Hee Received from Frier Simon de Sancto Quintino, One of the Foure Friers Sent . . . to the Tartars . . .', in **1873**, vol. 11, pp. 168–72. [**A.D. 1245–7.**]

1914 WILLIAM, *of Rubruck*. The Journey of William of Rubruck to the Eastern Parts of the World, 1253–55 . . . With Two Accounts of the Earlier Journey of John of Pian de Carpini. Translated from Latin and Edited by William W. Rockhill. (**1881**, Series 2, vol. 4.) L., 1900. Pp. lvi, 304. Bibl. William of Rubruck's Journey also in **1873**, vol. 11, pp. 5–149; **1879**, vol. 7, pp. 22–100; **1880**, vol. 1, pp. 161–261; **1894**, pp. 73–217; **1895**, pp. 89–220. [**A.D. 1253–5.**]

1915 POLO, MARCO. The Most Noble and Famous Travels of Marcus Paulus. (Trans. from Italian by John Frampton.) L., 1579. Pp. 167. [**A.D. 1271.**]

1916 POLO, MARCO. The Travels of Marco Polo : a Venetian in the Thirteenth Century . . . (Trans. from Italian by William Marsden.) L., 1818. Pp. lxxx, 782. [**A.D. 1271.**]

1917 POLO, MARCO. The Travels of Marco Polo . . . Translated by Hugh Murray. Edinburgh, 1844. Pp. 368. [**A.D. 1271.**]

1918 POLO, MARCO. The Travels of Marco Polo . . . Translation of Marsden Revised by Thomas Wright. L., 1854. Pp. xxviii, 508. Another Edition: L., N.Y., 1908. Pp. xvi, 461. [**A.D. 1271.**]

1919 POLO, MARCO. The Book of Ser Marco Polo, the Venetian, Concerning the Kingdoms and Marvels of the East. Edited and Translated by Sir Henry Yule. 2 vols. L., 1871. 2nd ed. 2 vols. L., 1875. 3rd ed. 2 vols. L., 1903. [**A.D. 1271.**]

1920 POLO, MARCO. The Travels of Marco Polo. Revised from Marsden's Translation by Manuel Komroff. L., 1928. Pp. 352. [**A.D. 1271.**]

1921 POLO, MARCO. 'Travels [etc.]', in **1873**, vol. 11, pp. 188–309 and **1880**, vol. 1, pp. 266–392. [**A.D. 1271.**]

1922 OLSCHKI, LEONARDO. Marco Polo's Asia: an Introduction to his *Description of the World, Called 'Il Milione'.* (Trans. from Italian.) U. of California P., 1960. Pp. ix, 459.

1923 HETHUM, *Prince of Korghos* (Haiton) (Hatto) (Hetoum). 'The Historie of Ayton, or Anthonie, the Armenian, of Asia and Specially Touching the Tartars', in **1873**, vol. 11, pp. 309–64. [**A.D. 1290.**]

1924 IBN BATTUTA (Muhammad Ibn Abd Allāh). The Travels of Ibn Batuta. Trans. from the Abridged Arabic Ms. . . . L., 1829. Pp. xviii, 243. [**A.D. 1325–54.**]

1925 IBN BATTUTA (Muhammad Ibn Abd Allāh). The Travels of Ibn Battuta, A.D. 1325–1354. Translated . . . from the Arabic . . . by H. A. R. Gibb. 2 vols. (**1881**, Series 2, vols. 110 and 117.) C.U.P., 1958–9. Bibl. [**A.D. 1325–54.**]

1926 SCHILDTBERGER, JOHANN. 'Travels . . . into Tartary in 1394', in **1880**, vol. 1, pp. 456–60. [**A.D. 1394.**]

1927 GONZALEZ DE CLAVIJO, RUY. Narrative of the Embassy of Ruy Gonzalez de Clavijo to the Court of Timour at Samarcand, A.D. 1403–6. Translated [from Spanish] . . . with Notes . . . and an Introductory Life of Timour Beg by Clements R. Markham. (**1881**, Series 1, vol. 26.) L., 1859. Pp. lvi, 200. [**A.D. 1403–6.**]

1928 GONZALEZ DE CLAVIJO, RUY. Embassy to Tamerlane,

1403–1406. Translated from Spanish by G. Le Strange. L., 1928. Pp. xv, 375. [**A.D. 1403–6.**]

1929 KLIMAS, PETRAS. Ghillebert de Lannoy in Medieval Lithuania ... N.Y., 1945. Pp. 96. Bibl. (Pbk.) [ca. **1413.**]

1930 BARBARO, JOSAFA *and* CONTARINI, AMBROGIO. Travels to Tana and Persia. (Trans. from Italian.) (**1881,** Series 1, vol. 49.) L., 1873. Pp. xi, 175. [**A.D. 1436.**]

1931 BARBARO, JOSAFA. 'Travels of Josaphat Barbaro, Ambassador from Venice to Tanna, Now Called Asof, in 1436', in **1880,** vol. 1, pp. 501–12. [**A.D. 1436.**]

1932 HERBERSTEIN, SIGISIMUND VON. Notes upon Russia: Being a Translation of the Earliest Account of that Country, Entitled: *Rerum Moscoviticarum Commentarii.* Translated and Edited by R. H. Major. 2 vols. (**1881,** Series 1, vols. 10 and 12.) L., 1851–2. [**A.D. 1517–26.**]

1933 HERBERSTEIN, SIGISIMUND VON. The Description of the Regions, People and Rivers Lying North and East from Moscovia ...', in **1872 b,** vol. 3, pp. 405–12. [**A.D. 1517–26.**]

1934 BEAZLEY, *Sir* RAYMOND. 'Herberstein's Russia', *Contemporary Review,* vol. 170, 1946, pp. 33–8, [**A.D. 1517–26.**]

1935 MENDEZ-PINTO, FERNAM. 'Observations of China, Tartaria and other Eastern Parts of the World ...', in **1873,** vol. 12, pp. 54–141. [ca. **1544.**]

1936 CABOT, SEBASTIAN. 'The Excellent Orders and Instructions ... Given to Sir Hugh Willoughby and his Fleete in their Voyage Intended for Cathay', in **1872 b,** vol. 2, pp. 195–205. [**A.D. 1553.**]

1937 'The Voyages of Sir Hugh Willoughby, Richard Chancellor and Others to the North Parts of Russia and Siberia', in **1879,** vol. 1, pp. 1–80. [**A.D. 1553–**]

1938 ADAMS, CLEMENT. Chancellor's Voyage to Muscovy: Being Clement Adams' *Anglorum Navigatio ad Muscovitas* (1630) ... Edited by Edmund Goldsmid. (Bibliotheca Curiosa, vol. 47.) Edinburgh, 1886. Pp. 78. Also in **1872 b,** vol. 2, pp. 239–70 and **1873,** vol. 11, pp. 615–21. [**A.D. 1553.**]

1939 CHANCELLOR, RICHARD (Chancellour). 'The Booke of the Great and Mighty Emperor of Russia and Duke of Moscovia . . .', in **1872 b**, vol. 2, pp. 224–38 and **1873**, vol. 11, pp. 595–615. [**A.D. 1553.**]

1940 'Certaine Instructions Delivered in the Third Voyage, Anno 1556, for Russia, to every Purser and the Rest of the Servants', in **1872 b**, vol. 2, pp. 317–22. [**A.D. 1556.**]

1941 BURROUGH, STEPHEN. 'The Navigation and Discoverie toward the River of Ob . . . Passed in the Yeere 1556', in **1872 b**, vol. 2, pp. 322–44. [**A.D. 1556.**]

1942 JOHNSON, RICHARD. 'Certain Notes . . . Written by Richard Johnson . . . Which was . . . with Steven Burrowe in the Serchthrift 1556 and Afterwarde among the Samoedes . . .', in **1872 b**, vol. 2, pp. 345–9. [**A.D. 1556.**]

1943 JENKINSON, ANTHONY. 'The Names of such Countries as I . . . have Travelled unto from the Second of October 1546 . . . untill . . . 1572, When I Returned Last out of Russia', in **1872 b**, vol. 3, pp. 195–6. [**A.D. 1557–71.**]

1944 'Voyages and Travels of Mr. Anthony Jenkinson from Russia to Boghar or Bokhara in 1557', in **1879**, vol. 9, pp. 386–94. [**A.D. 1557.**]

1945 JENKINSON, ANTHONY. 'The First Voyage . . . toward the Land of Russia, Begun the Twelfth of May in the Yeere 1557', in **1872 b**, vol. 2, pp. 413–25 and **1873**, vol. 11, pp. 623–49. [**A.D. 1557.**]

1946 'The Voyage Wherein Osep Napea, the Moscovite Ambassadour Returned Home . . . with his Entertainement at his Arrival at Colmogro . . .', in **1872 b**, vol. 2, pp. 425–37. [**A.D. 1557.**]

1947 HAWTREY, THOMAS. 'A Letter . . . to . . . Master Henrie Lane, Agent at Colmogro, Written in Vologda the 31 of Januarie 1557', in **1872 b**, vol. 2, pp. 392–4. [**A.D. 1558.**]

1948 JENKINSON, ANTHONY. 'The Voyage . . . from the Citie of Mosco in Russia to the Citie of Boghar in Bactria in the Yeere 1558', in **1872 b**, vol. 2, pp. 449–79 and **1873**, vol. 12, pp. 1–31. [**A.D. 1558.**]

1949 JOHNSON, RICHARD. 'Certaine Notes Gathered by Richard Johnson (Which was at Boghar with M. Anthony Jenkinson) of the Reports of Russes and other Strangers, of the Wayes of Russia to Cathaya, and of Divers and Strange People', in **1872 b**, vol. 2, pp. 480–4. [**A.D. 1558.**]

1950 'The Maners, Usages and Ceremonies of the Russes', in **1872 b**, vol. 2, pp. 438–48. [**A.D. 1558.**]

1951 GRAY, RICHARD. 'A Letter of Master Richard Gray, One of the First Agents of the Moscovie Companie, to Master Henrie Lane at Mosco, Written in Colmogro, the 19. of Februarie, 1558', in **1872 b**, vol. 2, pp. 394–6. [**A.D. 1559.**]

1952 JENKINSON, ANTHONY. 'A Letter . . . upon his Returne from Boghar to . . . Master Henrie Lane . . . Resident in Vologda, Written in the Mosco the 18. of September, 1559', in **1872 b**, vol. 2, pp. 400–1. [**A.D. 1559.**]

1953 ELIZABETH I, *Queen of England*. 'Letters to the Emperour of Russia, Requesting Licence and Safe Conduct for M. Anthony Jenkinson to Passe thorow his Kingdome of Russia into Persia . . .', in **1872 b**, vol. 3, pp. 1–8. [**A.D. 1561.**]

1954 RUSSIA COMPANY. 'A Remembrance Given . . . the 8 Day of May 1561 to our Trustie Friend Anthonie Jenkinson at his Departure towards Russia and so to Persia . . .', in **1872 b**, vol. 3, pp. 9–14. [**A.D. 1561.**]

1955 JENKINSON, ANTHONY. 'A Compendious and Briefe Declaration of the Journey . . . into the Land of Persia, Passing . . . thorow Russia, Moscovia and Mare Caspium . . . Begun the 14th Day of May, Anno 1561 . . .', in **1872 b**, vol. 3, pp. 15–38. [**A.D. 1561.**]

1956 CHEINIE, RICHARD. 'The Second Voyage into Persia Made by Tho. Alcock Who was Slaine there and by George Wren and Ric. Cheinie . . . in Anno 1563', in **1872 b**, vol. 3, pp. 40–4. [**A.D. 1563.**]

1957 EDWARDS, ARTHUR. 'Letters [Written on] the Thirde Voyage into Persia, Begun in the Yeere 1565 by Richard Johnson, Alexander Kitchin and Arthur Edwards', in **1872 b**, vol. 3, pp. 44–67. [**A.D. 1565–7.**]

1958 SOUTHAM, THOMAS. 'The Way Discovered by Water by Us Thomas Southam and John Sparke, from the Towne of Colmogro . . . into the Citie of Novogrod . . . Anno 1566', in **1872 b**, vol. 3, pp. 73–83. [**A.D. 1566.**]

1959   TURBERVILLE, GEORGE. 'Certain Letters in Verse, Written ... out of Moscovia ... 1568 ...', in **1872 b,** vol. 3, pp. 124–35. [**A.D. 1568.**]

1960   RANDOLFE, THOMAS. 'The Ambassage of ... Thomas Randolfe ... to the Emperour of Russia in the Yeere 1568 ...', in **1872 b,** vol. 3, pp. 102–8. [**A.D. 1568.**]

1961   CHAPMAN, LAURENCE. 'The Fourth Voyage into Persia Made by M. Arthur Edwards Agent, John Sparke, Laurence Chapman, Christopher Faucet and Richard Pingle in the Yeere 1568 ...', in **1872 b,** vol. 3, pp. 136–42. [**A.D. 1568.**]

1962   PLUMTREE, LIONEL. 'The Fift Voiage into Persia Made by M. Thomas Banister and Master Geofrey Ducket, Agents for the Moscovie Companie, Begun from England in the Yeere 1574 ...', in **1872 b,** vol. 3, pp. 150–7. [**A.D. 1568–74.**]

1963   JENKINSON, ANTHONY. 'A Note of the Proceeding of M. Anthonie Jenkinson, Ambassadour ... to the Emperour of Russia ... 26. of July 1571 until ... 23. of July 1572', in **1872 b,** vol. 3, pp. 170–95. [**A.D. 1571–2.**]

1964   HORSEY, *Sir* JEROME. 'Extracts out of Sir Jerome Horsey's Observations in 17 Yeeres Travels ... in Russia and other Countries Adioyning ...', in Purchas, Samuel. *Purchas his Pilgrimage; or, Relations of the World ...* 4th ed., L., 1626, pp. 973–92. Also in **1883.** [**A.D. 1573–90.**]

1965   BRONIOVIUS, MARTIN. 'Collections out of Martin Broniovius de Biezerfedea, Sent Ambassadour from Stephen King of Poland to the Crim Tartar ... (Trans. from Latin.)', in **1873,** vol. 13, pp. 461–91. [**A.D. 1579.**]

1966   BURROUGH, CHRISTOPHER. 'Advertisements and Reports of the 6. Voyage into the Parts of Persia and Media ... in the Yeeres 1579, 1580 and 1581 ...', in **1872 b,** vol. 3, pp. 214–48 and **1873,** vol. 12, pp. 32–48. [**A.D. 1579–81.**]

1967   HAYWARD, *Sir* ROWLAND *and* BARNE, GEORGE. 'Commission Given ... unto Arthur Pet and Charles Jackman for a Voyage by Them to be Made for Discovery of Cathay, 1580 ...', in **1872 b,** vol. 3, pp. 251–8. [**A.D. 1580.**]

1968   SMITH, HUGH. 'The Discoverie Made by M. Arthur Pet

and M. Charles Jackman of the Northeast Parts Beyond
the Island of Vaigatz . . . in the Yeere 1580', in **1872 b,**
vol. 3, pp. 282–303. [**A.D. 1580.**]

1969 FRAMPTON, JOHN. A Discoverie of the Countries of
Tartaria, Scithia and Cataya. L., 1580.

> Translated from Boemus via Francisco Thamara by Frampton.
> The only known copy extant is kept in the Lambeth Palace
> Library.

1970 'A Briefe Discourse of the Voyage of Sir Jerome Bowes,
Her Majesties Ambassadour to Ivan Vasilivich the
Emperour of Muscovia in the Yeere 1583', in **1872 b,**
vol. 3, pp. 315–29. [**A.D. 1583.**]

1971 BOWES, *Sir* JEROME. 'The Ambassage of Sir Hierome
Bowes to the Emperour of Moscovie, 1583', in **1872 b,**
vol. 3, pp. 463–85. [**A.D. 1583.**]

1972 FLETCHER, GILES. Of the Russe Common Wealth; or,
Maner of Gouernement by the Russe Emperour . . . with
the Manners and Fashions of the People of that Countrey.
L., 1591. Pp. 117. Other Editions, Entitled : The History of Russia [etc.] L., 1643. Pp. 280; L., 1657.
Pp. 280. Also in **1872 b,** vol. 3, pp. 357–405, 413–9;
1873, vol. 12, pp. 499–633 and **1883.** [**A.D. 1588.**]

> The most important English source for the period. See **1973–1975,**
> below, for the most recently published editions of this text.

1973 FLETCHER, GILES. The English Works of Giles Fletcher,
the Elder. Edited by L. E. Berry. U. of Wisconsin P.,
1964. Pp. xv, 546. [**A.D. 1588.**]

> Contains *Of the Russe Common Wealth* in the text of 1591 and
> *Israel Redux; or, The Restauration of Israel* [*with*] *an Essay
> upon Some Probable Grounds that the Present Tartars near the
> Caspian Sea are the Posterity of the Ten Tribes of Israel* . . .
> (1677 ed.) L., 1749.

1974 FLETCHER, GILES. Of the Rus Commonwealth. Edited
by A. J. Schmidt. (Folger Documents of Tudor and
Stuart Civilization.) Cornell U.P., 1966. Pp. xliv, 176.
[**A.D. 1588.**]

1975 FLETCHER, GILES. Of the Russe Commonwealth; 1591
Facsimile Edition with Variants. With an Introduction
by Richard Pipes. Harvard U.P., 1966. [**A.D. 1588.**]

1976 HAKLUYT, RICHARD. 'The Ambassage of M. Giles Fletcher
. . . Sent from Her Majestie to Theodor the Emperor of

Russia, Anno 1588', in **1872 b**, vol. 3, pp. 353–7. [**A.D. 1588.**]

1977 RANDOLFE, THOMAS *and* BANNISTER, THOMAS. 'A Commission Given ... unto James Bassendine, James Woodcocke and Richard Browne ... Appoint[ed] in a Voyage of Discovery ... from the River Pechora to the Eastwards ... Anno 1588, the 1st of August', in **1872 b**, vol. 3, pp. 119–24. [**A.D. 1588.**]

1978 VEER, GERRIT DE. A True Description of Three Voyages by the North East towards Cathay and China, Undertaken by the Dutch, in the Years 1594, 1595 and 1596 ... (Translated from Dutch.) (**1881**, Series 1, vol. 13.) L., 1853. Pp. cxlii, 291. 2nd ed., Entitled: The Three Voyages of William Barents to the Arctic Regions in 1594, 1595 and 1596. (**1881**, Series 1, vol. 54.) L., 1876. Pp. clxxiv, 289. Also in **1873**, vol. 13, pp. 35–162 and **1879**, vol. 1, pp. 81–130. [**A.D. 1594–7.**]

1979 PARRY, WILLIAM. A New and Large Discourse of the Travels of Sir Antony Sherley ... to the Persian Empire. L., 1601. Pp. (56). Facsimile Reprint in: Collier, J. P., *ed. Illustrations of Early English Popular Literature,* vol. 2, L., 1863; [reprinted] N.Y., 1966. Also Abridged Version in **1873**, vol. 8, pp. 442–9. [**A.D. 1599.**]

1980 SIR THOMAS SMITHES VOIAGE AND ENTERTAINMENT IN RUSHIA, with the Tragicall Ends of Two Emperors and One Empresse ... and the Miraculous Preservation of the now Raigning Emperor, Esteemed Dead for 18 Yeares. L., 1605. Pp. 92. [**A.D. 1604.**]

    Sometimes ascribed to George Wilkins.

1981 SMITH, *Sir* THOMAS. 'Occurrents of Principal Note which Happened in Russia in the Time while the Honorable Sir Thomas Smith Remayned there Embassador ...', in **1873**, vol. 14, pp. 132–57. [**A.D. 1604.**]

1982 GOURDON, WILLIAM. 'A Voyage Made to Pechora, 1611, Written by William Gourdon of Hull, Appointed Chiefe Pilot for Discoverie to Ob etc.', in **1873**, vol. 13, pp. 194–205. [**A.D. 1611.**]

1983 PURSGLOVE, WILLIAM (Poursglove). 'A Briefe Relation of a Voyage to Pechora and Wintering there, Began in the Yeere 1611', in **1873**, vol. 13, pp. 239–55. [**A.D. 1611.**]

1984 LOGAN, JOSIAS. 'The Voyage of Master Josias Logan to Pechora and his Wintering there with Master William Pursglove and Marmaduke Wilson, Anno 1611', in **1873**, vol. 13, pp. 222–38. [**A.D. 1611.**]

1985 FINCH, RICHARD. 'A Letter to ... Sir Thomas Smith ... and to the ... Companie of English Merchants Trading into Russia ...', in **1873**, vol. 13, pp. 205–22. [**A.D. 1611.**]

1986 KONOVALOV, SERGEY. 'Thomas Chamberlayne's Description of Russia, 1631', *OSP*, vol. 5, 1954, pp. 107–16. [ca. **1611.**]
   Includes text of Chamberlayne's: *A Relation of the Empire and State of Russia* from the unique MS. in the Public Record Office, London.

1987 GERARDUS, HESSELL. 'A Description of the Countries of Siberia, Samoieda and Tingoesia ... (Trans. from Latin and Abridged)', in **1873**, vol. 13, pp. 171–92. [**A.D. 1612.**]

1988 BRERETON, HENRY. Newes of the Present Miseries of Rushia, Occasioned by the Late Warre in that Countrey ... L., 1614. Pp. 56. Facsimile Reprint: Berlin, 1855. Also in **373**, pp. 69–150. [**A.D. 1614.**]

1989 GOURDON, WILLIAM. 'Later Observations of William Gourdon in his Wintering at Pustozera in the Yeeres 1614 and 1615. With a Description of the Samoyeds' Life', in **1873**, vol. 13, pp. 255–65. [**A.D. 1614–15.**]

1990 TRADESCANT, JOHN. 'Diary of a Voyage to Russia, June–September 1618. (Edited by Serge Konovalov)', *OSP*, vol. 2, 1951, pp. 130–41.
   See also **629**.

1991 SMITH, JOHN. The True Travels, Adventures and Observations of Captaine John Smith in Europa, Asia, Africa and America ... 1593 to 1629. L., 1630. Pp. x, 60. Also in **1873**, vol. 8, pp. 334–42 and **1874**, vol. 2, pp. 371–402. [**A.D. 1625.**]

1992 BARBOUR, PHILIP L. 'Captain John Smith's Route through Turkey and Russia', *William and Mary Quarterly*, Series 3, vol. 14, 1957, pp. 358–69. [**A.D. 1625.**]

1993 OLEARIUS, ADAM. The Voyages and Travels of the Ambassadors Sent by Frederick, Duke of Holstein, to the Great Duke of Muscovy ... Begun in the Year 1633 and Finished in 1639 ... (Trans. from German by J. Davies.) 2 pts. L., 1662. Pp. xxii, 424. 2nd ed. 2 pts. L., 1669. [**A.D. 1633–9.**]

1994 DE LA MARTINIÈRE, PIERRE M. A New Voyage into the Northern Countries: Being a Discription of the Manners, Customs ... [etc.] of the Norwegians, Laponians, Kilops, Borandians, Siberians, Samojedes ... [etc.] (Trans. from French.) L., 1674. Another Edition: L., 1706. Pp. viii, 153. [**A.D. 1647.**]

1995 PAUL, *of Aleppo*. The Travels of Macarius, Patriarch of Antioch, Written by his Attendant, Archdeacon Paul of Aleppo in Arabic. (Trans. by F. C. Belfour.) 9 pts. in 2 vols. L., 1829–36. Also Abridged Edition: O.U.P., 1936. Pp. xi, 125. [**A.D. 1652–60.**]

1996 'An Account of Two Voyages: the First of Feodor Iskowitz Backhoff the Muscovite Envoy into China ...', in **1874**, vol. 2, pp. 545–51. [**A.D. 1654.**]

1997 BEAUPLAN, GUILLAUME LE VASSEUR, *Sieur de*. 'A Description of Ukraine ... (Trans. from French)', in **1874**, vol. 1, pp. 571–610 and in **1875**, 3rd ed., vol. 2, pp. 516–20. Facsimile Reprint of 3rd English ed. of 1744 (i.e. in no. **1874**), N.Y., 1959. Pp. xiii, 445–81. [ca. **1659.**]
    Rev.: Ya. Slavutych in *ASEER*, vol. 19, 1960, pp. 463–464.

1998 SICHYNSKY, VOLODYMYR. 'A French Description of Ukraine 300 Years Ago', *Ukr Qly*, vol. 6, 1950, pp. 57–64. [ca. **1659.**]
    Commentary on **1997**.

1999 COLLINS, SAMUEL. The Present State of Russia in a Letter to a Friend at London ... L., 1671. Pp. xx, 141, ii. [**A.D. 1659–67.**]
    The author was employed as a physician to Peter the Great's Father—Alexei.

2000 LOEWENSON, LEO. 'The Works of Robert Boyle and "The Present State of Russia" by Samuel Colins (1671)', *SEER*, vol. 33, 1954–5, pp. 470–85. [**A.D. 1659–67.**]

2001 GORDON, PATRICK. Passages from the Diary of General

Patrick Gordon of Auchleuchries, A.D. 1635–1699. (Spalding Club.) Aberdeen, 1859. Pp. xxxvi, 244. [**A.D. 1661–99.**]

The author was an intimate of Peter the Great and had served under his father and the regent Sophia. The original diary in 6 quarto volumes has never been published in its entirety and is preserved in Russia. See also **583**.

2002 BUKSGEVDEN, *Baroness* Sofiya K. (Buxhoevden). A Cavalier in Muscovy [i.e. General Patrick Gordon]. L., 1932. Pp. xiv, 325. Bibl. [**A.D. 1661–99.**]

2003 MIÈGE, GUY. A Relation of Three Embassies from His Sacred Majestie, Charles XII, to the Great Duke of Muscovie . . . Performed by the . . . Earl of Carlisle in the Years 1663 and 1664. L., 1669. Pp. 461. Another Edition, Entitled: A Journey to Russia in 1663. Edited by H. M. Margoliouth. L., 1926. Pp. v, 90. [**A.D. 1663–4.**]

2004 TAVERNIER, JOHN B. The Six Voyages of John Baptista Tavernier . . . through Turky into Persia . . . Finished in the Year 1670 . . . (Trans. from French.) 2 pts. and annexes (in 1.) L., 1678. [**A.D. 1665–70.**]

Includes travels in Georgia and Armenia.

2005 A SHORT DESCRIPTION of all the Kingdoms which Encompass the Euxine and Caspian Seas . . . (Annex to **2004.**) L., 1677. [ca. **1665.**]

2006 STRUYS, JAN J. The Perillous and Most Unhappy Voyages of John Struys through Italy, Greece, Lifeland, Moscovia, Tartary . . . [etc.] (Trans. from Dutch by John Morrison.) L., 1683. Pp. xxii, 378, ix. Another Edition, Entitled: The Voyages and Travels of John Struys . . . L., 1684. Pp. iv, 378, xxv. [**A.D. 1668–70.**]

2007 LOEWENSON, LEO. 'E. G. von Berge, Translator of Milton and Russian Interpreter (1649–1722)', *SEER*, vol. 34, 1955–6, pp. 281–91. [**A.D. 1670–78.**]

Ernst Gottlieb von Berge was at one time tutor in the home of Patrick Gordon.

2008 'A Voyage to the North, Containing an Account of . . . the . . . Muscovite Laplands, Borandia, Siberia, Samojedia . . . .', in **1875**, 3rd ed., vol. 2, pp. 457–92. [**A.D. 1670.**]

2009 CHARDIN, *Sir* JOHN. The Travels of Sir John Chardin into Persia and the East Indies. Vol. 1. The Author's

Voyage from Paris to Ispahan. L., 1686. Pp. xii, 154, v. Also in **1875**, 3rd ed., vol. 2, pp. 862–76. [**A.D. 1672.**]
Travels in the Caucasus.

2010   CHARDIN, *Sir* JOHN. Sir John Chardin's Travels in Persia. (Editor: N. M. Penzer.) L., 1927. Pp. (xxx, 287).

2011   PAUL, R., ed. 'Letters and Documents Relating to Robert Erskine, Physician to Peter the Great, Czar of Russia, 1677–1720', *Miscellany of the Scottish History Society*, vol. 2, [i.e.] *Publications of the Scottish History Society*, vol. 44, 1904, pp. 371–430. [**A.D. 1677–1720.**]

2012   AVRIL, PHILIPPE. Travels into Divers Parts of Europe and Asia, Undertaken by the French King's Order to Discover a New Way by Land into China ... (Trans. from French.) L., 1693. Pp. viii, 191 + 178. [**A.D. 1686.**]
Caucasus and Central Asia.

2013   FOY DE LA NEUVILLE. An Account of Muscovy as it Was in the Year 1689 ... (Trans. from French.) L., 1699. [**A.D. 1689.**]
Rare work cited in **4** and **1871**.

2014   BRAND, ADAM. A Journal of the Embassy from their Majesties John and Peter Alexievitz, Emperors of Muscovy etc. Overland into China through the Provinces of Ustiugha, Siberia, Dauri and the Great Tartary to Peking by Everard Isbrand, their Ambassador ... (Trans. from German). L., 1698. Pp. 134. [**A.D. 1692–5.**]

2015   IDES, EVERT YSBRANTS (Isbrants). Three Years Travel from Moscow Over-land to China thro' Great Ustiga, Siriania, Permia, Sibiria, Daour, Great Tartary etc. to Peking ... (Trans. from German.) L., 1706. Pp. x, 210. Also in **1875**, 3rd ed., vol. 2, pp. 918–60. [**A.D. 1692–95.**]
cf. **2023.**

2016   'A Description of Moscovy ...', in **1876**, vol. 1, pp. 239–50. [ca. **1698.**]

2017   A NEW AND EXACT DESCRIPTION OF MOSCOVY ... L., 1698. Pp. 28.

2018   PERRY, JOHN. The State of Russia under the Present Czar ... L., 1716. Pp. 280. Facsimile Reprint L., 1967. Pp. 280. [**A.D. 1698–1712.**]

An interesting account by an engineer employed in the building of St. Petersburg.

2019 CRULL, JODOCUS. The Antient and Present State of Muscovy ... 2 vols. L., 1698. [**A.D. 1698.**]

2020 CRULL, JODOCUS, *ed*. The Present Condition of the Muscovite Empire till the Year 1699 ... With the Life of the Present Emperour of China by J[oachim] Bouvet. L., 1699. Pp. 111. [**A.D. 1699.**]

2021 KORB, JOHANN G. Diary of an Austrian Secretary of Legation at the Court of Czar Peter the Great. (Trans. from Latin.) 2 vols. L., 1863. [**A.D. 1698–9.**]

2022 PITTON DE TOURNEFORT, JOSEPH. A Voyage into the Levant ... Containing ... the Coasts of the Black Sea, Armenia, Georgia ... (Trans. from French.) 2 vols. L., 1718. Another Edition: 3 vols. L., 1741. [ca. **1700.**]

2023 BRUIN, CORNELIS DE (Cornelius Le Brun) (Bruyn). Voyage to the Levant and Travels into Moscovey ... (Trans. from French). 3 vols. L., 1720. Another Edition, Entitled: Travels into Muscovy, Persia and Part of the East Indies. To which is Added an Account of the Journey of Mr. Isbrants through Russia and Tartary to China ... 2 vols. L., 1737. Also: A New and More Correct Translation ... [by M. Powis] of Mr. Cornelius Le Brun's Travels into Muscovey, Persia [etc]. L., 1759. Pp. 343. Abridged Version in **2028**. [**A.D. 1701.**]

2024 BRUCE, PETER H. Memoirs of ... a Military Officer in the Services of Prussia, Russia and Great Britain, Containing an Account of his Travels in Germany, Russia, Tartary ... [etc.] also Several ... Private Anecdotes of the Czar, Peter I of Russia. L., 1782, Dublin, 1783. Pp. x, 446. [**A.D. 1710–.**]

2025 WHITWORTH, CHARLES, *1st Baron*. An Account of Russia as it was in the Year 1710. Strawberry Hill, 1758. Pp. xxiv, 158. [**A.D. 1710.**]

2026 DE LA MOTTRAYE, AUBRY (De La Motraye). Travels through Europe, Asia [etc.] With an Historical Account of ... the Engaging of the Russian and Turkish Armies on the Banks of the Pruth. 3 vols. L., 1723–32. [ca. **1711–27.**]

2027 CHANCEL, A. DORIACK. A New Journey over Europe

from France thro' Savoy, Switzerland, Germany ...
Muscovy, Poland ... [etc.] L., 1714. Pp. xvi, 256, viii.
[ca. **1713**.]

> Traveller's guide book. The information on Russia is sketchy and
> probably secondhand.

2028   WEBER, FREIDRICH C. The Present State of Russia ...
1714 to 1720. (Trans. from German.) 2 vols. L., 1722–3.
[**A.D. 1714–20.**]

2029   LANGE, LORENZ. 'Journal of Laurence Lange's Travels to
China', in **2028**, vol. 2, pp. 3–36. [**A.D. 1715—.**]

2030   MUELLER, JOHN B. 'The Manners and Customs of the
Ostiacks ... with some Curious Remarks on the Kingdom
of Siberia ...', in **2028**, vol. 2, pp. 37–92. [**A.D. 1716.**]

2031   BELL, JOHN, *of Antermony*. Travels from St. Petersburg
in Russia to Diverse Parts of Asia. 2 vols. Glasgow, 1763.
Reprinted L., 1764. Another Edition: Dublin, 1764.
New Edition: Edinburgh, 1788. Reprinted 1806. Also in
1879, vol. 7, pp. 271–516. New Edition, Entitled: A
Journey from St. Petersburg to Pekin, 1719–22. Edited
by J. L. Stevenson. Edinburgh U.P., 1965. Pp. x, 248.
[**A.D. 1719–22.**].

> The 1965 edition is based on the text of the Glasgow edition of
> 1763. The text in Pinkerton (published 1811) is based on that of
> the 1788 edition.

2032   'A Distinct Account of Part of the North-East Frontier of
the Russian Empire, Commonly Called the Country of
Kamschatka ...', in **1875**, 3rd ed., vol. 2, pp. 1016–41.
[**A.D. 1725.**]

2033   MANSTEIN, CHRISTOPHER H. VON. Memoirs of Russia:
Historical, Political and Military from the Year 1727 to
1744 ... (Trans. from French.) L., 1770. Pp. viii, 432.
2nd ed. L., 1773. 3rd ed., Entitled: Contemporary
Memoirs of Russia [etc.]. L., 1856. Pp. xv, 416.
[**A.D. 1727–44.**]

2034   STRAHLENBERG, PHILIP J. VON. An Historico-Geograph-
ical Description of the North and Eastern Parts of Europe
and Asia, but more Particularly of Russia, Siberia and
Great Tartary ... (Trans. from German.) L., 1736. Also
L., 1738. Pp. xii, 463. [ca. **1727–8.**]

2035   KEITH, JAMES. A Fragment of a Memoir of Field-Marshal
James Keith, Written by Himself. (Publications of the

Spalding Club, vol. 8.) Edinburgh, 1843. Pp. xv, 124.
[**A.D. 1728–.**]

2036 RONDEAU, *Lady* JANE (*Mrs.* Jane Ward) (*Mrs.* Jane
Vigor). Letters from a Lady Who Resided Some Years
in Russia to her Friend in England ... L., 1775. Pp.
viii, 207. 2nd ed. L., 1777. Pp. viii, 207. [**A.D. 1728–
39.**]

2037 LOEWENSON, LEO. 'Lady Rondeau's Letters from Russia,
1728–1739', *SEER*, vol. 35, 1956–7, pp. 399–408.
[**A.D. 1728–39.**]

2038 DASHWOOD, *Sir* FRANCIS. 'Sir Francis Dashwood's Diary
of his Visit to St. Petersburg in 1733. Introduction and
Notes by Betty Kemp', *SEER*, vol. 38, 1959–60, pp. 194–
222. [**A.D. 1733.**]

2039 COOK, JOHN. Voyages and Travels through the Russian
Empire, Tartary and Part of the Kingdom of Persia. 2
vols. Edinburgh, 1770. [ca. **1736.**]

2040 JUSTICE, *Mrs.* ELIZABETH. A Voyage to Russia, Describing the Laws, Manners and Customs of the Great Empire
as Governed at this Present by that Excellent Princess
the Czarina ... York, 1739. Pp. xvi, 59. 2nd ed. L.,
1746. [ca. **1738.**]

On the author's erring spouse, see P. Gaskell, 'Henry Justice: a
Cambridge Book Thief', *Transactions of the Cambridge Bibliographical Society*, vol. 1, 1952, pp. 348–357.

2041 ALGAROTTI, *Count* FRANCESCO. Letters ... to Lord
Hervey and the Marquis Scipio Maffei Containing the
State of the ... Russian Empire ... (Trans. from Italian).
2 vols. L., 1769. [**A.D. 1739.**]

2042 SPILMAN, JAMES. A Journey through Russia into Persia
by Two English Gentlemen, Who Went in the Year 1739
... L., 1742. Pp. 74. [**A.D. 1739.**]

2043 BENIOWSKI, *Count* Maurice A. (Móric A. Benyovszky).
The Memoirs and Travels of Mauritius Augustus, Count
de Benyowsky in Siberia, Kamchatka, Japan [etc.].
(Trans. from his Ms. (1741–1771) by Wm. Nicholson,
1790). 2 vols. L., 1790. Other Editions: 2 vols. Dublin,
1790; L., 1893. Pp. 399; L., 1904. [**A.D. 1741–71.**]

Exaggerated and unreliable.

2044 HANWAY, JONAS. An Historical Account of the British

Trade over the Caspian Sea. With a Journal of Travels from London through Russia into Persia . . . 4 vols. (in 3). L., 1753. 2nd ed. 2 vols. L., Dublin, 1754. 3rd ed. 2 vols. L., 1762. [**A.D. 1743–50.**]

2045 PUGH, JOHN. Remarkable Occurrences in the Life of Jonas Hanway, Esq. . . . Comprehending an Abstract of Parts of his Travels in Russia and Persia. L., 1787. Pp. x, 262. Bibl. [**A.D. 1743–50.**]

2046 N., N. A Letter from a Russian Sea-Officer to a Person of Distinction at the Court of St. Petersburgh . . . Translation Edited by Arthur Dobbs. L., 1754. Pp. 83. [ca. **1753.**]
    Relates to new Russian discoveries in the Far East.

2047 CHAPPE d'AUTEROCHE, JEAN. A Journey into Siberia, Made by Order of the King of France . . . (Trans. from French). L., 1770. Pp. xiii, 395. [**A.D. 1761.**]

2048 The ANTIDOTE; or, An Enquiry into the Merits of a Book, Entitled: *"A Journey into Siberia, Made in 1761 . . ."* and Published . . . by . . . Chappe d'Auteroche . . . (Trans. from French). L., 1772. Pp. iv. 202. [**A.D. 1761.**]
    Variously attributed to Catherine II and the Countess Dashkova.

2049 GILCHRIST, PAUL. A Genuine Letter to Mr. Saunders. . . Giving a Particular and Circumstancial Account of the Great Revolution in Russia and the Death of Peter III . . . L., 1762. [**A.D. 1762.**]

2050 'A New Account of Samoiedia and the Samoiedes', in **1879,** vol. 1, pp. 522–34. [ca. **1762.**]

2051 MACARTNEY, GEORGE, *Earl Macartney.* An Account of Russia, 1767. L., 1768. [**A.D. 1767.**]
    cf. **599.**

2052 MARSHALL, JOSEPH. Travels through Holland, Flanders, Germany, Denmark, Sweden, Lapland, Russia, the Ukraine and Poland in the Years 1768, 1769 and 1770 . . . . 3 vols. L., 1772. 2nd ed. 3 vols. L., 1773. [**A.D. 1768–70.**]
    Russia and the Ukraine are covered in volume 3.

2053 RICHARDSON, WILLIAM. Anecdotes of the Russian Empire. In a Series of Letters Written a Few Years Ago from St. Petersburg. L., 1784. Pp. xvi, 478. [**A.D. 1768–72.**]

2054 KING, JOHN G. A Letter to the Right Reverend the Lord Bishop of Durham Containing Some Observations on the Climate of Russia ... L., 1778. Pp. 23. [ca. **1770.**]

2055 TOTT, FRANÇOIS DE, *Baron.* Memoirs Containing the State of the Turkish Empire and the Crimea during the Late War with Russia ... (Trans. from French.) 2 vols. L., Dublin, 1785. Another Edition: 2 vols. L., 1786. [ca. **1773.**]

2056 STAEHLIN–STORCKSBURG, JACOB VON. An Account of the New Northern Archipelago Lately Discovered by the Russians in the Seas of Kamtschatka and Anadir. (Trans. from German). L., 1774. Pp. 118. [ca. **1773.**]

2057 WRAXALL, *Sir* NATHANIEL W. Cursory Remarks Made in a Tour through some of the Northern Parts of Europe Particularly Copenhagen, Stockholm and Petersburgh. L., 1775. 2nd ed., Entitled: A Tour through some of the Northern Parts of Europe [etc.]. L., 1775. Another Edition: Dublin, 1776. Pp. iv, 268. 3rd ed. L., 1776. 4th ed., Entitled: A Tour round the Baltic [etc.]. L., 1807. [ca. **1774.**]

2058 RICHARD, JOHN. A Tour from London to Petersburgh, from thence to Moscow ... L., 1780. Pp. xiv, 222. Another Edition: Dublin, 1781. Pp. xv, 222. [ca. **1774.**]

2059 OBSERVATIONS ON THE PRESENT STATE OF DENMARK, RUSSIA AND SWITZERLAND ... L., 1784. Pp. xvi, 423. [**A.D. 1777.**]

2060 TRUSLER, JOHN. A Descriptive Account of the Islands Lately Discovered in the South Seas ... with some Account of the Country of Camchatca ... L., 1778. Pp. vii, 303, viii. [ca. **1777.**]

2061 COXE, WILLIAM. Travels into Poland, Russia, Sweden and Denmark ... 2 vols. and 3 vols. L., 1784. 2nd ed. 3 vols. L., 1785–90. 3rd ed. 5 vols. L., 1787–91. 4th ed. 5 vols. L., 1792. 5th ed. 5 vols. L., 1802. 6th ed. 3 vols. L., 1803. Also in **1879**, vol. 6, pp. 570–913. [**A.D. 1778–9.**]

2062 HARRIS, *Sir* JAMES, *1st Earl of Malmesbury.* Diaries and Correspondence ... Containing an Account of his

Missions to the Courts of Madrid, Frederick the Great, Catherine the Second ... [etc.] 4 vols. L., 1844. 2nd ed. 4 vols. L., 1845. [**A.D. 1778–83.**]

See also **604–605**.

2063 BENTHAM, *Lady* MARIA S. Life of Brigadier-General Sir Samuel Bentham. L., 1862. Pp. xiv, 322. [**A.D. 1779–91.**]

2064 ANDERSON, MATTHEW S. 'Samuel Bentham in Russia, 1779–1791', *ASEER*, vol. 15, 1956, pp. 157–72. [**A.D. 1779–91.**]

2065 KIRCHNER, WALTHER. 'Samuel Bentham and Siberia', *SEER*, vol. 36, 1957–8, pp. 471–80. [**A.D. 1779–91.**]

2066 PLESHCHEEV, SERGEY. Survey of the Russian Empire According to its Present Newly Regulated State ... (Trans. from Russian by James Smirnove). L., 1792. Pp. xxiv, 358. [ca. **1785.**]

The author spent 3 years in the British Navy and later became a friend of Samuel Bentham. This is the first general survey of Russia by a Russian to be translated into English.

2067 FORSTER, GEORGE. A Journey from Bengal to England ... and into Russia by the Caspian Sea. 2 vols. L., 1798. [**A.D. 1782.**]

Not inspected.

2068 SINCLAIR, *Sir* JOHN. General Observations Regarding the Present State of the Russian Empire. L., 1787. [ca. **1785.**]

2069 SAUER, MARTIN. An Account of a Geographical and Astronomical Expedition to the Northern Parts of Russia ... Performed by ... Joseph Billings in the Years 1785 to 1794. L., 1802. Pp. xxvi, 332 + 58. [**A.D. 1785–94.**]

2070 M., M. M. '[The Peninsula of the Krim, or Krimea]', *Gentleman's Magazine*, vol. 56, 1786, pp. 643–8. [**A.D. 1786.**]

2071 CRAVEN, *Lady* ELIZABETH (Elizabeth Berkeley) (Elizabeth Margravine of Anspach). A Journey through the Crimea to Constantinople in a Series of Letters ... Written in the Year 1786. L., 1789. Pp. 327. 2nd ed., Entitled: Letters during her Travels through France, Germany and Russia in 1785 and 1786. L., 1814. [**A.D. 1786.**]

2072 LEDYARD, JOHN. Journey through Russia and Siberia, 1787–1788 : the Journal and Selected Letters. Edited by S. D. Watrous. U. of Wisconsin P., 1966. Pp. xiv, 293. Bibl. [**A.D. 1787–8.**]

2073 DVOICHENKO-MARKOV, EUFROSINA. 'John Ledyard and the Russians', *Rus R*, vol. 11, 1952, pp. 211–222. [**A.D. 1787–8.**]

2074 LESSEPS, JEAN B. B. DE (De Lesseps). Travels in Kamtschatka during the Years 1787 and 1788. (Trans. from French). 2 vols. L., 1790. Also in **1878**, vol. 2, pp. 146–94. [**A.D. 1787–8.**]

2075 CHANTREAU, P. N. Philosophical, Political and Literary Travels in Russia during the Years 1788 and 1789. (Trans. from French). 2 vols. Perth, L., 1794. [**A.D. 1788–9.**]

2076 SWINTON, ANDREW. Travels into Norway, Denmark and Russia in the Years 1788, 1789, 1790 and 1791. L., 1792. Pp. xxvii, 506. [**A.D. 1788–91.**]

2077 STRUVE, JOHANN C. VON. Travels in the Crimea : a History of the Embassy from Petersburg to Constantinople in 1793 ... L., 1802. Pp. (vi, 393). [**A.D. 1793.**]

2078 PALLAS, PETER S. Travels through the Southern Provinces of the Russian Empire in the Years 1793 and 1794. (Trans. from German). 2 vols. L., 1802–3. Also 4 vols. L., 1803 (i.e. vols. 5–8 of Francis W. Blagdon's *Modern Discoveries* in 8 vols., L., 1802–3). 2nd ed. 2 vols. L., 1812. [**A.D. 1793–4.**]

2079 NIEMCEWICZ, JULIAN U. Notes of My Captivity in Russia in the Years 1794, 1795 and 1796. (Trans. from French). Edinburgh, L., 1844. Pp. xxiii, 251. [**A.D. 1794–6.**]

2080 GUTHRIE, *Mrs*. MARIA. A Tour Performed in the Years 1795–6 through the Taurida or Crimea, the Antient Kingdom of Bosphoros ... L., 1802. Pp. xxiv, 446. [**A.D. 1795–6.**]

2081 JACKSON, JOHN. 'A Journey from India towards England in the Year 1797 ... Particularly through Curdistan, Diarbekr, Armenia ...', in **1878**, vol. 2, pp. 619–48. [**A.D. 1797.**]

ADDENDA

The following list represents material published between 31 July 1967 and 31 December 1968. Items in this section are arranged alphabetically by author and are not included in the index.

A 1   ALPATOV, MIKHAIL V. Art Treasures of Russia. (Trans. from French.) L., 1968. Pp. (178).

A 2   BERRY, LLOYD E. *and* CRUMMEY, ROBERT O., *ed*. Rude and Barbarous Kingdom: Russia in the Accounts of Sixteenth Century English Voyagers. U. of Wisconsin P., 1968. Pp. xxiii, 391.

A 3   BOBA, IMRE. Nomads, Northmen and Slavs: Eastern Europe in the Ninth Century. (Slavo-Orientalia, Bd. 2.) The Hague, 1967. Pp. 138.

A 4   BÖRTNES, JOSTEIN. 'Frame Technique in Nestor's Life of St. Theodosius', *Scando-Slavica*, vol. 13, 1967, pp. 5–16.

A 5   BUZZI, GIANCARLO. The Life and Times of Peter the Great. (Trans. from Italian.) L., 1968. Pp. (75).

A 6   CAHEN, GASTON. History of the Relations of Russia and China under Peter the Great, 1689–1730. Orono, Me., 1967. Pp. (128).

A 7   CARMICHAEL, JOEL. A Cultural History of Russia. L., 1968. Pp. 272.

A 8   CHERNIAVSKY, MICHAEL. 'Ivan the Terrible as Renaissance Prince', *Slavic Rev*, vol. 27, 1968, pp. 195–211.

A 9   CHRISTIAN, R. F. 'A Recently Discovered 17th—Century Russian Manuscript', *SEER*, vol. 46, 1968, pp. 195–209.

A10   COOPER, LEONARD. Many Roads to Moscow: Three Historic Invasions. L., 1968. Pp. (xiii, 240). Bibl.

A11   CRANMER-BYNG, J. L. 'Russian and British Interests in the Far East, 1791–1793', *Canadian Slavonic Papers*, vol. 10, 1968, pp. 357–75.

A12 DMYTRYSHYN, BASIL, *ed.* Imperial Russia: a Source Book, 1700–1917. N.Y., L., 1967. Pp. (x, 435).
cf. **86**.

A13 DONNELLY, ALTON S. The Russian Conquest of Bashkiria, 1552–1740: a Case Study in Imperialism. Yale U.P., 1968. Pp. (214).

A14 DOSSICK, JESSE. 'Doctoral Dissertations on Russia, the Soviet Union, and Eastern Europe Accepted by American, Canadian, and British Universities, 1966–1967', *Slavic Rev,* vol. 26, 1967, pp. 705–12.
cf. **18–19**.

A15 DREW, W. J. 'Sino-Russian Relations in the 17th Century', *CAR,* vol. 16, 1968, pp. 136–46.
Abstract of **764**.

A16 DUKES, PAUL. Catherine the Great and the Russian Nobility: a Study Based on the Materials of the Legislative Commission of 1767. C.U.P., 1967. Pp. xi, 269. Bibl.

A17 DURANT, MARY. 'Catherine's Boat Ride', *Horizon,* vol. 8, no. 4, 1966, pp. (98–104).
Article on Catherine II's tour of the Crimea in 1787.

A18 EDGERTON, WILLIAM B. 'Recent Anthologies of Eighteenth-Century Russian Literature: a Review Article', *SEEJ,* vol. 12, 1968, pp. 59–78.
Reviews **A63**.

A19 FENNELL, JOHN L. I. The Emergence of Moscow, 1304–1359. L., 1968. Pp. 352. Bibl.

A20 FENNELL, JOHN L. I. 'The *Slovo o Polku Igoreve:* the Textological Triangle', *OSP,* New Series, vol. 1, 1968, pp. 126–37.

A21 FINE, JOHN V. A. 'Fedor Kuritsyn's *Laodikijskoe Poslanie* and the Heresy of the Judaisers', *Speculum,* vol. 41, 1966, pp. 500–4.
cf. **341**.

A22 GORDON, PATRICK. Passages from the Diary of General Patrick Gordon of Auchleuchries in the Years 1635–1699. (Russia through European Eyes, no. 3.) Aberdeen, 1859; reprinted L., 1968. Pp. xxxvi, 244.
Facsimile reprint of **2001**.

A23 HAMEL, JOSEPH VON. England and Russia: Comprising

the Voyages of John Tradescant the Elder etc. (Russia through European Eyes, no. 6.) L., 1854; reprinted L., 1968. Pp. xi, 422.

Facsimile reprint of **1885**.

A24 HELLIE, R., *comp.* Readings for Introduction to Russian Civilization, Muscovite Society. (Trans. from Russian.) Chicago, 1967. Pp. (320).

A25 HINGLEY, RONALD. The Tsars: Russian Autocrats, 1533–1917. L., 1968. Pp. (313).

Collective biography.

A26 HOOD, GARY A. 'A Bibliography of Works Dealing with the Relationship between Baltic and Slavic', *Lituanus,* vol. 13, no. 2, 1967, pp. 38–46.

A27 HORAK, STEPHEN M. 'Michael Hrushevsky: Portrait of an Historian', *Canadian Slavonic Papers,* vol. 10, 1968, pp. 341–56.

A28 HOWES, ROBERT C., *ed.* The Testaments of the Grand Princes of Moscow. (Trans. from Russian.) Cornell U.P., 1967. Pp. xvii, 445. Bibl.

A29 KAPLAN, HERBERT H., *ed.* Russia and the Outbreak of the Seven Years' War. U. of California P., C.U.P., 1968. Pp. (xi, 165). Bibl.

A30 KEENAN, EDWARD L. 'Muscovy and Kazan: Some Introductory Remarks on the Patterns of Steppe Diplomacy', *Slavic Rev,* vol. 26, 1967, pp. 548–58.

A31 KEIM, JEAN A. Russian Icons. L., 1967. Pp. (16).

A32 KLIMAS, ANTANAS. 'Balto-Slavic, or Baltic and Slavic? The Relationship of Baltic and Slavic Languages', *Lituanus,* vol. 13, no. 2, 1967, pp. 5–37.

A33 KOCHAN, MIRIAM. Life in Russia under Catherine the Great. L., 1969. Pp. (x, 182). Bibl.

A34 KONOVALOV, SERGE. 'England and Russia: Two Missions, 1666–1668', *OSP,* vol. 13, 1967, pp. 47–71.

A35 KONOVALOV, SERGE. 'Sixteen Further Letters of General Patrick Gordon', *OSP,* vol. 13, 1967, pp. 72–95.

A36 KORB, JOHANN G. Diary of an Austrian Secretary of Legation at the Court of Czar Peter the Great. (Trans. from Latin.) 2 vols. (in 1). (Russia through European Eyes, no. 8.) L., 1863; reprinted L., 1968.

Facsimile reprint of **2021**.

A37 LEEMING, H. 'Russian Words in Sixteenth-Century English Sources', *SEER,* vol. 46, 1968, pp. 1–30.

A38 LEWANSKI, R. C., *and others.* The Literatures of the World in English Translation: a Bibliography. Vol. 2. The Slavic Literatures. (New York Public Library.) N.Y., 1967. Pp. xiv, 630.

A39 LEWITTER, L. R. 'Russia, Poland and the Baltic, 1697–1721', *Historical Journal,* vol. 11, 1968, pp. 3–34.

A40 LIKHACHEV, D. S. 'The Authenticity of the *Slovo o Polku Igoreve:* a Brief Survey of the Arguments', *OSP,* vol. 13, 1967, pp. 33–46.

A41 LIKHACHEV, D. S. 'The Type and Character of the Byzantine Influence on Old Russian Literature', *OSP,* vol. 13, 1967, pp. 14–32.

A42 LIPSKI, ALEXANDER. 'A Russian Mystic Faces the Age of Rationalism and Revolution: Thought and Activity of Ivan Vladimirovich Lopukhin', *Church History,* vol. 36, 1967, pp. (170–88).

A43 LUNDEN, SIRI S. 'Some Lexical Groups in Russian Thematic Vocabularies of the 16th and 17th Centuries,' *Scando-Slavica,* vol. 14, 1968, pp. 157–64; Bibl.

A44 LYONS, M., *ed.* The Russian Imperial Army: a Bibliography of Regimental Histories and Related Works. Stanford U.P., 1968. Pp. (188).

A45 MANSTEIN, CHRISTOPHER H. VON. Contemporary Memoirs of Russia from the Year 1727 to 1744. (Trans. from French.) 2nd [i.e. 3rd] ed. (Russia through European Eyes, no. 7.) L., 1856; reprinted L., 1968. Pp. xv, 416.
Facsimile reprint of 2033.

A46 MORREN, DOUGLAS G. 'Donald Mackenzie Wallace and British Russophilism, 1870–1919', *Canadian Slavonic Papers,* vol. 9, 1967, pp. 170–83.

A47 NEBEL, HENRY M. N. M. Karamzin: a Russian Sentimentalist. The Hague, 1967. Pp. (190). Bibl.

A48 OINAS, FELIX J. 'Legends of the Chuds and Pans', *SEEJ,* vol. 12, 1968, pp. 184–98.

A49 OLEARIUS, ADAM. The Travels of Olearius in Seventeenth-Century Russia. Translated [from German] and

Edited by Samuel H. Baron. Stanford U.P., 1967. Pp. xvii, 349. Bibl.

cf. **1993**.

A50　PAPMEHL, K. A. 'Samuel Bentham and the *Sobesednik*, 1783', *SEER*, vol. 46, 1968, pp. 210–9.

A51　PARKER, W. H. An Historical Geography of Russia. U. of London P., 1968. Pp. 416. Bibl.

A52　PELENSKI, JAROSLAW. 'Muscovite Imperial Claims to the Kazan Khanate', *Slavic Rev*, vol. 26, 1967, pp. 559–76.

A53　PENNINGTON, A. E. 'Future Periphrases in 17th-Century Russian: Some Evidence from Translated Material', *SEER*, vol. 46, 1968, pp. 31–47.

A54　PERRY, JOHN. The State of Russia under the Present Czar ... (Russia through European Eyes, no. 1.) L., 1716; reprinted L., 1967. Pp. 280.

Facsimile reprint of **2018**.

A55　PHILLIPS, EUSTACE D. The Mongols. (Ancient Peoples and Places, vol. 64.) L., 1969. Pp. (208). Bibl.

A56　POLONSKA-WASYLENKO, NATALIA D. Two Conceptions of the History of Ukraine and Russia ... L., 1968. Pp. 79.

A57　PRITSAK, OMELJAN. 'Moscow, the Golden Horde, and the Kazan Khanate from a Polycultural Point of View', *Slavic Rev*, vol. 26, 1967, pp. 577–83.

A58　RAEFF, MARC, *comp*. Plans for Political Reform in Imperial Russia, 1730–1905. Englewood Cliffs, 1966. Pp. (xi, 159).

A59　RAHUL, R. 'Russia's other Boundaries', *Australian Journal of Politics and History*, vol. 11, no. 1, 1965, pp. (23–40).

Article on Russia's boundaries with Iran, Turkey and Afghanistan.

A60　RICHARDSON, WILLIAM. Anecdotes of the Russian Empire in a Series of Letters ... (Russia through European Eyes, no. 5.) L., 1784; reprinted L., 1968. Pp. xvi, 478.

Facsimile reprint of **2053**.

A61　ROZEMUND, KEETJE. 'An Old Russian Passage of Dionysius the Areopagite', *SEER*, vol. 46, 1968, pp. 192–4.

A62　SEAMAN, GERALD R. History of Russian Music. Vol. 1.

From its Origins to Dargomyzhsky. O., 1967 [i.e. 1968].
Pp. (xv, 351). Bibl.

A63   SEGEL, HAROLD B., *comp*. The Literature of Eighteenth
Century Russia : an Anthology . . . (Trans. from Russian.)
2 vols. N.Y., 1967. Bibl. (Pbk.)

A64   SHEEHY, ANN. 'Russia and China in the Pamirs : 18th
and 19th Centuries', *CAR*, vol. 16, 1968, pp. 4–14.

A65   SHEVCHENKO, IHOR. 'Muscovy's Conquest of Kazan :
Two Views Reconciled', *Slavic Rev*, vol. 26, 1967, pp.
541–7.

A66   SIMMONS, JOHN S. G. 'Theses in Slavonic Studies
Approved for Higher Degrees by British Universities,
1907–1966', *OSP*, vol. 13, 1967, pp. 133–59 [and statistical conspectus].

A67   SMITH, ROBERT E. F., *comp*. The Enserfment of the
Russian Peasantry. (Trans. from Russian.) C.U.P., 1968.
Pp. xii, 180. Bibl.
       cf. **889**.

A68   SOKOLOV, YURI M. Russian Folklore. (Trans. from
Russian.) New Introduction and Bibliography by Felix
J. Oinas. Hatboro, Pa., 1966. Pp. (760).
       Reissue of **1081**.

A69   SØRENSEN, HANS C. 'The So-Called Varangian-Russian
Problem', *Scando-Slavica*, vol. 14, 1968, pp. 141–8.

A70   STADEN, HEINRICH VON. The Land and Government of
Muscovy : a Sixteenth-Century Account. Translated
[from German] and Edited by Thomas Esper. Stanford U.P., 1967. Pp. xxiii, 142.

A71   STEVENS, HENRY C., *comp*. Russian Folk Tales. Translated [from Russian] and Retold . . . L., 1967. Pp.
(140).

A72   SULIMIRSKI, TADEUSZ. Corded Ware and Globular
Amphorae North-East of the Carpathians. L., 1968. Pp.
(xxiii, 281).

A73   SULLIVAN, J. *and* DRAGE, C. L. 'Poems in an Unpublished Manuscript of the *Vinograd Rossiiskii*', *OSP*, New
Series, vol. 1, 1968, pp. 27–48.

A74   SZAWLOWSKI, RICHARD *and* TERLECKA, HANNA. 'Western
Research on Russia until 1939, I : Developments up to

1914', *Canadian Slavonic Papers,* vol. 9, 1967, pp. 145–69.

A75 TAYLOR, NORMAN W. 'Adam Smith's First Russian Disciple', *SEER,* vol. 45, 1967, pp. 425–38.
A study of the 18th century Russian economist, Ivan Andreevich Tret'yakov.

A76 TEODOROVICH, N. 'Monasteries of the Russian Orthodox Church', *Bulletin of the Institute for the Study of the U.S.S.R.* (Munich), vol. 13, no. 9, 1966, pp. 3–12.

A77 THOMPSON, A. H. 'The Legend of Tsarevich Dimitriy: some Evidence of an Oral Tradition', *SEER,* vol. 46, 1968, pp. 48–59.

A78 VOYCE, ARTHUR The Art and Architecture of Medieval Russia. U. of Oklahoma P., 1967. Pp. (432).

A79 WALLACE, ROBERT, *and others.* The Rise of Russia. N.Y., 1967. Pp. (184).

A80 WEBER, FRIEDRICH C. The Present State of Russia. (Trans. from German.) 2 vols. (Russia through European Eyes, no. 2.) L., 1722–3; reprinted L., 1968.
Facsimile reprint of **2028.**

A81 WEIGH, KEN S. Russo-Chinese Diplomacy, 1689–1924. 2nd ed. Orono, Me., 1967. Pp. (xxi, 382).

A82 WORTH, GERTA H. 'Church Slavonic Elements in Russian', *OSP,* New Series, vol. 1, 1968, pp. 1–11.

A83 WREN, MELVIN C. The Course of Russian History. 3rd ed. N.Y., 1968. Pp. (750).
cf. **223.**

INDEX

The index is a combined name and subject index. References are to item and not page numbers. Filing is word-by-word. Names with prefixes and hyphenated words are filed as if written as one word. Title entries are only given for books of anonymous or hidden authorship or those which may be known chiefly by their titles. Title entries are distinguished by italics. Russian and other foreign terms for which there is no exact English equivalent are also italicized. Items listed in the Addenda are not represented in the index.

P